LARGE PRINT
CROSSWORDS

LARGE PRINT
CROSSWORDS

THUNDER BAY
P·R·E·S·S
San Diego, California

Thunder Bay Press
An imprint of Printers Row Publishing Group
10350 Barnes Canyon Road, Suite 100, San Diego, CA 92121
www.thunderbaybooks.com • mail@thunderbaybooks.com

All notations of errors or omissions should be addressed to Thunder Bay Press, Editorial Department, at the above address. All other correspondence (author inquiries, permissions) concerning the content of this book should be addressed to Arcturus Holdings Limited, 26/27 Bickels Yard, 151-153 Bermondsey Street, London SE1 3HA, info@arcturuspublishing.com

Thunder Bay Press
Publisher: Peter Norton
Associate Publisher: Ana Parker
Publishing/Editorial Team: April Farr, Kelly Larsen, Kathryn C. Dalby
Editorial Team: JoAnn Padgett, Melinda Allman, Traci Douglas

ISBN: 978-1-64517-127-0
AD007413US

Printed in China
23 22 21 20 19   2 3 4 5 6

1

Across

1 Part of a church that contains the altar
5 Monte Carlo attraction
11 Busiest
12 Daniel Webster, for one
13 "Chariots of Fire" finale
14 Puddinglike dessert
15 Be at fault
16 Revolved
17 Goo
19 Brown ermine
23 "Crouching Tiger, Hidden Dragon" director
24 Like "Lost" episodes
25 "For Your ____ Only"
27 "__, please" ("I like mine still mooing")
28 Igneous rock, originally
30 Chicken Little's mother, e.g.
31 ____ shooting
32 ____ Allan Poe
35 Lion's "meow"
37 Major time period
38 Star sign
41 Chum, e.g.
42 Taken
43 Empty
44 Lets out, say
45 "Story of My Life" Mike

Down

1 ____-ski
2 Steinbeck opus, with "The"
3 Gross irreverence
4 Barely get, with "out"
5 Provide for free, informally
6 Incite, as passion
7 Strolled
8 "____ just what I wanted!"
9 #s
10 State that "Portlandia" is filmed in: abbr.
16 "Get it?"
18 Spellbind
20 Citrus drink
21 "____ Force One" (1997 Harrison Ford film)
22 Driving need
25 Common couple?
26 Animal whose name also means "to talk nonstop"
29 Penitent
30 "____ Town Too" (1981 hit)
33 Seed coverings
34 Gives a five, maybe
36 Assists
38 Fed. construction overseer
39 "Electric" creature
40 Cambridge sch.
41 Recycling ____

2

Across

1 Bad-mouth
4 Aquatic shocker
7 Piece of equipment for a rock band: abbr.
10 Application question, often
11 ___ Day
12 Road, in Rome
13 Distance from one side to the other
16 Creep
17 Eastern wrap: var.
18 Morality subject
21 "Fudge!"
22 Like some muscles
24 Hood's gun, shortly
25 Merry-go-round
28 "Catch-22" pilot
29 Certain pickle
30 G.M. or G.E.
32 Slightest amounts
36 Skoal, e.g.
38 Links rental
39 Better-known name of Phoebe Moses: 2 wds.
42 Broccoli or spinach, for short
43 Juliet, to Romeo
44 Bud
45 "Able was I ___ …"
46 "Don't give up!"
47 Downed a sub, say

Down

1 Flax-like fiber
2 "The X-files" extra
3 Dilly
4 Australian non-flyer
5 Audience
6 Caustic cleaners
7 Garden-variety
8 Quartz or borax, e.g.
9 Clear
14 Bake in individual dishes, as eggs
15 "Cheap" satire magazine
19 128 cubic feet
20 Mar
23 Christmas
25 Bing Crosby, for one
26 Bracket
27 Remiss
28 Harmonious interval
31 Telepathy, e.g.
33 Minute floating marine creature
34 Milk-Bone biscuit, e.g.
35 Do a do
37 Makeup, e.g.
40 "___ Gang"
41 "___ calls?"

3

Across

1 Medieval war clubs
6 Arguments
11 "The Gift of the Magi" device
12 Army attack helicopter
13 Capital of Tanzania: 3 wds.
15 "The ___ Daba Honeymoon"
16 Folk song "Jolly Roving ___"
17 Have a bit of, as brandy
18 "Well, ___ be a monkey's uncle!"
19 Taconite, e.g.
20 Addition
21 Spring (from)
23 "___ quam videri" (North Carolina's motto)
24 Freetown currency unit
26 "Yo!" alternative
29 Gusto
33 Short sleep phenomenon?
34 1-1 game, say
35 "The Matrix" character
36 Victorian, for one
37 Big roll, as of cash
38 ___ cross
39 Garden center purchases
42 Pennies, sometimes
43 Present
44 Plagued, as by problems
45 Teens who wear black makeup, e.g.

Down

1 Above ground level
2 Fit for farming
3 Reef components
4 Chemical suffix
5 Part of a heartbeat
6 Alarm
7 Sen. or Rep.
8 Loses prestige
9 Park features
10 Taste
14 Relating to tailoring
22 Last, for short
23 1997 Koji Yakusho film, with "The"
25 Short of
26 Factory-made, as housing
27 Calm
28 Common sense
30 Absorbed
31 "___ me!"
32 Colonials and split-levels, e.g.
34 Chubby Checker's dance
40 Pipe joint
41 Lion's home, maybe

4

Across

1 End of "Coriolanus": 2 wds.
5 "Way of the gods," literally
11 "Boss Lady" star Lynn
12 ___ hearts (red playing card): 2 wds.
13 Pennsylvanian city known as "The Gem City"
14 Pontiac, e.g.
15 Workout wear
17 Geological ridge
18 Cool eyewear
21 Cutlet?
25 Coffee-to-go need
26 Ballerina's pivot point
27 Acted like
29 Auteur's art
32 Finnish architect Alvar ___
34 Bruce Willis film: 2 wds.
39 Latin-American dances
40 "Able was I ___ saw Elba": 2 wds.
41 Adjust
42 Cash advance
43 Chemical cousin
44 First video game

Down

1 Biblical shepherd
2 Attention
3 H.S. math
4 Watched
5 Underwater toons of the 1980s
6 Words to a blackjack dealer: 2 wds.
7 Unpaid worker, often
8 Impending
9 Drags
10 "Son ___ gun!": 2 wds.
16 Widow in "Peer Gynt"
18 Hearst kidnap grp.
19 Edgy
20 Drink suffix
22 Mineral suffix
23 Dot follower
24 Mauna ___, Hawaii
28 "Consarn it, ye varmint!"
29 Deal maker
30 BBC rival
31 Useless
33 All together: 2 wds.
34 Bowlers, e.g.
35 "___us a son…"
36 Slangy suffix for "buck"
37 Withdraw gradually
38 Card in a royal flush
39 "___-Pan" (1966 novel)

5

Across

1 Portuguese territory
6 The Underworld, to Ancient Greeks
11 Lab gels
12 Scrub, NASA-style
13 Having a key center
14 Finnish steam room
15 Manhattan Project goal: hyph.
17 Plead for a treat, dog-style
18 Hospital fixtures
20 Ring, as bells
22 Self-proclaimed psychic Geller
23 Eternal
26 Iranian money
28 Cheesy snack
29 Bible book
31 Hold up
32 Defeated
33 Spinning toys
34 Eggs
36 Second-year students, for short
38 Type measurements
40 Artist's support
43 Bread spread
44 "___ Mine" (1985 sci-fi movie)
45 Cool, lustrous fabric
46 As such: 2 wds.

Down

1 Pin cushion?
2 From long ___
3 Breakfast buffet choice: 2 wds.
4 Ishmael's people
5 1952 Olympics host
6 Ex-stars: hyph.
7 J.D.'s org.
8 Two-timer: hyph.
9 Coastal raptor
10 Like bachelor parties
16 Gas-guzzling stat.
18 Town, informally
19 Lake that feeds Niagara Falls
21 French menu phrase: 2 wds.
23 Hired killer
24 Boutique
25 Breaks down, in a way
27 "I Hope You Dance" singer ___ Ann Womack
30 City in Japan
33 Macbeth, for one
34 Fiery gemstone
35 King Henry ___
37 Birdcall
39 Ginger ___ (soft drink)
41 Bad ___, German spa
42 Caustic chemical

6

Across

1 Fills out
6 Hole that an anchor rope passes through
11 Dismay
12 "___ not amused!": 2 wds.
13 Payment alternative to checks: 2 wds.
15 Part of Q & A, briefly
16 Goes off, in a way
17 ___ Fjord
18 He had the first billion-view YouTube video
21 Throw in, as a question
23 Racer Ricky
25 Guitarist Phil
26 Where goods are displayed
30 Reaction to Niagara Falls, often
31 ___ of Spain, Trinidad
32 "___ Colors" (Cyndi Lauper chart-topper)
33 Pro-Bowl defensive end Umenyiora
36 "Spin City" actor: 3 wds.
40 C.S. Lewis' lion
41 "Ditto!": 3 wds.
42 Mockery, of a sort
43 Prefix meaning "nine" that can precede -gram

Down

1 Ole Miss rival
2 ___ reflection
3 Hospital carers, initially
4 Actor Hakeem ___-Kazim, Colonel Iké Dubaku in "24"
5 Least ingenuous
6 Intense shock
7 "No ifs, ___ …"
8 Little, in Scotland
9 "Certainly, ___!"
10 Letter before "tee"
14 Heraldic border
17 French wave
18 Rhymer's writing
19 Draft org.
20 "Uh-huh"
21 Doing nothing
22 Connive
23 Pretoria's country letters
24 Dennis Williams' org.
27 Jumped (out)
28 Don Juan, e.g.
29 End of a threat: 2 wds.
32 Word after "greater" or "lesser"
33 In the blink ___ eye: 2 wds.
34 "___ Like It Hot"
35 Ornamental plant
36 Calf's cry
37 Initially, you'll need one to get online
38 151, to Nero
39 ___ Stewart, former host of "The Daily Show"

7

Across

1 Pop's kin
4 Dance bit
7 "___ Kapital" (Karl Marx)
10 ___ ammoniac
11 Augmented fourth in music
13 Scented sheet used in a storage area: 2 wds.
15 Daughter of King David
16 "Endymion" poet
17 German drinking salutation
19 AT&T competitor
21 Sachet holding leaves for infusion: 2 wds.
25 Up to me: 3 wds.
28 Whiskey made from potatoes
29 First president of South Vietnam, ___ Dinh Diem
30 The ___ State (Connecticut nickname)
33 Sketch comedy series inspired by a magazine: 2 wds.
36 Scale
39 Country entertainment: 2 wds.
41 Actor Kurt
42 Band associated with Elvis Presley
43 Water___ (flosser)
44 Cpl.'s superior
45 The ___ Glove (hot surface mitt)

Down

1 DOT, alternatively
2 Japanese capital (710–84)
3 "Beverly Hillbillies" name
4 Wing (prefix)
5 Abbr. on some sheet music
6 More smooth
7 Spanish lady
8 Without ___ (dangerously): 2 wds.
9 Sun. talks?
12 Cravat pin: var.
14 Armed conflict
18 Daring film feat
19 Econ. measure
20 ___ many irons in the fire
22 Meet head on: 2 wds.
23 H.S. class
24 Shine, in ad-speak
26 Gossips at the synagogue?
27 Outputs of artists
31 Onetime Golden Arches' offering
32 Highest note in Guido's scale
33 Fig. on a car sticker
34 Here, in Spain
35 Time of long shadows
37 1205, to Romans
38 Lilith's portrayer on "Cheers"
40 Finnish-American actress and dancer Taina

8

Across

1 Barbecue fuel
6 Ladies of the house, informally
11 "___ Road" (Beatles album)
12 Call off, at Cape Canaveral
13 Daniel Boone, notably
15 Little bird
16 Big belly
17 Certain tropical cuckoo
18 "Do the Right Thing" director Spike
19 Dig up dandelions, maybe
20 Churchill's "so few," initially
21 Bounds
23 African fly
25 "Oklahoma!" aunt
27 Edible legume
30 Cut
34 Gasteyer of "Mean Girls"
35 Do film work
37 Monetary unit of Romania
38 Cook Co.'s home
39 Drops in the morning meadow
40 Container's top
41 Tiny time period
44 OH- or Cl-, chemically
45 Part of a spur
46 Cardinal flats
47 Band on the run?

Down

1 Kine
2 "Access Hollywood" cohost
3 Died Down
4 "Fantasy Island" prop
5 Slender woman
6 Lap dog
7 Legal letters
8 "Amadeus" composer
9 Rupp, Arco, et al.
10 Friction
14 Footwear securers
22 Back-to-school mo.
24 .0000001 joule
26 Warm-up acts: hyph.
27 Alligator's cousin
28 Surfing, perhaps
29 "Casablanca" producer
31 Concedes
32 Fishing nets
33 Powwow
36 Dweeb
42 Auction offering
43 Pigeon English?

9

Across

1 Olden drum
6 Garbage
11 In the know
12 Perfume
13 "At the Center of the Storm" author George
14 Bus alternatives
15 Campus quarters
17 Dermatologist's concern
18 Clover site
20 Bounce, as from a bar
22 Sea eagles
24 "Memoirs of a ___" (Arthur Golden novel)
28 Certain fraction
30 Manages
31 Bracing coastal atmosphere: 2 wds.
33 Stoolie
34 Cold cuts, e.g.
36 Good buddies use them, initially
37 0.5 fl. oz.
40 Bit
42 Put in the cup
44 Having a cupola
47 Gloss over, like a syllable
48 Wing-shaped
49 "Ahoy ___!"
50 Dive (for)

Down

1 Body art, for short
2 Cause of speechlessness
3 Colorful neckerchief: var.
4 100+-year-old cookie
5 Backward-looking, in fashion
6 Avena sativa grain
7 Half or quarter, e.g.
8 Cunning
9 "The Folks That Live On The Hill" author
10 Endure
16 Coffee holder
18 Contact, e.g.
19 Shallowest of the Great Lakes
21 Part of a min.
23 Rush of frightened animals
25 Astronaut
26 Basil, e.g.
27 Calls for
29 Get going
32 Aries animal
35 ___ wave (tsunami)
37 Opponents of "us"
38 Gaucho's weapon
39 Open, as an envelope
41 Balsam used in perfumery
43 "L.A. Law" actress Susan
45 Unit of energy
46 Make a different color, like hair

10

Across

1. ____-loading (pre-marathon activity)
6. Chuck
10. TV soldiers of fortune: hyph.
11. Below-the-belt
12. Darn it!
14. "Wheel of Fortune" buy: 2 wds.
15. "Fancy that!"
16. Yoko born in Tokyo
17. Ofc. computer link
18. "We ____ to please"
19. Certain digital watch face, for short
20. Bed board
22. Pried
24. Failed to be
26. Muzzle
28. Primordial matter, to physicists
32. Aegean, Red or Adriatic, e.g.
33. Bachelor's home
35. Popeye's "Positively!"
36. Body part that also means "cool"
37. Absorbed, as a cost
38. Big Apple attraction, with "The"
39. Not removable (of a right)
42. Like some consonant sounds
43. Down producer
44. ____ brat
45. Bugle sounds

Down

1. Intrigues
2. Hard on the ear, maybe
3. Focal point
4. "____ humbug!" (Scrooge's shout)
5. 1980s Olds clone of Chevrolet Citation
6. Black-throated ____ (Asian bird)
7. Black, white and orange bird
8. Blotto
9. Church assembly
11. Evil spirit: var.
13. Restore control, say
21. "____ Buck Chuck" (Charles Shaw)
23. Chester White's home
25. Domestic: 2 wds.
26. Fisherman with a net
27. Flamethrower fuel
29. Greek consonant
30. Button holder
31. Gauges
32. Hindu deity
34. Star in Cygnus
40. Produce, as an egg
41. Have what's "going around"

11

Across

1 Datebook entry: abbr.
5 Attacks: 2 wds.
10 Clean up, in a way
12 Beneficial: 2 wds.
13 African language
14 ___ Carlo
15 Little pest
16 Ogles offensively: 2 wds.
18 Less likely to fall over
20 Princess, initially
21 Magnetic induction unit
22 Suffix for gran and graph
23 Beat the pants off
25 Stayed in a lodge
27 Howard of "Happy Days"
28 Scene of W.W. I fighting
30 Initially a port
31 Binds together: 2 wds.
34 Vulture's dinner?
36 "___ la la…"
37 Special way of doing something
38 Being broadcast: 2 wds.
40 Arise
41 Jottings
42 Irritates
43 Sandwich retailer

Down

1 Mahmoud ___, president of Palestine after Yasser Arafat
2 Industrial building
3 Senior military staff: 2 wds.
4 Vietnamese lunar New Year
5 Bart, Lisa and Maggie's dad: 2 wds.
6 Gets an ___ effort: 2 wds.
7 Florida: 2 wds.
8 Phoenician goddess of love and fertility
9 Grew biters
11 Go to live elsewhere: 3 wds.
17 Suffix with adopt or address
19 Suddenly
23 Long-distance driver
24 "Silverado" actress Arquette
26 Long-running UK music mag.
29 Alliance created in 1948, initially
32 Poem by Ralph Waldo Emerson
33 Adherent of Zoroastrianism
35 Bra size: 2 wds.
39 Affirmative action

12

Across

1 Willing to face danger
6 Aircraft controller
11 Wise words
12 Accused's need
13 Criminal mobs
14 Fey
15 "The L Word" actress Daniels
16 Beer amount
17 Warm dry mountain wind: var.
19 Adept
22 Horse, to a child: hyph.
24 Criticize
25 "Rumor ____ it..."
26 Place for a cat, often
28 Gay Nineties, e.g.
29 "Humanum ____ errare"
30 Decorative bunch of cords
32 ____ Aquarids (meteor shower associated with Halley's Comet)
33 Like many Poe stories
34 Boris Godunov, for one
36 Misdeals, e.g.
39 Cream and The Police, for two
41 Blacksmith's block
42 ____ dark space (region in a vacuum tube)
43 Give extreme unction, once
44 Clichéd
45 Ran quick

Down

1 Plum variety
2 Jewish calendar's sixth month
3 Appearance in bodily form, as of a ghost
4 Christmas drink
5 "Absolutely!"
6 Song of joy
7 Pollution, poverty, etc.
8 Flotation device: 2 wds.
9 "Kill Bill" sash
10 Only three-letter element
16 Crook
18 Fish that can be "electric"
20 Collector's guide adjective
21 Girasol, e.g.
22 Clarified butter in Indian cookery
23 "____ of Eden"
27 Golf course score
31 Burnt ____ (Crayola color)
33 Artist's stand
35 Pop, to some
37 Anger, with "up"
38 "Mush!" shouter's vehicle
39 Bill
40 Part of a cell nucleus, briefly
41 "How very nice!"

13

Across

1 Indian nursemaid
5 Mirror ____
10 Archeological find
12 Afflictions
13 "Farewell, mon ami"
14 "Reversal of Fortune" star
15 Oversized
16 Flower-shaped decoration
18 Third generation Japanese-American
20 Egg layer
21 Like Death's horse, in Revelations
23 Org. until 1993
24 Raised mark on the skin
27 Country great Haggard
29 Paddle's cousin
30 Part of a leaf, perhaps
32 Female gametes
33 Classic theater name
37 Abandons
40 Hemingway book "The Old Man and the ____"
41 Purple shade
42 Bake, as eggs
44 Correspond, in grammar
45 Alpine air?
46 Extremely: 2 wds.
47 "Bill & ____ Excellent Adventure"

Down

1 Keffiyeh wearers
2 News shows, newspapers, etc.
3 Adjust, in a way
4 Make haste
5 Nile bird
6 Filly's mother
7 Repeat order at the bar
8 Refined
9 Gist
11 Solution to any problem: hyph.
17 "Texas tea"
19 Day ____ (place for a pedicure)
22 Diplomatic mission
24 Tree feller
25 Try it out: 3 wds.
26 Operation with a pencil
28 Sushi ingredient, often
31 Reject, with "out of"
34 "All kidding ____..."
35 Waxed, old style
36 Counts, now
38 All square
39 Thatch bit, perhaps
43 Sweltering

14

Across

1. "Great Expectations" hero
4. "Dirty dog"
7. Chemical ending
10. Egg-shaped instrument
12. Campaigner, for short
13. City in Israel
14. Eggs, in biology
15. Abominable Snowman
16. Goat's snack, in many cartoons
17. ____ case scenario
20. Didn't just aah
22. "Exodus" hero
23. Ague cousin
24. Arboreal rodent: 2 wds.
30. Point, in baseball
31. "____ rang?"
32. Brown shade
35. What "yo mama" is
37. "____ Maria"
38. Add punch to the punch
40. Ballpoint, e.g.
41. Amos Oz, for one
45. "Lord of the Rings" bad guy
46. Building where livestock are fattened up
47. "The Catcher in the ____"
48. Nautical lurch
49. A hallucinogen, initially

Down

1. Ale holder
2. Diamonds, slangily
3. Bosom buddy
4. Cat-like mammal
5. Condo, e.g.
6. It's filled at the market
7. Age
8. Stars that increase in brightness, then fade
9. Dik-dik's kin
11. Beams
17. Major event of 1812
18. Molybdenite, e.g.
19. Free from, with "of"
21. "____ Father"
23. A good time
25. Relative of "Reverend"
26. Make more specific
27. Shag rug made in Sweden
28. Eternity, seemingly
29. Carry around, as a set of golf clubs
32. Flavor
33. "____ Heartbeat" (Amy Grant hit)
34. British coins
35. "The Turn of the ____"
36. Advantage, in sports
39. Fishing, perhaps
42. Letter after kay
43. "____ Olvidados" (1950 Luis Buñuel film)
44. "____ be a pleasure!"

15

Across

1 Some Italian cars, for short
6 Clenched hands
11 Sierra ___
12 Jellied garnish
13 Like ghost stories
14 100 kobo in Nigeria
15 Breaks off
17 Part of a list
18 Avoid
19 Alternative to a fence
21 Voting "nay"
22 Deliberately invalid but ingenious argument
25 Exist en masse
26 "That means ___!"
27 Prefix with classical
28 Takes back a former statement
30 Serengeti grazer
31 "That hurt!"
32 Commend
33 Macbeth, for one
35 Hindu religious teacher
37 Caulking fiber
39 Arboreal animal
41 Word before suspect or rate
42 Earnings
43 Exhausted, as resources
44 Grave marker

Down

1 Draft choice
2 Coast that the wind blows on: 2 wds.
3 Baked dough cake containing a prediction: 2 wds.
4 Charged particle
5 Percolate
6 Buff
7 "Two Concepts of Liberty" author Berlin
8 Exact double of another: 2 wds.
9 Radial, e.g.
10 Dishonest way to make money
16 Irons out creases
18 Animated Disney villain
20 Big production
22 Coordinate
23 Guard
24 Grimace of discontent
29 Fall in Britain
32 Diamond weight
33 Soaks (up), as with a paper towel
34 Gripe
36 Impresses greatly
38 Came Across
40 Fed. property overseer

16

Across

1 Switches
6 "Desire Under the ___"
10 It used to be Pleasant Island
11 Change, chemically
13 Actor, singer, dancer, e.g.
15 Pilot's announcement letters
16 ___ Alamos, N.M.
17 African antelope
18 Go one of two opposite directions
19 "___ what?!"
20 "Do the Right Thing" director
21 Biblical paradise
23 Ashes, e.g.
25 Bloodless
27 Desserts, to many dieters
29 Roll-top, for one
33 ___ Remo, Italy
34 Finish, with "up"
36 "___-Pan" (James Clavell novel)
37 Mission control, for short
38 Dash lengths
39 Attila the ___
40 Right of the accused: 2 wds.
43 Even if, briefly
44 Neighborhood
45 ___ Mix
46 Like a teen's room, stereotypically

Down

1 Allergic reaction
2 Classified: hyph.
3 Power ___
4 Grand ___ ("Evangeline" setting)
5 Bad-tempered
6 Kind of mark
7 Hawaiian wreath
8 Fabric press
9 Movie parts
12 "___ Grit" (1969 John Wayne film)
14 Delicious
22 Masefield play "The Tragedy of ___"
24 Beatles tune, with "The"
26 By hook or by crook
27 Flamethrower fuel
28 Like some inspections: hyph.
30 High standards
31 Hot spots
32 Royal
33 Living room piece
35 Biblical poem
41 Density symbol
42 Sushi topping, sometimes

17

Across

1 Long-range weapon, briefly
5 Animals
10 Daughter of Zeus and Demeter in Greek mythology
11 Dressed (up)
12 Month before Nisan
13 Channeled
14 Brewer's kiln
15 Boston's Liberty Tree, e.g.
16 Caspian and Caribbean
18 Not yet final, at law
22 Accomplishments
24 Rock band equipment
25 "___ got a golden ticket…"
26 Air hero
28 Fraternity members
29 Give or take, e.g.
31 Bug
33 Length x width, for a rectangle
34 Cattail, e.g.
35 ___ de Triomphe
37 Baby-talk characteristic
40 Kind of number
43 Animal shelter
44 Right, in a way
45 Volcano in Verne's "Journey to the Center of the Earth"
46 It can give a golfer a lift
47 Take five, say

Down

1 Aviation org.
2 Closing passage
3 Woman's garment
4 Sable kin
5 April honoree
6 Barnard graduate, e.g.
7 Final: abbr.
8 French word in wedding announcements
9 Continue
11 Formal theater area: 2 wds.
17 Ottoman officer
19 Straightaway
20 Blueprint item, briefly
21 "___ It Romantic?"
22 Prima donna
23 Frequent word from ham operators
27 Opposite WSW
30 Giving a bleat
32 Buyer's counterpart
36 ___ Against the Machine (rock-rap group)
38 Breaks a commandment
39 Duff
40 Cutter
41 Party time, maybe
42 Cabernet color

18

Across

1 Chilean range
6 Enlarge: 2 wds.
11 "No ___ Bob!"
12 Beau
13 Edwin with the 1970 #1 hit "War"
14 Eyes
15 ___ Haven, CT
16 Astronomer Bart
18 "Argo" director Affleck
19 ___ Lanka
20 Groenland, par exemple
21 Bathroom, in Bristol
22 Amateur sports grp.
24 Fam. tree member
25 Append: 2 wds.
27 De ___
28 In the past, in the past
29 Red or Brave, for short
30 "Take a chair!"
31 Washington, e.g.: abbr.
32 Ben-Hur was chained to one
35 Est., once
36 "Bah!"
37 157.5 degrees from N.
38 Military camp
40 Figure skater Cohen
42 Disorderly
43 "On ___ to know basis": 2 wds.
44 Aides: abbr.
45 Billiard shot

Down

1 Clubs: abbr.
2 Fertilizer component
3 Way to randomly choose a person for an unpleasant task: 2 wds.
4 Always, in verse
5 Like tennis star Novak Djokovic
6 Came to
7 Disney dwarf
8 Betrays: 2 wds.
9 Bony fish
10 River to the Atlantic
17 Motor suffix, commercially
23 Army bed
24 Actor Daniel ___ Kim
25 Mosaic piece
26 British blue-bloods: abbr.
27 Refuse
29 "The Matrix" hero
31 "___ Anatomy"
33 "Angela's ___" (1996 best seller)
34 Aptly named English novelist
39 May hrs., in Modesto
41 Gasteyer formerly of "SNL"

19

Across

1 Composed
6 ____ Lee cakes
10 Big house occupant?
11 Sink fitting: hyph.
12 "Is that good ____?": 2 wds.
13 Suffix for di or pan
14 TV show set in Massachusetts: 2 wds.
16 "____, you noblest English!": 2 wds.
17 Composer Kern
21 Amorphous food
25 Tiny time unit: abbr., 2 wds.
26 South Seas starch
27 Mil. prep. course
28 Pakistani city
30 Eye askance
32 Changing digits
39 German town
40 Fur source
41 Eye sores
42 Actress Téa
43 Briny bodies
44 Nothing to it: 2 wds.

Down

1 Messy dresser
2 Novice
3 F-16's homes, initially
4 "____ my peas with honey…": 2 wds.
5 Archenemy of the Fantastic Four: 2 wds.
6 Intensity
7 As limp as ____: 2 wds.
8 Hindu deity
9 "Come on, be ____!": 2 wds.
11 Ball-and-mallet game
15 Hurricane dir.
17 Dad's namesake: abbr.
18 That, in Tijuana
19 Done working: abbr.
20 Blocks
22 "7 Faces of Dr. ____"
23 Hockey legend Bobby
24 "The Bells" poet
28 Med. country
29 Anatomical ring
31 Ambulance staffers, for short
32 Blog feeds, initially
33 Major ending?
34 Bottled spring water brand
35 Hwys.
36 Have ____ good authority: 2 wds.
37 1980s German pop star
38 Film crew member

20

Across

1 Couples
6 Bacteria
11 Blue hue
12 Common daisy
13 Began to smoke: 2 wds.
14 Botherer
15 Eastern ties
17 Absorbs, with "up"
18 Animal represented in the zodiac by Aries
20 An empty bottle is full of it
22 Athletic supporter?
23 "Shoo!"
25 Study (with "over")
27 Festivals
29 Ball game
32 "___ of the Dead" (Karloff film)
34 Plane, e.g.
35 Cul-de-___
37 Be a chatterbox
39 "Yes" indication
40 Chesapeake Bay creature
42 Assay or essay, perhaps
44 Burning
46 They may have abs of stone
49 "Hello ___!"
50 Cool
51 Class
52 Hangs out

Down

1 City in Tex.
2 Action film staple
3 In an unthinking way
4 Clobber
5 Brown-tinted photo
6 Pan, e.g.
7 Donald and Ivana, e.g.
8 Channel changer: 2 wds.
9 Mr. Magoo, for one
10 "That makes no ___!"
16 Little bit, as of coffee
18 "A Yank in the ___" (1941 film)
19 Amaze
21 Bassist Wasserman
24 "Without question!"
26 "Baloney!"
28 Arch
30 Bill and ___
31 Antiquity, in antiquity
33 "___, drink, and be merry"
35 A lot
36 Cant
38 "She loves me not" determiner
41 ___ weevil
43 Aria, e.g.
45 English river
47 Another word for the Sun
48 Conditions

21

Across

1 Greek portico
5 Coffin-carrying car
11 Charged particles
12 Flunky: hyph.
13 Racecar servicing areas
14 Searched for water
15 K-12, in education: hyph.
16 Big TV maker
17 Boston Bruins Line
19 At no time, poetically
23 Covets
26 Big D.C. lobby letters
27 ____ Amin, former dictator of Uganda
28 Bullring "Bravo!"
29 Largest city in Mich.
30 Abet
31 Most cheeky
33 Hair removal brand
35 Actor Michael of "Year One"
36 D.C. summer clock setting
38 Hertz competitor
41 Non-scary ghost
44 Bit
45 Noble Italian family name
46 "Star Trek" counselor, Deanna
47 Bitter tasting
48 IRS IDs

Down

1 Thin slit in a tire tread
2 Trouble's partner, in Shakespeare
3 Served separately from the main dish: 3 wds.
4 Birthplace of a saint
5 Like some dams
6 Anti-discrimination group, initially
7 It's upstream from Luxor
8 Apt. ad info
9 Manuscript encl.
10 Discontinue
18 Support, with "up"
20 Tries hard
21 "____ tú" it's you, in Spain
22 "Infestation" rock group
23 Anthropologist Fossey
24 Adams of "Up in Smoke"
25 All dried up
32 Distinguishing characteristics
34 Lukewarm
37 Prefix meaning one tenth
39 Lay ____ the line (gamble): 2 wds.
40 "Je ne ____ quoi"
41 Nashville-based awards org.
42 N.R.C. predecessor
43 "Star Wars" project of the 1980s

22

Across

1 Canned ham glaze
6 Magicians' rods
11 Negation mark in logic
12 Require salting, maybe: 2 wds.
13 Elevate
14 Skin (suffix)
15 Bait
17 Band's vehicle, often
18 ____ Lanka (Asian island nation)
20 "The Faerie Queene" division
22 Traveled over water, in a way
24 Part of Marty Feldman's Igor costume
27 Palatal pendant
28 Amount-and-interval numbers
29 Moore of "Disclosure"
30 Has faith in
31 One over par in golf
33 "... seen nothin' ____ "
34 Sun, to Domingo
36 Bridge positions
38 Beyond's partner
40 Good thing to buy in Monopoly
43 Loudness units
44 Alpha's opposite
45 Maze wall, sometimes
46 Brit's service discharge

Down

1 Absorbed, as a loss
2 Deep-____ (get rid of)
3 Pale hair color: 2 wds.
4 Between assignments
5 Order of whales and dolphins
6 Gain some unnecessary weight
7 Crack pilot
8 Body network sending signals: 2 wds.
9 Russian assembly
10 Attention ____
16 Blue
18 Ballistic missile not known for its accuracy
19 Top review
21 Old-school word for "you"
23 A little of this and a little of that
25 Allocate, with "out"
26 "Hey … over here!"
28 Without getting one's footwear wet: hyph.
30 Cha, in England
32 "Silly" birds
34 Obi, e.g.
35 "An ill wind that nobody blows good"
37 Big book
39 ____ out (really relax, in slang)
41 I, to Claudius
42 "Frankenstein" setting

23

Across

1 Sum up, for short
6 Wheat grown as stock feed
11 Love, in Lourdes
12 Beauty pageant wear
13 Low-grade wool
14 Attachment: hyph.
15 Brewski, slangily
17 Perform John Cage's "4'33"," e.g.
18 ___ War
20 Alter a "Life" sentence?
22 Be human, perhaps
23 Journal
26 Al Green, e.g.
27 ___ Today
28 "Gee whiz!"
29 "___: make my day!": 2 wds.
31 Barely get by (with "out")
32 Relate, as a story
33 Brit. tax system, initially
34 Gas leak evidence
36 "___ is the last straw!"
38 Wet, weatherwise
40 Deck out
43 Papal court
44 Commotion
45 Crosswise, on deck
46 Barely visible to the naked eye

Down

1 Ewe's mate
2 "Down under" fowl
3 College of arts
4 Foreshadow
5 Egg on
6 Pilot's announcement, briefly
7 Central vein of a leaf
8 Bespoke: 3 wds.
9 "Aeneid" figure
10 Let off steam, maybe
16 Condiment from the deep: 2 wds.
18 "Lulu" composer
19 Cookie with a "Double Stuf" variety
21 Tennis doubles team, e.g.
23 Face-off
24 Like some Chardonnay
25 "Trick" joint
30 Rupture
33 Arouse, as anger
34 "Free Willy" creature
35 Smear, like paint
37 Bulk
39 It's like a sweet potato
41 Physicist's study
42 ___ into (be nosy about)

24

Across

1 Cutter with a broad blade
4 "20/20" network
7 Aardvark's tidbit
10 Cousin of rage
11 One who plays for a living
12 Anonymous John
13 Calendar abbr.
14 Blood poisoning
16 Heroic poem
18 Asian persimmons
19 Second shot
21 Chemical compound suffix
23 One-eyed, long-bearded Norse god
24 Ten-cent coin
25 "2001" computer
27 Your, in the Bible
29 Salon offering
30 Beers
32 ____ Ham, London suburb
34 Delhi wrap
35 Lacking moral sense
38 Shaving need
40 "Road" film destination
41 General pardon
43 Wine cask
44 Merry mo.
45 "Titanic" actor DiCaprio
46 Like an antique
47 "____ on a Grecian Urn"
48 Eccentric
49 Beam

Down

1 Pointer
2 Hang
3 Non-acceptance of antisocial behavior: 2 wds.
4 Pertinent
5 Full of sorrow: hyph.
6 Hip joint
7 Business manager
8 Harmful
9 ____ Party Nation
15 Managed, with "out"
17 Down
20 Christopher Carson, familiarly
22 Court decision
25 Owns
26 Fearful
28 Thanksgiving side dish
31 Small, medium or large
33 Have a bawl
36 "Be-Bop-____" (1956 Gene Vincent hit): hyph.
37 Swing dance, ____ Hop
39 Munch Museum's locale
41 Time-wasting bother
42 Smallest Hebrew letter

25

Across

1 ____ and seek
5 Murders: sl., 2 wds.
11 "Ain't it the truth!"
12 Ancient ascetic
13 Get rid of pent-up energy: 3 wds.
15 ____ premium: 2 wds.
16 "Love Story" composer Francis
17 ____-Foy, Que.
18 Framework
20 ____ longa, vita brevis
21 2007 Tao Lin novel "Eeeee ____ Eeee"
22 Two, to Otto
23 Rusty of "Make Room for Daddy"
26 Gets bested
27 ____ end (over): 2 wds.
28 Suffix with cash
29 Slowing, in mus.
30 Judge
34 Tire meas.
35 Robert Burns' "The Bonnie ____ Thing"
36 "____ Ng" (They Might Be Giants song)
37 Bay of Naples attraction: 3 wds.
40 Numbers puzzle
41 Big house in Britain
42 Prickly plant
43 IRS identifiers

Down

1 Label for Arab meat dealers
2 "...____ man with seven wives...": 3 wds.
3 Coup ____
4 "Another Green World" composer
5 Scratch up
6 Actor Davis of "Do the Right Thing"
7 "C'____ la vie!"
8 Goes up and Down
9 Hanging out up high, like a bird: 3 wds.
10 Batman, to the Joker
14 Ace
19 Adolescent
22 Japanese thonged sandal
23 One pulling strings?
24 Under debate: 2 wds.
25 "Waltzing ____"
26 Mountain Community of the Tejon Pass, Calif.
28 Angry
30 Began to stir
31 ____ bar
32 "____: The Smartest Guys in the Room" (2006 documentary)
33 Berates
38 Aurora, to the Greeks
39 Mukasey and Ashcroft, for short

26

Across

1 Mine roof prop
6 Starchy foodstuff used in making puddings
10 Beauty queens' crowns
12 Flamboyance
13 With hands on hips
14 Theater section
15 Craving
16 But
18 Random wreckage
21 Au courant
23 Towards the back, on a ship
26 Creature fought by Harry Potter
27 Cries of sorrow and grief
29 Navigator's need
30 Rider's foot support
32 Syndicate
33 Italian sausage
36 Mischievous one
39 Birthright-for-pottage trader
40 ___ Babies (popular dolls)
43 Conclusion starter
44 First-born
45 Jekyll's alter ego
46 Customs

Down

1 Dog command
2 ___'s Peak, one of Colorado's 53 fourteeners
3 It can fall from the sky
4 Coat part
5 Go on and on
6 Exchanges for money
7 Cream additive
8 Comedian's stock
9 Singles
11 Becomes unpleasant
17 Birdbrain
19 Moray, e.g.
20 Certain fir
21 Cash dispenser, initially
22 Car grille protector
23 Frequent flier
24 Bird ___
25 80 minims: abbr.
28 "___ you joking?"
31 Cheyenne, Chippewa or Cherokee
32 Reason
33 Actor Green of the "Austin Powers" series
34 Far from ruddy
35 Extol
37 ___-en-scène
38 Animals at home
41 "Slippery" tree
42 Shakespeare's "Much ___ About Nothing"

27

Across

1 Put into words
4 "Come at me, ___" ("Jersey Shore" tag line)
7 Dirty digs
10 It's cold, regardless of climate
11 Church title, for short
12 It's Japanese for "carp"
13 Compensation
16 In a cool manner
17 Protection in a secure place
23 Music Appreciation, for one
24 Exodus commemoration
25 "American Gladiators" co-host Laila
26 Bitter feeling
27 Connections
30 Heat source
32 Expected hopefully
34 Contents of some cartridges
35 Noisy quarrel
41 Round, green vegetable
42 Blackguard
43 "___, four, six, eight, who do we appreciate?"
44 Element in a "Wizard of Oz" character's name
45 Brief time periods
46 Undertake, with "out"

Down

1 "Dear" one
2 Trick taker, often
3 "Amen!"
4 Building blocks
5 Adjust, as laces
6 Small eggs
7 Compete in the Winter Olympics, maybe
8 "___ bad!"
9 Yang's counterpart, to the Chinese
14 Associations
15 Label A or B, e.g.
17 La ___
18 Beat: 2 wds.
19 Get the vapors and fall Down
20 Dostoyevsky novel, with "The"
21 Audacity
22 Midas's undoing
28 Charlie Brown had trouble flying one
29 Burn
30 Catches, in a way
31 Bakery buy
33 Rack up, as debt
35 Quick, as a pupil
36 "Fantasy Island" neckwear
37 "Baywatch" complexion
38 Of a thing
39 "I ___ you one"
40 "___ a chance"

28

Across

1 Church service
5 Figures of speech
11 ____ du jour (dish of the day)
12 Hardly, if ever
13 Angel's headwear
14 Call for
15 Common chord
17 One with a beat
18 Creatures from outer space
20 Fractional ending
21 Give a bad review to
22 Instinctive
24 Artist's asset
25 Bobby of Boston Bruins fame
26 86,400 seconds
29 Oolong, for one
30 Choler
31 Curative waters locale
34 Computer devices: hyph.
36 Spring Break souvenir, maybe
37 Absolute
38 Mom's sister
40 Drone, e.g.
43 Milk and water, e.g.
44 Mosque V.I.P.
45 Boneless piece of fish
46 Forbidden: var.

Down

1 Dashboard inits.
2 Montgomery is its cap.
3 Soup cracker
4 Target, for one
5 Pirate hoard: 2 wds.
6 "We the Living" author Ayn
7 Food scrap
8 Christmas wish, for many
9 "Four Quartets" poet
10 Imaginary spirit of the air
16 Bullion unit
18 Gibbon, for one
19 Ballad
23 Business
26 Miniature 3D scene with figures
27 Chair part
28 "Without a doubt!"
31 Employees
32 St. ____ Girl, Beck's Brewery offering
33 Make void, as a marriage
35 Send, as payment
37 Fries, often
39 "Shop ____ you drop"
41 DNA testing facility
42 Ostrich look-alike

29

Across

1 Boom box abbr.
4 Barcelona bear
7 Sarah Palin, e.g.
9 Baltic or Bering
12 Like a gridiron
13 "Fantastic Mr. Fox" director Anderson
14 "Damages" actor Donovan
15 High-priority
17 More sore
19 Zap
20 "Idylls of the King" character
21 "Joy of Cooking" instruction
22 700 to Nero
24 "China Beach" setting, in short
26 Wanna-____ (poseurs)
27 Morlock morsels in "The Time Machine"
29 Korea Bay feeder
31 Butts
32 Caught
35 Breakfast cereal
37 French girl, briefly
38 Tally (up)
39 Hardest on the eyes
41 "Law," in Spanish
42 Destroy
43 "Quietly Brilliant" phone company letters
44 Orlando to Miami dir.

Down

1 Gozo Island is part of it
2 ____ artery
3 "Cut the jokes!": 3 wds.
4 River to the Volga
5 "____ at the movies": 2 wds.
6 Dilly
8 Greet and seat: 2 wds.
9 Drip with fear: 2 wds.
10 Minuscule: var.
11 Common flowers
16 Fast sports cars, for short
18 "… ____ Berliner"
22 Skin-related
23 Composer Debussy
25 Baby goat sound
28 Magazine: abbr.
30 55 miles an hour, maybe
33 "Someone ____ America" (1996 film)
34 Raison ____
36 Elbow-bender
40 Anita Brookner's "Hotel du ____"

30

Across

1. Evelyn ___, "Brideshead Revisited" writer
6. Captures via VCR
11. Breathing problem
12. Said rude words
13. Drinker's accident
14. Chubby
15. Two-seater
17. Agitation
18. "The Lord of the Rings" figure
19. Orange tuber
21. Genetic material, initially
22. Grubby guy
24. Loafer doodad
26. Knock: hyph.
28. Musket accessory
30. Guinea pigs, maybe
33. Historical period, or a detergent brand
34. Elephant's weight, maybe
36. Character used in density
37. "Hamlet" has five
39. ___ coaster
41. Posts
43. Bring up, as a child
44. Brief stanza
45. Cooper cars
46. Oceanic abysses
47. Anxiety

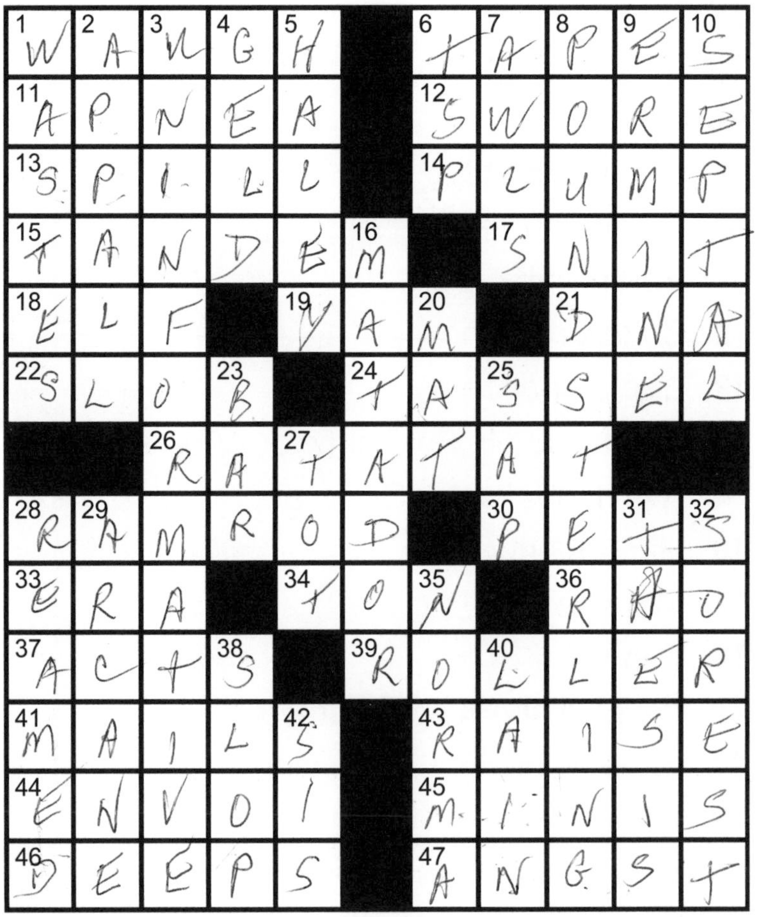

Down

1. Doesn't use
2. Horrify
3. Giving few or no details
4. Money: Ger.
5. "Roots" writer
6. Prescribed amt., sometimes
7. Bookbinder's tools
8. Brit. currency: 2 wds.
9. Fine fur
10. Of a partition
16. One who accepts charges?
20. "Welcome" site?
23. Place for a drink
25. Drain, as someone's energy
27. "Sesame Street" watcher
28. Didn't just criticize
29. Esoteric
31. Argument
32. Most mad
35. Actress Shearer
38. Food for pigs
40. (Had) reclined
42. Certain sibling, slangily

Grid (handwritten answers):

Row 1: W A U G H | T A P E S
Row 2: A P N E A | S W O R E
Row 3: S P I L L | P L U M P
Row 4: T A N D E M | S N I T
Row 5: E L F | Y A M | D N A
Row 6: S L O B | T A S S E L
Row 7: R A T A T A T
Row 8: R A M R O D | P E T S
Row 9: E R A | T O N | R A T O
Row 10: A C T S | R O L L E R
Row 11: M A I L S | R A I S E
Row 12: E N V O I | M I N I S
Row 13: D E E P S | A N G S T

31

Across

1 Curve shapes
6 Southern lady
11 Biblical possessive
12 ___ flu
13 Big artery
14 Russian-born conductor Koussevitzky
15 Largest city in California: 2 wds.
17 In a cool manner
18 Like hot goods
21 Ponytail locale
25 Bumper sticker letters
26 Catering dispenser
27 Rocky peaks
29 Concealed, like someone's face
32 Spot broadcast, often
34 Inspect with close attention
39 Pamper
40 Israeli statesman, ___ Ben Gurion
41 Ski trail
42 Easel, e.g.
43 Chipped in some chips
44 How lemonade tastes

Down

1 And others, for short: 2 wds.
2 "Out!"
3 Knights' titles
4 Consist of
5 Rap session?
6 Swiss city
7 "Brideshead Revisited" author, ___ Waugh
8 Former capital of Italy?
9 Falls behind
10 Denver to Detroit dir.
16 Martini ingredient
18 Did nothing
19 "___-te-Ching"
20 Blade
22 Arctic diving bird
23 Grand ___, Nova Scotia
24 Armageddon
28 Fairy
29 Clever comment
30 During
31 Beethoven's "Moonlight ___"
33 Made a decision, as a judge
34 "Wheel of Fortune" choice
35 Dealer's price
36 First tsar of Russia 1547–84
37 Animation
38 Boating hazard
39 Place for a manicure or a massage

32

Across

1 Not quick to catch on: var.
5 Proprietors
11 ___-bodied
12 Abominate
13 Follow-up injection: 2 wds.
15 Elderly spinster: 2 wds.
16 Discover
21 Machine's sound
25 Aquarium fish
26 "___ Man of Constant Sorrow": 3 wds.
27 German John
28 Blue cartoon figure
30 Helpers: abbr.
31 Kind of penguin
33 "Eureka!": 3 wds.
38 Modern breakfast food: 2 wds.
42 Gentle wind
43 Cottontail's tail
44 They're boring
45 Hardy character

Down

1 Actress Olivia
2 Ancient Greek coin
3 Slog
4 Subservient response: 2 wds.
5 Fatty liquid
6 Expressed
7 "If I Ruled the World" rapper
8 Addis Ababa's land: abbr.
9 Plato's "P"
10 6-3 or 6-4, in tennis
14 Bull: prefix
17 Contented sighs
18 Cell messenger letters
19 Hair colorer
20 "Bonanza" brother
21 Smart and seasoned
22 Gold medalist in gymnastics at the 2004 Olympics
23 "It's my turn!": 2 wds.
24 Choice
29 Architectural feature
30 Egyptian, often
32 "But of course!": 2 wds.
34 Expansive
35 "___ homo"
36 Notes for those in debt, initially
37 Some explosives, initially
38 Cable inits.
39 Coffee holder
40 Classic car
41 "___-plunk"

33

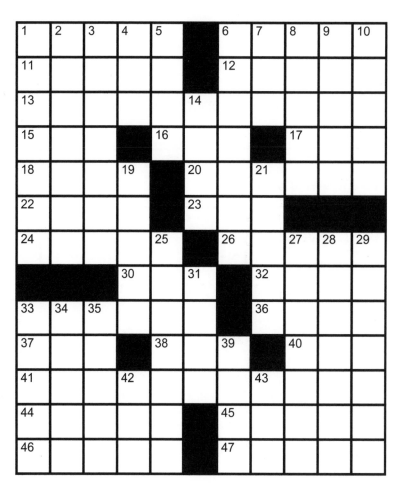

Across

1 Cornrow's place
6 Proto or ecto suffix
11 Dearest
12 From now onward
13 Performer
15 Bar stock
16 Big part of a hare
17 Black cuckoo
18 Anderson and Bowersox
20 Medicinal pill
22 Coil of thread
23 Peruvian money
24 Assassinated
26 Brought on board
30 Knock off
32 All's alternative
33 Carved figure
36 Mouthful
37 Close one
38 Double-crosser
40 "Yes, ___!"
41 Resourceful, enterprising
44 Era
45 Hair for lions
46 A deadly sin
47 "Keep Out" and "Danger"

Down

1 Arab chiefs: var.
2 Hide
3 Bug part
4 Bruce of martial arts
5 Combustible heap
6 Ruler in ancient Egypt
7 It's made of flowers in Hawaii
8 One year's record
9 Embarrassing public fight
10 ___ badge (boy scout's award)
14 Makes lace
19 Tutu, for one
21 Flashy jewelry, slangily
25 Feed
27 Stirring up
28 Animate
29 Bring down
31 Seed in a pod
33 Meat skewers
34 Dravidian language
35 "Remember the ___!"
39 Highland toppers
42 Come into possession of
43 ___ chi (martial art)

34

Across

1 "Brandenburg Concertos" composer
5 Ride, so to speak
11 Begrimed with soot
12 "Lawrence of ___"
13 Command
14 Converted, in a way
15 Animal house?
16 Amount in a Brylcreem slogan
17 Fall tool
19 Doctrines
23 Getting blocked with fine sand
26 "Stupid ___ Tricks" (Letterman bit)
27 Less cordial
28 Built round?
30 Big brute
31 Patella
33 C, for one
35 Fungal spore sacs
36 Bon ___
38 Boys
41 Elk
44 A little of this and a little of that dish
45 City north of Lisbon, Portugal
46 Arm bone
47 ___ Rockefeller, vice president under Ford
48 Gray remover, perhaps

Down

1 Event attended by Cinderella
2 Floating, perhaps
3 One way to get up a mountain
4 Supply water
5 Gel
6 Carpet layer's calculation
7 Browning's Ben Ezra, e.g.
8 Blood-typing letters
9 "Can I help you, ___?"
10 ___ Juan, P.R.
18 "Star Trek" captain
20 In particular
21 Elevated flat top, or an Arizona city
22 "___ lively!"
23 "Da Vinci Code" priory
24 U.N. flight agency
25 Says, to a teen
29 Make less visible, old-style
32 Land
34 Eastern V.I.P.s
37 "Beetle Bailey" barker
39 Banquet
40 Go paragliding, say
41 Came in first
42 Class clown, often
43 Party planner, for short?

35

Across

1 Heckler's hoot
4 Country rtes.
7 Lawyer's gp.
10 Wine: prefix
11 Ample shoe width
12 "___ wise guy, eh?": 2 wds.
13 One tenth of a sen
14 Suffix with differ
15 Kind of camera, initially
16 Hawaii
19 Variety, as of an animal
20 Protective garment
23 Harder to locate
27 "Polythene ___" (Beatles song)
28 Corn holder
29 Ogee shapes
32 Bridges
34 "Blame It on Me" singer Davis
36 Drink made with cream of coconut and rum: 2 wds.
41 "___ for apple": 2 wds.
42 Alt. spelling
43 Block
44 Emeritus: abbr.
45 Before, for Burns
46 Super Bowl highlights, for many
47 Parts of finan. portfolios
48 Certain sibling, affectionately
49 Pollen carrier

Down

1 When doubled, a South Pacific island
2 Eye, to Pierre
3 "Step ___ pets" (popular palindrome): 2 wds.
4 Win back, as trust
5 Heavy, like bread
6 Irish ___ (breed of dog)
7 ___ prof.
8 Tree trunk
9 Rhine feeder
17 "Curb Your Enthusiasm" network
18 Holly Hunter in "The Piano"
20 Gorilla, e.g.
21 Dance step
22 Real estate ad abbr.
24 Camcorder brand letters
25 Long, long time
26 Tony Dorsett, John Riggins, etc.
30 Suffix with Jacob
31 Breaks one's back
32 Sleeping sounds
33 Cohort
35 Some mites
36 Motley
37 Adherents: suffix
38 Basic verse option
39 Miami-___ County
40 "As I Lay Dying" father
41 ___ welder

36

Across

1 "Big ____" (Notorious B.I.G. hit)
6 Son of Jacob and Zilpah
11 "The Little Mermaid" mermaid
12 Fifth wheel
13 Embroidery on canvas
15 Carbonated quaff
16 Hidden
17 Distort
19 Bar
22 Approached the bench?
25 Reform-minded
28 Congressional measure
29 Couch
30 Harness racer
32 "____ Street" (famous kids' show)
35 Europe's most active volcano
39 Dread, misgiving
41 Buenos ____
42 All-too-public tiff
43 Chicago's NFL team
44 Chronic nag

Down

1 Balance parts
2 ____ balls (chocolate covered treats)
3 ____ Piper
4 Educator
5 "Is that ____?"
6 In accordance with: 2 wds.
7 Go bad
8 Hearty hello
9 Coastal flyer
10 Given up working: abbr.
14 Disappeared gradually
18 Oslo's country: abbr.
19 Feature of a nice hotel
20 Leap across a gap, electrically
21 "Thanks a ____!"
22 Be in session
23 Many a D.C. road
24 Ball raiser
26 "It's right over there!"
27 Duration
30 "____ or plastic?"
31 Awry
32 "I'll take a ____ at it"
33 Northernmost Pennsylvania county
34 It comes twice after "Que" in a song
36 Layer, as of a wedding cake
37 "With malice toward ____ …" (Lincoln)
38 "I Found ____ Baby": 2 wds.
40 Onager, e.g.

37

Across

1 Musical "repeat" sign
6 Homes for doves
11 Roots used in the Hawaiian dish poi
12 "Two Women" star
13 Golf bag items
14 Midwest hub
15 Modern-sounding creature?
16 Letters seen in red, white and blue
18 Old style "For shame!"
19 Door sign
20 Arctic bird
21 Casbah headgear
22 Venomous snakes
24 Not looking good, to say the least
25 What a crossword clue might be
27 A lot of ice
29 Puts up
32 Director ___ Howard
33 Hereditary material, initially
34 Actor Holm
35 "Them!" creature
36 Bizarre
37 Bar order
38 Compassion
40 Cry of surrender
42 Leave via ladder, maybe
43 Amber or umber
44 Singer Bob
45 Decorative jugs

Down

1 Bad mark
2 Made, as money
3 "___ to Major Tom …" Bowie line
4 ___ compos mentis
5 Urn for bones
6 Disguise
7 "Amazing!"
8 Road junction with a central island: 2 wds.
9 More inexplicable
10 Need a tissue
17 Dangle, hang
23 "___ Time transfigured me": Yeats
24 Boneshaker's cube
26 Slander
27 Incriminated, set up
28 Deserted
30 Former U.S. president Zachary
31 Bad looks
33 Experienced leader
39 Bean counter, for short
41 "Right this instant!"

38

Across

1 Dads
6 Bamm-Bamm's foursome
9 Circulatory chamber
11 Apple product
12 Cooking fuel
13 Bag of chips, maybe
14 Bill collector?
15 Hot Wheels toy company
17 Asia's Trans ___ mountains
18 Fortune 500 company based in Moline, Ill.
19 Cut, as a log
20 Desperate: 2 wds.
21 Big pitchers for water
23 Hebrew letters
26 Bavarian river
30 CB, for one
31 Batmobile "garage"
32 Marcos of the Philippines
34 Counterfeiters' nemeses: hyph.
35 Prefix with -phile
36 Damon, to Pythias
38 Agitated state
39 Taoism founder: hyph.
40 Non-Rx, initially
41 ___ more (several): 2 wds.

Down

1 Tortellini, rigatoni, etc.
2 ___ the Hun
3 Like some undergrad studies
4 Bad job for an acrophobe: 2 wds.
5 Closest star to Earth, with "the"
6 Acted badly
7 Capital of Lesotho
8 Drag
10 ___-and-pop store
11 Meeting place
16 It's after Shebat
20 "___ a Liar" (song by the Bee Gees)
22 "___ I Be?" Shrek song
23 Melodic
24 Keen
25 Blissful
27 Reproductive cell
28 "Be that as it may…": 2 wds.
29 Furnish
33 I.W.W. rival
37 P.V. Narasimha ___, 1990s Indian P.M.

39

Across

1 Kuwaiti, e.g.
5 Come-ons
11 1995 earthquake city
12 Tired person's utterance: 2 wds.
13 Emphatic type: abbr.
14 Blue
15 Vintner's prefix
16 Bass, e.g.
17 "Rebecca of Sunnybrook Farm" director Allan
19 Home of four ACC teams: abbr., 2 wds.
23 Ranch add-on
25 Milan opera house: 2 wds.
27 Hawaiian porch
29 Race of Norse gods
30 More lithe
32 "Get it?"
33 ___ -de-camp
34 Angelou or Lin
36 Univ. in Troy, N.Y.
38 ___ 'acte
41 Dr. Seuss egg hatcher
44 "Zip-___-Doo-Dah"
45 "Remington ___" (1980s show)
46 Way around London, once
47 Frozen cause of water blockage: 2 wds.
48 "The Odd Couple" director

Down

1 Sony co-founder Morita
2 Automatic
3 Left
4 In steerage, say
5 European capital
6 Actor Jannings
7 Lack
8 Et ___ (and the following): abbr.
9 ___ Claire, Wis.
10 ___-Anne-des-Plaines, Quebec
18 Came down to earth
20 Daughter of the Trojan king Priam
21 "I cannot tell ___": 2 wds.
22 Like the first issue of "Action Comics"
23 "Born Free" lioness
24 First name in raga
26 "___ Smile" (1976 hit)
28 Gave a heads-up to
31 "8 Mile" actor
35 "Sailing to Byzantium" poet
37 Silents star Negri
39 Deck material
40 Radiation dosages
41 Fu-___ (legendary Chinese sage)
42 Stock page heading, initially
43 Riddle-me-___ (rhyme)

40

Across

1 Main stem of a tree
5 Struck
10 Call from the flock
11 Avid
12 Book that has been bought by many people
14 Disturb the composure of
15 U.S. medical research agcy.
16 Increase, with "up"
20 Canceled, as of a correction or deletion
24 Speed along
25 Montezuma, e.g.
26 Accustom (to)
28 Cool
29 Iodine, chrlorine, or bromine, e.g.
31 Radio and Disco, e.g.
33 Go for the gold?
34 Terminates a debate by calling for a vote
39 Way to get rid of second-hand goods: 2 wds.
41 Plant used in the making of tequila
42 River that flows through Hamburg
43 Home of the brave
44 Be a bookworm

Down

1 Hindu title of respect
2 Black cat, to some
3 Amount to make do with
4 Rapprochement
5 Boil
6 Large shopping area
7 Gives the eye
8 Course requirement?
9 Foul up
13 Sew
17 Criminal
18 Ireland, to the Irish
19 Hammer end
20 Out of reach
21 Former Russian ruler: var.
22 Volcano in Sicily
23 Enlarge
27 Teetotaler, e.g.: hyph.
30 Opposite of perigee
32 ___ metal
35 Bathe
36 Rattling sound
37 Island of Napoleon's exile
38 Future flower
39 Gangster's sidearm
40 Lady's secret, perhaps

41

Across

1 Financial newspaper, for short
4 Special effects used in "Avatar," e.g.
7 Fair hiring letters, for short
8 ____ Magnon
9 Chest muscle, for short
12 Aboveboard
14 Make bigger, like a photo: abbr.
15 Algae bed?
16 Fatherland, to Flavius
18 Do away with
20 Those things, in Tijuana
21 ____ Stadium (D.C. United's home)
22 Flightless bird
24 Stores
26 Georgia O'Keeffe Museum city: 2 wds.
28 FDR home loan org.
31 Put up, as a picture
32 Crams
34 "In ____ and out the other": 2 wds.
36 Archeology venue, at times
37 Make sense, with "up"
38 "It's Too Late Now" autobiographer: 3 wds.
40 Scottish novelist Josephine
41 Broke bread
42 A limited number of
43 Sound of satisfaction

Down

1 Niobe, e.g.
2 Start a trip: 2 wds.
3 35th President: 3 wds.
4 New Deal agcy.
5 Henry Fonda film of 1940, with "The": 3 wds.
6 Seat of Allen County, Kan.
9 Arm of the Arabian Sea: 2 wds.
10 Early supercomputer
11 Conflict
13 "High Sierra" actress Lupino
17 Austin of "Knots Landing"
19 Barry Manilow song locale
23 Certain surgeon's "patient"
25 Homeowner's regular pymt.
26 Young hog
27 "Biography" network: 3 wds.
29 "Die Lorelei" poet
30 Good ____: 2 wds.
33 Soft & ____ (Gillette brand)
35 Battery for small devices, initially
39 "I'm not real impressed"

42

Across

1 Boor
4 Window hangings
10 ___ of Evil
12 Aggregate
13 Exec's note
14 Exposure unit?
15 False start?
17 ___ down (sheds weight)
19 Chemistry suffix
22 Louisville Slugger, e.g.
24 Karlsbad, for one
25 "… borrower ___ a lender be"
26 Sartre's "The Transcendence of the ___"
27 Keats's "still unravish'd bride of quietness"
28 Sporty British car, for short
29 Attention
30 "I told you so!"
31 "I get it now!" sounds
32 Before, before
33 Emerson's "Circles," for instance
35 Layers
38 African trip
43 Alpine transport: hyph.
44 Slowly, to a conductor
45 Meager
46 Infatuated with: 2 wds.
47 "Tarzan" star Ron

Down

1 Place for a tent
2 Cancels
3 Place to buy cheap goods: 2 wds.
4 ___ chamber, for deep-sea divers
5 Cell stuff, initially
6 Bank letters
7 Quiche, e.g.
8 Blow one's lines, e.g.
9 View from the deck, perhaps
11 Aretha's genre
16 Neglect
18 Least crazy
19 Delightful
20 Wyle of "ER"
21 Units of energy
22 Answering machine sound
23 Biology lab supply
34 "The Seven Lively ___" (Gilbert Seldes)
36 Detective, at times
37 Ground force
38 Lack muscle tone, perhaps
39 "Without further ___ …"
40 Ardent admirer
41 "The ___ of Innocence"
42 "___ Bravo" (John Wayne film)

43

Across

1 Goes back, like the tide
5 Homeopathy predisposition MIASM
10 Bearded animal
11 Hanna-Barbera cartoon character: hyph.
12 Capital of Norway
13 Eager
14 "The Paris of the Orient"
16 Shepherd's locale
17 Eat or drink quickly or greedily, slangily
21 Great quantity
23 Casa dweller
24 "The Rumble in the Jungle" victor
25 Leaves in a cup
26 "Holy cow!"
29 Externalize, in a way
31 Defeat soundly, in slang
32 PC linkup
33 Picnic sporting event: 2 wds.
37 Strip of meat in a Tex-Mex treat
40 Spin like ___: 2 wds.
41 Charm
42 Be slack-jawed
43 Certain recesses
44 Ultimatum ender

Down

1 Driving forces
2 "Poppycock!"
3 Russian guitar
4 Removed the pits from
5 Bog MORASS
6 Mild antiseptic
7 "How to Succeed in Business Without Really Trying" librettist Burrows
8 Ham, to Noah
9 Witticism
11 Companion of "humbug"
15 Auto-tank filler
18 Before birth
19 Some bucks
20 Brotherhood, for short
21 "___ who?"
22 Cut short
27 Store, as corn
28 Pair seen in winter
29 Animal found in Finland
30 Car house
34 Alley animal
35 Officers
36 Fencing sword
37 Airline overseer, initially
38 Fuse abbreviation
39 Au ___ (served in its own gravy)

44

Across

1 "Concentration" puzzle
6 Word meaning determiner, usually
11 Nitrogen compound
12 Amalgamated
13 In good working order
15 Office computer system
16 Diminish
17 One pill, maybe
20 "C'est la ___!"
22 Tokyo, once
23 Blasted
27 Reflection: 2 wds.
29 "ER" extras
30 Brothers and sisters, e.g.
31 Casual attire
32 Abstain from food
33 Does a hit man's job
36 Light source
38 Frank
43 1,000 kilograms
44 "Gladiator" setting
45 Hard work
46 Good to have around

Down

1 Brit. bombers
2 Australian bird
3 Coal carrier
4 "I give up!"
5 ___ good example: 2 wds.
6 Spaceship, maybe
7 Shaft of light
8 Katmandu's continent
9 Fellow, for short
10 Add a fringe to
14 Scottish city
17 Moore of "G.I. Jane"
18 Chief Norse god
19 Separate by color, say
21 "Under the Net" author Murdoch
23 Hardly the life of the party
24 "We'll ___ kindness yet, for auld lang syne…" (Robert Burns): 2 wds.
25 Auspices
26 Mar, in a way
28 Greek wine
32 "La Traviata" mezzo
33 Chooses, with "for"
34 Course
35 Church, poetically
37 Brightly colored food fish
39 Ball stopper, sometimes
40 "Mad Men" account executive Cosgrove
41 "Parade's ___" (Ford Madox Ford tetralogy)
42 "I'm against the motion"

45

Across

1 Ball girls?
5 Old counter
11 Baseball's Hershiser
12 Everlasting, to the bard
13 Everywhere at once
15 Dabbling duck
16 Comic strip cry
17 ____ the other: 2 wds.
18 Evening hour, in Madrid
19 "____ XING" (street sign)
20 Completely: 2 wds.
23 Peacenik's phrase: 2 wds.
24 Frozen cause of water blockage: 2 wds.
26 AOL alternative
29 Brit. decorations
30 Toothpaste advertised by Bucky Beaver in the 1950s
32 O.T. book, for short
33 Election loser: hyph.
35 Soldier's award
37 Sonnet section
38 Drug carrier across the border
39 Black Sea port
40 "Grand" ice cream maker

Down

1 "Duke of Earl" or "Book of Love," stylistically: hyph.
2 Regal fur
3 On ____ knee (proposing marriage, perhaps)
4 County next to Mayo
5 Prefix with -drome
6 Bingo call: 2 wds.
7 1950s political inits.
8 Tapestry yarn
9 Detach with a hammer's claw
10 Actor Green and author Godin
14 Sentence stopper
18 Big ____, Calif.
21 Dr. Dre's old group
22 Starve
23 Super ____ (GameCube predecessor)
24 Gave out
25 Consisting of large grains or particles
26 Pillage and plunder
27 Tough to comb
28 1598 French edict city
29 Alcoholic, for short
31 Verse, in Paris
33 Some beers
34 "____ smile be your umbrella" (Bing Crosby): 2 wds.
36 Goals, e.g.: abbr.

46

Across

1 Dead, as an engine
6 Emulate a litterbug
11 ____ Jeane Baker (Marilyn Monroe's real name)
12 ____ rhythm, brain waves pattern
13 All thumbs
14 Indemnify
15 Gumshoe, for short
16 More even
18 ____ of Langerhans
20 ____ grass
23 Emulated running mates?
25 "Great" dog
26 Rains hard
27 Post-skiing beverage, for some
28 "____ Street" ("Annie" song)
29 Hawaiian welcomes
30 "Star Trek" rank: abbr.
31 Cold-weather wear
32 ____ pole
34 "La Femme Nikita" network
37 Exceeding
39 Sweater material
41 Corporal punishment inflictor
42 Fixed the pilot
43 In that place
44 What's in, in fashion

Down

1 Jersey, e.g.
2 Top-grade: hyph.
3 Emerald or sapphire, e.g.
4 Short strike caller?
5 Rats
6 Pompous walk
7 "With this ring, I ____ wed"
8 In a reproving manner
9 H, to Homer
10 Kind of station
17 Color on China's flag
19 Active
21 Relative of the buffalo
22 Green and herb, e.g.
23 Foil alternative
24 Advance
25 "Let's Make a Deal" offering
27 Blares
29 Great serve, in tennis
31 About 1.3 cubic yards
33 "One Flew ____ The Cuckoo's Nest" (1975)
35 Agronomy concern
36 A chip, maybe
37 Appear
38 "____, humbug!"
40 Abbr. after some generals' names

47

Across

1 Oscilloscope part, initially
4 Male sheep, in Britain
7 Conned
10 Catalyst for Pinocchio
11 Retrovirus component, initially
12 "___ moment, please"
13 100 percent
14 Pop-ups, usually
15 Blaster, initially
16 Small smoked sausages
18 "I told you so!" laugh
19 Category
20 Blunder
21 Spenders' binges
23 Blood letters
24 Fla. neighbor
25 Fraternity letter
27 Mafia boss
28 Afternoon break, perhaps
29 Fuse unit
31 Degree in math?
32 Hair holder
33 "That's painful!"
34 Kind of gland
37 Cuckoo bird
38 "Flying Down to ___"
39 Big time
40 Elton John, e.g.
41 Dash widths
42 Break a Commandment
43 Cubes in the freezer
44 Conceit
45 Down in the dumps

Down

1 Dog's scratcher
2 Anger
3 Message carrier once: 2 wds.
4 Apprentice
5 Comprehension
6 Antiquated
7 Impetuosity
8 Michegan city: 2 wds.
9 Oust
17 French word before a maiden name
21 Hindu religious mendicant
22 Passionless
26 Type of sweetened sherry
30 Author Edgar Allan ___
32 Ranee's wrap: var.
35 Diva's song
36 About 30% of the earth's surface

48

Across

1 Before, in poetry
4 Former airline letters
7 "Oedipus ___"
8 "To each ___ own"
9 Ending for capital or social
12 Deed
13 Better
15 Collected
17 "I had no ___!"
18 ___ cheese
19 Fire starter
20 What's left
23 ___ gestae
24 Proportionately: 2 wds.
26 Adept
28 Steams up
31 Indy entrant
33 Baikal is the world's deepest
34 Bearded bloomer
35 Began
37 Motor elements
39 Follow
40 Elver's elder
41 "___ dead, Jim" ("Star Trek" line)
42 Ecru, e.g.
43 Bon ___ (witticism)
44 On ___ own terms

Down

1 Desk item
2 Go back, as a hairline
3 Exceptionally good: hyph.
4 "After that …"
5 Beaujolais, e.g.
6 ___ blond
9 Daughter of Nehru: 2 wds.
10 Brouhaha
11 Butchers' offerings
14 Afflict
16 Arabic for "commander"
19 "Nothing is more despicable than respect based on ___" (Camus)
21 Live wire, so to speak
22 Samovar, e.g.
25 A fisherman may spin one
26 Come up, as a subject
27 Bill of fare
29 Barely make: 2 wds.
30 Marsh plants
32 Abbr. on a city limit sign
35 ___ O's (discontinued Post cereal)
36 "Hey there!"
38 Omega, to an electrician

49

Across

1 Mined materials
5 Former Turkish bigwig
10 Habit
11 Lasso
12 "And that's a ____!"
13 Common food, or its color
14 Fingerboard ridge
15 Confederate soldier, for short
16 2007 role for Depp
18 "A Day in the ____": Beatles
22 Kind of monkey
24 Arab bigwig
25 "____ Miss Brooks"
26 Pick, with "for"
28 Con balancer
29 No angel
31 Alcove
33 "If all ____ fails…"
34 Jewish month
35 Dump
37 Great Plains home for an Indian: var.
40 Bandage
43 Contemptible one
44 Charlatan
45 Break
46 Niches with crucifixes
47 Catch a glimpse of

Down

1 "Carmina Burana" composer Carl
2 Big laugh
3 Additional unspecified odds and ends
4 Scraps: hyph.
5 Take off the peel, as an apple
6 Like farmland
7 Absolution cause
8 Appearance-challenged woman
9 Broke bread
11 "Our Father" (Sermon on the Mount, Matthew 6: 9–13): 2 wds.
17 Batman and Robin, say
19 Domineering
20 Christmas trees, often
21 Archer with wings
22 "Harry Potter" garb
23 Throw forcefully
27 "Hazel" cartoonist Key
30 End-of-semester student, often
32 Ranch beasts
36 As an example
38 Spider's sense organ
39 How a slacker sits there
40 Day ____
41 Doo-____ (1950s music style)
42 Beast of burden

50

Across

1 Shot, for short
5 Compliment
9 ____ Tower
11 Claim as one's own, as land
13 Pelvic bones
14 "The Italian Job" actor Michael
15 ____ Grove Village, Ill.
16 Gangster's gun, for short
18 252 wine gallons
19 Bow
20 Before, in poems
21 Native of Benin, Nigeria
22 "Buona ____" (Italian greeting)
24 Depress
26 Level
28 "The ____ of Swat"
30 Ailurophobe's fear
33 "48 ____" (Eddie Murphy movie)
34 Lobster eater's garb, for some reason
36 Definite article word
37 "Go team!"
38 Cold cubes
39 Anger
40 Not fitting
42 Single-master
44 Anatomical sac
45 Metric weight
46 "Laugh-In" segment
47 "Previously owned," in ad-speak

Down

1 Ledger column
2 South African maize plant
3 Porbeagle: 2 wds.
4 "Bobby Hockey"
5 Milky
6 Alicia of "Falcon Crest"
7 Organization of countries set up in 1945: 2 wds.
8 Strip away, as a forest
10 Astute
12 Air component
17 Element #33
23 Behave
25 Elmer, to Bugs
27 Home
28 Poison oak, e.g.
29 Distant planet
31 Seat of power
32 Oozed
35 #1
41 Telekinesis, e.g.
43 "Skip to My ____"

51

Across

1 Slot machine symbol
4 Anatomical pouch
7 Beer variety, initially
8 Creative drive
9 When doubled, a Teletubby
12 Poppy derivatives
14 Breed of dog, for short
15 Puncture sound
16 Blood's partner
17 "A Passage to India" heroine
19 Eyelid maladies
20 "Bleak House" girl
21 Sedate
23 J.J. Pershing's command in W.W. I
24 Different ending?
25 Bleat
28 Auto pioneer Citroën
30 Suffix with Ecuador
31 Actress Anouk
33 Geometric ratios
35 ____-a-brac
36 Art class feedback session, slangily
37 ____ Harbour, Florida
38 Followers of a Chinese philosophy
41 King in Spain
42 Enero to enero
43 "The Raven" author's monogram
44 "Kapow!"
45 Codebreaking arm of govt.

Down

1 High school class, for short
2 Software program, briefly
3 Bring up kids: 3 wds.
4 Reserves: 2 wds.
5 Gets on in years
6 Corporations: abbr.
9 Four-term senator from Texas: 2 wds.
10 Alpine river
11 Shinzo ____, prime minister of Japan
13 Be laid up
16 Volkswagen model
17 Good credit rating letters
18 Ike, initially
19 Where goods are displayed
22 Road crew supply
26 Dental org.
27 Years, to Yves
29 Japanese computer giant, initially
31 Short form, for short
32 "Dies ____"
34 It's three, on some clocks
36 Marriage site in John 2:1–11
38 Bill at a bar
39 Professor's helpers, initially
40 Facial business

52

Across

1 Small meal served with alcoholic drinks
5 Scare
11 "___ Brockovich"
12 More like mortar
13 ___ beans
14 Slow movement, in music
15 Balance sheet item
16 "Cats" showstopper
17 Broadcaster
19 Short-tailed lynx
21 "The Little Red Book" writer
24 Deviation
25 "___ will be done"
27 Supplement (with "to")
28 "… ___ he drove out of sight"
29 Aid to loading a muzzle
31 Hitchcock classic
32 Intolerant
36 Conical tent: var.
39 Zebra, e.g.
40 "Once ___ a time…"
41 Kind of school
42 Captain, e.g.
43 Diminishes
44 Aims

Down

1 Blend
2 "15 miles on the ___ Canal"
3 Country, capital Harare
4 On the mother's side
5 Weapons that spray out burning fuel: hyph.
6 Equestrian
7 Mosque figure
8 "Junk begets junk" (rule in computing, initially)
9 Prince of Wales, e.g.
10 "Iliad" city
18 "Dirty" tattletale
19 "Bon voyage!"
20 Propel, in a way
21 Almond confection
22 "Much ___ About Nothing"
23 Strange
26 Talk and talk and talk
30 Turn red, perhaps
31 Laser printer powder
32 Home, informally
33 Band with the hit "Barbie Girl"
34 Beef cut
35 "The ___ of the Ancient Mariner"
37 Duck's home
38 Signs, as a contract

53

Across

1 Rebels
8 ABC morning show, for short
11 Oath
12 "You dirty ___!"
13 Mole: 2 wds.
15 Holdings
16 Decorative case
17 Angry, with "off"
18 Shaquille of the N.B.A.
19 Group of schools in one area, for short
20 Ape's cousin
22 Infant's illness
23 Anon
26 Dracula, at times
29 Actor Quinn
30 Gem that can be carved
31 Dudley Do-Right's org.
32 ___ dictum
34 Tony Danza sitcom
36 Department of eastern France
37 Accord
38 Marked a ballot, maybe
39 "Guys and Dolls" composer/lyricist Frank

Down

1 Additional data on a news story
2 Non-poetic writing forms
3 Stirred up
4 Fix firmly: var.
5 Bank deposit?
6 Mexican men, colloquially
7 "Twenty Thousand Leagues Under the ___"
8 Humperdinck heroine
9 Owner's guidebook
10 Emperor who died on his wedding night
14 Photo finish?
18 At first: abbr.
20 Thug
21 Former name of the cable network Versus, initially
22 Applauds
23 Swab target
24 Fonzie's red-haired pal
25 Dumas's Dantès
26 Marching band sticks
27 "___ Fideles"
28 Less verbose
30 Agrees
32 "Yikes!": 2 wds.
33 Jean Renoir film "La ___ Humaine"
35 Address book no.

54

Across

1 Passbook abbr.
4 WWW pop-ups, e.g.
7 Snow, in Scotland
10 France's Belle-____
11 Cubs play here
12 Half a score
13 Hillshire Brands company: 2 wds.
15 Average: abbr.
16 Go (through), as evidence
17 Break away
19 Foe
21 Heaven's opposite
22 Calendar abbr.
23 Fairy tale figures
26 Maria ____, (1717–80) Archduchess of Austria
28 Criticize maliciously
30 End-of-the-century year
33 Carpenter's wedge
34 Field Marshal of World War II, ____ von Bock
36 Diners
39 Mötley ____ (Nikki Sixx's band)
40 Mil. decoration
41 Part of London that includes the Docklands: 2 wds.
43 Extreme
44 Constellation near Scorpius
45 Pou ____, standing place
46 Carried out
47 "Greetings" org.

Down

1 Put down, slangily
2 "Ishtar" director May
3 Ability to reproduce a musical note accurately: 2 wds.
4 Jewish org. founded in 1913
5 Bad marks
6 Bygone blade
7 Application info: 2 wds.
8 Sewing item
9 Heavenly messengers
14 Cash cache initials
18 Xs to the Greeks
20 River of Belgium
24 Couples, briefly
25 Atoll protector
27 Blood pigment
28 Geopolitical org. that includes The Philippines and Brunei
29 Part of a column between the base and the capital
31 Recites numbers in ascending order
32 Statements of belief
35 Outside: prefix
37 Go through volumes
38 Draped dress
42 Feeling low

55

Across

1 Hack
4 "Rings" found in a tree
7 Available, with "on"
10 Calif., Fla., Ill., etc.
11 Autograph seeker, perhaps
12 "___ Of Destruction"
13 Casual tops: hyph.
15 "Holy smokes!"
16 "I Saw Three Ships Come Sailing In," e.g.
17 A.T.M. need
18 Husky breaths
21 In a fitting way
23 "Surfer," so to speak
24 Eggs, to a scientist
25 Protector on the gridiron: 2 wds.
30 "Dear old" guy
31 Substantial, as a sum
32 Cash or gold coins, e.g.
35 Jenny Lind, e.g.
36 "Aren't you ___ one who always said…"
37 "Hey, what's the big ___?"
39 Once around the track
40 Music genre
44 "Wheel of Fortune" purchase: 2 wds.
45 "Slippery" tree
46 Program, for short
47 Calypso offshoot
48 Caribbean, e.g.
49 Congratulations, of a sort

Down

1 "Stop shooting!"
2 Jesus's mount, in John
3 "A Christmas Carol" outburst
4 Big dos
5 Airplane boarding place
6 Put in irons
7 Act the siren
8 Be of service to
9 Marshall of "Awakenings"
14 Gate-crash
18 Boil fluid
19 Bat wood
20 "The Matrix" role
22 Approaching but not reaching: 2 wds.
24 "That's ___ …"
26 Milky plant fluids
27 Pandowdy, e.g.
28 Annex
29 ___ job
32 Book of maps
33 Meat cut
34 Brownish pigment
35 1965 King arrest site
38 "Over" follower in the first line of "The Caissons Go Rolling Along"
41 Father, to Huck Finn
42 "Fat" farm
43 Decide to leave, with "out"

56

Across

1 Plane store
7 Gallery display
10 God of light
11 Boom or gaff
12 Razor sharpeners
13 "What've you been ___?": 2 wds.
14 Type of gingham
16 Oktoberfest dance
19 "What Am ___ You?" (2004 Norah Jones single): 2 wds.
20 "A Lesson From ___" (play)
21 Lower-level gods in Hinduism and Buddhism
24 It may say "stop" or "yield"
25 Agitate
26 Trunks
28 "Ninotchka" director Lubitsch
29 Pick a candidate, say
30 Former Nigerian capital
31 Good luck charm
34 Accomplished
35 Comfy: 2 wds.
39 Audiotape holder
40 Pressure: 2 wds.
41 Anomalous
42 Attached, in biology

Down

1 Consumes
2 Apropos
3 "…___ a lender be"
4 German percussion instrument
5 Top dogs
6 ___ Parks of the civil rights movement
7 Giving sanction to
8 ___-tat-tat: hyph.
9 2004 Brad Pitt film
11 Below ground
15 ___-Atlantic
16 After the hour
17 Gallimaufry
18 Traded votes in politics
22 In addition
23 Adjusts, as an alarm clock
27 "__ true!"
28 Flying high
31 Poi source
32 Lying, maybe
33 ___ fide (law)
36 Santa ___, California
37 Heavy drinker
38 NYC to Boston dir.

57

Across

1 Invitation request, initially
5 Aquarium owner's bane
10 Safe, on board
11 ____ Field, Mary Todd Lincoln in the 2012 movie "Lincoln"
12 Extensive: hyph.
14 Hook shape
15 Lentil, e.g.
16 Gets on film
18 "____ on Down the Road" ("The Wiz")
22 More, to a minimalist
24 Arrow partner
25 Barter
28 Decrease
30 Costa del ____
31 Baby's first word, maybe
33 Equal
35 Body
39 Beethoven work
41 Balloon filler
42 Labor saver
45 Big-eyed bee
46 Albatross, figuratively
47 Circe, for one
48 "Same time ____ week"

Down

1 Rapid series of short loud sounds
2 Cut drastically, as prices
3 Even-numbered page
4 Hard throw, in baseball
5 Appraise
6 Negligee material
7 Clearing
8 Every little bit
9 Reversible body part, as it were
13 Favor
17 "____ Black Magic"
19 Camel-hair coat
20 Barfly
21 Dolly, for one
23 Indian turnover
25 1/6 fl. oz.
26 Anonymous Wade opponent
27 Microbrew, frequently
29 Block passage through
32 Insight
34 Chopper blade
36 "Common Sense" pamphleteer
37 Crazy Horse, e.g.
38 "Lunar Asparagus" sculptor Max
40 Corn ____
42 Magazine pages, often
43 Altdorf is its capital
44 Heavyweight boxer "Two ____" Tony Galento

58

Across

1 Attired
5 Pirate costume part
11 Apiary feature
12 ____ borealis
13 Bypass
14 "Two ____ don't make a right"
15 Temporary insurance certificates: 2 wds.
17 Hope or community follower
18 "____ through the tulips"
21 Fall gemstone
25 High card, in many games
26 Eggs, to a biologist
27 Grizzly, e.g.
29 Like many nuts
32 Northern Spy, for one
34 Concerned
39 Bookstore section
40 Calcutta coverup
41 Chilling, so to speak: 2 wds.
42 "____ Go Bragh!" (Irish)
43 Fish of the perch family
44 Lobster and beluga products

Down

1 Ice cream flavor, for short
2 Airport pickup
3 Tel ____, Israel
4 Discern
5 Oklahoma Indian
6 Coins featuring Pope Benedict XVI
7 Blue ____, sea cave of Capri
8 "The ____ Ranger"
9 Shifting dunes in deserts such as the Sahara
10 Delight, to a hipster
16 P, to Pythagoras
18 Bar bill
19 Diamonds, to hoods
20 "The Princess and the ____"
22 Beer belly
23 Broadway, e.g.
24 'A Shropshire ____' (A.E. Housman work)
28 Drum sound: hyph.
29 More nimble
30 Amber, e.g.
31 Inferior
33 In itself: 2 wds.
34 Greek letter, or a tiny bit
35 Poetic contraction
36 Hawaiian tuber
37 Pennsylvania city on Presque Isle Bay
38 Rackets
39 Cushion

59

Across

1 Blood component
7 ___ talk
10 Wealth
11 Pivot
12 Sung dramas
13 Container weight
14 Lift
16 Senior person
18 African animal
19 Egghead
23 He shrugged, in an Ayn Rand title
26 Gumdrop flavor
27 Uncertainties
29 Choose (with "for")
30 Due to
33 Alert
36 Western blue flag, e.g.
37 Cooking directions
41 Camera piece
42 Bewitch
43 Account
44 Parti-colored

Down

1 In favor of
2 Griffin Dunne comedy, "___ Service"
3 Serve right on the T, often
4 Bit
5 Breakfast, lunch and dinner
6 Pluses
7 ___ du jour
8 100 cents, sometimes
9 ___-reviewed journals
11 Keep food from
15 Butcher's offering
16 "I'm ___ you!" ("You don't fool me!")
17 "Little" comic strip character
18 "Crikey!"
20 "Famous" cookie guy
21 "Forget it!"
22 Letters that are Wile E. Coyote's undoing, often
24 "The Sound of Music" figure
25 Hasenpfeffer, e.g.
28 Chicken
31 Hippodrome, e.g.
32 Open, as a bottle
33 "___ 'er up!"
34 Sundae topper, perhaps
35 Ali's milieu
38 Dennis the Menace, e.g.
39 Running expert, for short
40 "...I'll be there ___ long" (Cohan lyric)

60

Across

1 Traditional theme, motif
6 Greek portico
10 ___ in (overflowing with)
11 Evil spirit
12 Seat of Greene County, Ohio
13 Became an issue
14 Certain system of highways
16 Turn red or yellow, say
17 Historical periods
20 Maker of chic shades
24 Toothed tool
25 African grazer
26 Before, before
27 Britney of pop
29 ___ moss
30 Supermodel Campbell
32 Restrained
37 Persian Gulf emirate
38 At hand
39 Seed coverings
40 Nigerian language
41 "All ___ are off!"
42 "As You Like It" setting

Down

1 2004 Queen Latifah movie
2 John Irving's "A Prayer for ___ Meany"
3 Breathe hard
4 Some willows
5 Emmy-winning Lewis
6 Got smaller
7 Horn sound
8 Any of three English rivers
9 Drink on draft
11 Rich cake
15 Champion
17 Biblical beast
18 Clothing store, with "The"
19 Green grass eater
21 "Malcolm X" director
22 Geologic time period
23 Anyhow
25 Free
28 Historical records
29 Means of support
31 Chocolate-coffee flavoring
32 Fix, as a medical condition
33 Brief bio, on parting
34 Clear's partner
35 To be, in old Rome
36 Torvill's skating partner
37 Apply gently

61

Across

1 Mideast native
6 "___ sow, so shall…": 2 wds.
10 Ancient: hyph.
12 Code in which many Web pages are written, initially
13 Spicy condiment
14 Circus crowd's sounds
15 "Don't get any funny ___!"
17 Scottish "no"
18 Crash site?
20 Rodrigo Díaz de Vivar: 2 wds.
22 Certain plaintiff, at law
24 Like tears
27 Flip-flop
29 Phone corporation (1984–97)
30 Spanish sirs
32 Earthy prefix
33 "Maria ___" (Jimmy Dorsey #1 hit)
35 Mount Olympus dweller
36 Infomercials, e.g.
38 Well-known knife brand
40 Brainy sort
42 Soap ingredient
45 Fit
46 1924 gold medal swimmer
47 Comic book dog barks
48 Back, in a way

Down

1 Adage
2 Turkish for "lord"
3 Irrational (with worry, grief, etc.): 2 wds.
4 Course
5 "A Delicate Balance" playwright
6 "Bingo!"
7 Acting as a sentinel: 2 wds.
8 Jewish youth org.
9 "Anything ___?"
11 Disappearing phone features
16 Digitize a picture
18 Calls' partner
19 "A Hard Road to Glory" author Arthur
21 ___ Ulyanov, Vladimir Lenin's father
23 Chem. ending
25 Famous fiddler
26 Biblical bk.
28 Kinnear of "The Kennedys"
31 Long-billed wading bird
34 It's marked by a "-" on a battery
36 Eastern pooh-bah
37 "___ me!"
39 "Nana" star Anna
41 "Star Trek: Voyager" character
43 ___ Poke (caramel sucker)
44 Cut, as a tree

62

Across

1 ____ Sorvino, Amy Whelan of "Intruders"
5 Diminish
10 Aces, sometimes
11 Feline crossbreed
12 Sticky fragrant resin of the terebinth tree
14 Pension supplement, for short
15 Concede
16 North African fox
18 Greek and Roman, e.g.
21 Alliance
23 U.N. agcy. concerned with working conditions
24 Brute follower
27 Polynesian rain dances
29 "Die Meistersinger" heroine
30 Ivan the Terrible, for one
32 Goes off course
34 Baroque
38 Gave out
40 Rossini's "La Donna ____ Lago"
41 Item seen in court?: 2 wds.
43 Alleviated
44 Appropriately named fruit
45 Hammock cords
46 Bungle, with "up"

Down

1 Recurring theme
2 Accustom
3 Aired again
4 Death on the Nile cause, perhaps
5 Magnet alloy (trade name)
6 Angler's hope
7 Good at gymnastics, maybe
8 Ivy feature
9 Bard's "before"
13 Hole in your shoe
17 "30 Rock" network
19 C.S.A. state
20 "Rescue me!" letters
22 Sailor's maps
24 Tina of "30 Rock"
25 Egg cells
26 Injustice: 2 wds.
28 Big container
31 Stripes' counterparts, in pool
33 Hearing, taste or touch
35 "Time is money," e.g.
36 Leaks
37 Island in New York Bay
39 For the second time, say
41 Magnum, for one, slangily
42 Work shirker

63

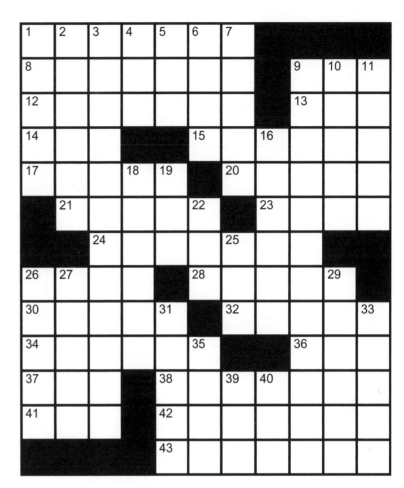

Across

1 Buffaloed: 3 wds.
8 Nut
9 Get down on one's knees
12 Relating to the sole of the foot
13 "Earth Girls ___ Easy" (Julie Brown song)
14 Big success
15 Long vowel mark
17 Greenfly, e.g.
20 Analyze, in a way
21 Fatty secretion
23 Flower fanciers
24 Barely enough
26 Health resorts
28 Blood bank patron
30 Eminent
32 Exposed
34 Come to light
36 African antelope
37 Casbah headgear
38 Composer Aaron
41 Finish, with "up"
42 Property recipient, at law
43 Migratory grasshoppers

Down

1 First letter, to Greeks
2 Dutch export
3 Curse or declare to be evil
4 PC linkup
5 Giant slugger Mel
6 "The King and I" locale
7 Tiny bit, as of food
9 Calliope cousins: 2 wds.
10 Jagged, as a leaf's edge
11 Inheritance, of a sort
16 Beach shelter
18 Wading birds
19 Dark horse
22 Central, in combinations
25 Protesters, sometimes
26 Big mess, slangily
27 Skin openings
29 Milk curdler
31 Sticker on a windshield
33 Bros
35 ___ contendere (court plea)
39 Snapshot, for short
40 Money in Moldova

64

Across

1 Buffalo hockey player
6 Ginger cookies
11 More unwell
12 Apocryphal Old Testament book
13 La ____, Argentinian port
14 Daughter of Juan Carlos I
15 Financial security: 2 wds.
17 Drudges
18 Bull fight matador
21 "Did You Ever ____ Lassie?": 2 wds.
25 Feeling blue
26 Letters on a Cardinal's cap
28 Hemingway's "The Old Man and the ____"
29 Blog feeds, initially
31 Living room piece
33 Ralph of "The Waltons"
35 Machine replacement pieces: 2 wds.
40 Game with numbered balls
41 Helvetica alternative
42 Clinging plants
43 Wedge-shaped bones
44 "Fiddle-____!": 2 wds.
45 Expressionless

Down

1 Onetime football quarterback Brian
2 "It was ____ huge mistake!": 2 wds.
3 "Gil ____" (Alain-René Lesage novel)
4 Enter again, as data
5 Back-to-school purchases
6 Area to the rear
7 At least: 2 wds.
8 As busy as ____: 2 wds.
9 Blood-donation amount
10 Railroad stop: abbr.
16 Hoffman movie of 1982
18 Dungeons & Dragons game co., initially
19 Grp. founded in Bogotá
20 Ave. cousins
22 Extreme ending
23 Shoebox letters
24 Tooth-doctors' org.
27 Allow to overtake: 2 wds.
30 "Way down upon the ____ River…"
32 Attack: 2 wds.
34 Appeared
35 Golfer Ballesteros
36 Handed over money
37 "Little Caesar" role
38 Mountain pool
39 Kill, in the Bible
40 Signal at auction

65

Across

1 Al Capone henchman Frank
6 Encouraged, with "on"
11 Lake Geneva spa
12 Eddy who made money in the 1950s and 1960s
13 Johnston McCulley literary creation
14 Not too hot, like a burner: 2 wds.
15 Sufficient, informally
17 Women, to a buckaroo
18 Bassist Claypool
20 Avatar of Vishnu
22 Acknowledge
24 Calm
28 Player
30 Best Actor of 1958
31 "Just a mo!": 2 wds.
33 "Revenge" getter of film
34 Heavy, durable furniture wood
36 Phone six letters
37 Architect Mies van der ____
40 ____ double take (looked again): 2 wds.
42 "What now?!"
44 Pamplona runners
47 Actress Oberon
48 Attempts
49 Class that doesn't require much studying: 2 wds.
50 "Golden ____" (David Bowie song)

Down

1 ____ Percé
2 Literature Nobelist Andric
3 Dreadfully dull
4 Glacier-formed lake
5 "Peace ____ time"
6 Tokyo, formerly
7 Kipling classic
8 Inaugural ball, e.g.
9 Carbon compound
10 Moistens, in a way
16 Mis followers
18 Titicaca, por ejemplo
19 "____ Almighty" (2007 film)
21 Checkers, e.g.
23 Like some winds
25 Rosary recital: 2 wds.
26 Seabird that can be "sooty"
27 Prefix meaning "within"
29 Riddle-me-____
32 Blackguard
35 Baby cat
37 "Ben Hur" setting
38 Roman "olive"
39 ____ de combat
41 Scale start: 2 wds.
43 Crime-busters' grp.
45 Done, to Donne
46 Barbecue sound

66

Across

1 Geisha's girder
4 Draper of "Mad Men"
7 Pen
9 Golf score
12 Clad
13 ___ Victor
14 20–20, e.g.
15 Shipping hazard, briefly
16 Ad headline
18 Showy flowers
20 Be indisposed
21 Playing marble
22 Poetic palindrome
23 "Honor ___ father"
24 Apprehend
27 Coagulates
29 Make a knot
30 Prearranged situations: hyph.
32 "There is nothing like a ___"
33 Central point
34 Tugboat sound
36 Ortiz, Hilda of 'Ugly Betty'
37 Kind of law
40 "The Fresh Prince of ___-Air"
41 Toward the land: 2 wds.
42 Toil and trouble
43 Angler's catcher

Down

1 Wood sorrel
2 Computerized task performer
3 Highbrow type
4 ___ straits (serious trouble)
5 Short-term affair: hyph., 2 wds.
6 Aussie outlaw Kelly
8 Number of digits on one hand
9 Demonstration
10 A lot of lot
11 Riches preceder, sometimes
15 Small amount
16 Freelancer's enc.
17 Epitome of lightness
19 Sunbeams
21 Above
25 Ability to hit a target
26 Buzzer
28 Neighbor of Ger.
30 Strikebreaker
31 Fish-eating eagle
32 "The lady ___ protest too much"
35 Estimator's phrase: 2 wds.
37 Extinct flightless bird
38 "___ you for real?"
39 Release, with "out"

67

Across

1 Bite-the-bullet type
6 Biting
11 ___ cotta
12 "Dream ___" (1959 Bobby Darin hit)
13 American dogwood: red ___
14 Cover, in a way
15 All-purpose truck, for short
16 Bass, for one
18 Animal that says "moo"
19 Discussion
21 "What's the ___?"
22 Fond du ___, Wis.
23 Act
24 Norway and Germany, for example
27 Bring tranquility to
28 Ring bearer, maybe
29 "… hmm"
30 From England, Wales, or Scotland, e.g.
34 Alter, in a way
35 Bob Newhart, as Dick Loudon, ran one
36 ___-eyed
37 Mom's relative
39 Spherical objects
41 Less emotional
42 Double-S curves
43 Gives advice
44 Not better

Down

1 Basin for holy water
2 Head, in Italy
3 Architectural projection
4 Bad thing to raise
5 Parade
6 Birch relative
7 ___ anglais (English horn)
8 One leaving before a storm
9 Uses a couch, maybe
10 Like tea
17 Stand
20 Booster, perhaps
23 Embarrassing info, to the tabloids
24 Fall in pitch of the voice
25 Elderly spinster: 2 wds.
26 Colorful arc seen after a storm
27 Estate sharer
30 Coffin holders
31 Do-nothing
32 They're underfoot
33 "Demian" author
38 Tiger's start, in two different ways
40 "Give it ___!"

68

Across

1. Functions
6. Assist in a crisis, with "out"
10. Farewells
12. "___ and the King of Siam"
13. Presenting in a new way
15. H.S. class
16. Be entertaining
19. Crown
23. George W., to George
24. In layers
26. Cooking gadgets, e.g.
29. Easy to don shoe: hyph.
30. Pull behind, as a boat
31. Delight, slangily
32. Adhesive
34. Building-blocks name
36. Creeping shrub of eastern North America
43. Graphical user interface feature
44. French cake
45. 2012 presidential candidate Gingrich
46. Remove further material from (a movie)

Down

1. Armed conflict
2. Thomas Hood's "Autumn," e.g.
3. "Let 'er ___!"
4. "Ode to a Nightingale" poet
5. Bolivian capital
6. Grocery store container
7. "Wheel of Fortune" request: 2 wds.
8. Setting for TV's "Newhart"
9. Fall behind
11. Enjoy the Alps, maybe
14. "Not ___!"
16. Says "When?"
17. Slaves
18. Sammy Kaye's "___ Tomorrow"
20. Cathedral fixture
21. Daughter of Mnemosyne
22. Canon competitor
24. King's equal in blackjack
25. Wet, as morning grass
27. Tax pro, for short
28. Argument settler, often
32. Actress Samantha
33. ___-cochere (carriage entrance)
35. Energy unit
36. Acquire
37. Bar stock
38. At once
39. Blaster, initially
40. Common Market inits., once
41. Évian, e.g.
42. Big devotee

69

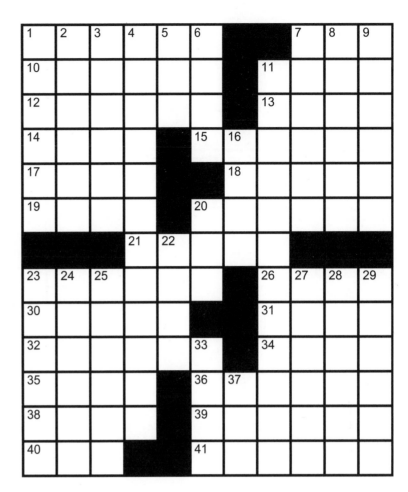

Across

1 Criticizes harshly or violently

7 Some Heisman Trophy winners, initially

10 Lean against: 2 wds.

11 Fuel in Ireland

12 Ancient meeting places

13 90 degrees from norte

14 Boy, to his madre

15 Heir's concern

17 Finish off: 2 wds.

18 Conger catcher

19 Fly in the ointment

20 Kitchen gadgets

21 Jumps (out)

23 Boxers' warnings

26 Those things in Tijuana

30 1988 Olympics locale

31 Cabbage

32 Familiarize

34 Trevi filler, once

35 Complete: 3 wds.

36 Mario Puzo best seller

38 Be defeated

39 Look over again, as an article

40 ___-Cat (winter vehicle)

41 Determine

Down

1 Uses a hot iron, as on cattle

2 Host

3 Tone deafness

4 6 on the Beaufort Scale: 2 wds.

5 ___ fault (overly): 2 wds.

6 Old dagger

7 Secondhand transaction

8 One up

9 Beef on the hoof

11 "Pink Panther" actor: 2 wds.

16 Close, as an envelope

20 Table-shaped Greek letters

22 Actor Rickman in "Harry Potter and the Sorcerer's Stone"

23 Oslo toasts

24 Ed of "The Honeymooners"

25 Melodic passage

27 Evening do

28 Main arteries

29 Places

33 When said three times, a W.W. II film

37 My, in Marseilles

70

Across

1 Taking part in a game: 2 wds.
7 100 lb. units
11 ___ oil (cologne ingredient)
12 Guitarist Phil
13 Drift off
14 Sitar music
15 ___ room
16 Ancient
18 North Carolina capital: abbr.
19 Go-aheads
21 "Raging Bull" star
23 Wishy-___
25 Two hrs. to midnight: 2 wds.
26 Figure out
27 S.A. country
28 Passover month
30 Bread for breakfast
33 Heads off
35 Fast fliers, initially
36 Damage or deface
37 Cut ___ paste
39 Collected
40 One of the deadly sins
42 More chichi
44 Furniture chain
45 Stew cooked in a shallow pan
46 Wyndham Lewis novel
47 "Sophie's Choice" Oscar winner

Down

1 ___ Lloyd Webber
2 Mother ___
3 Writ deliverer: 2 wds.
4 Depressed
5 Not to mention
6 Highway sign
7 Jelmar product, initially
8 Grinning: 3 wds.
9 John Irving hero: inits., 2 wds.
10 Hebrew "peace"
17 Coup ___
20 Fleece
22 Peter and Franco
24 Buttinsky
28 "I'll do anything!": 2 wds.
29 Trump daughter
31 Writer Shelby
32 Woman's shoe: hyph.
34 Cracks sharply
38 "Fiddlesticks!"
41 Shostakovich's "Babi ___" Symphony
43 Dutch painter Gerard ___ Borch

71

Across

1 Common connector
4 Little troublemaker
7 Elvis's record label, initially
10 Nuclear plant building
12 Curved shape
13 Surrender of a person from one country to another
15 Appropriate
16 Large house
17 Hints, warnings
19 Declassify
22 Old Chinese money
24 Baby food
25 Forty winks
27 Soapmaker's need
28 Animal fat
30 Cell centers
32 Two-wheeled vehicle
34 "I've Got My Mind ___ You," George Harrison song: 2 wds.
35 Move, in a way
39 Be involved in
41 Athenian vowel
42 French writer of novels about women
43 "Runaway" singer Shannon
44 Maa in "Babe"
45 Brick-carrying trough

Down

1 Mars, to the Greeks
2 Dismissive call
3 Anniversary, e.g.
4 Language spoken in Florence
5 "The ___ Squad" TV series of 1968–73
6 Awesome, in slang
7 Annual climatological statistic
8 Type of squint: hyph.
9 Face cream target
11 Box
14 1920s chief justice
18 Garden store purchase
19 "What Can Brown Do For You?" company
20 Revolt
21 Phantom
23 Flowers around your neck, in Hawaii
26 Childish
29 Honk the horn
31 Brunch serving
33 Where a skater likes to be: 2 wds.
34 Hightailed it
36 Approach
37 Sgt. Snorkel's bulldog in "Beetle Bailey"
38 Began, with "off"
40 Bully

72

Across

1 Central, in combinations
4 Bikini top
7 ____-Wan Kenobi (Alec Guinness role)
8 Ballad ending
9 Ashen
12 Book, as a table in a restaurant
14 Fuss, in a Shakespeare title
15 Gasket used to seal a joint against high pressure: hyph.
16 Lit
18 ____ function
19 Creole cuisine staple
20 "Dig in!"
21 Lot
24 Jubilance
26 Asian shrines
28 Neon, e.g.
31 Color from the French for "unbleached"
32 Invitation request, initially
33 Begin
35 ____ nut
36 Day care candidate
37 Canned fish
39 Galena or bauxite
40 Become better, like cheddar
41 Act as a prompter
42 Pistol, slangily
43 Jennings of "Jeopardy!" fame

Down

1 Down in the dumps
2 1968 James Michener novel
3 Fall to pieces
4 Ice in the sea
5 Gun, as the engine
6 Length times width, for a square
9 Aid to getting along: 2 wds.
10 Bejewel, e.g.
11 Not at all: 2 wds.
13 Organic suffix
17 Head for: 2 wds.
21 Family man
22 Flight board letters
23 "Pretty sneaky, ____" (line from an old ad for the game Connect Four)
25 Scowl
26 Basil sauce
27 Tom Cruise or John Travolta
29 Park, for one
30 Immune system organ
32 Color in Russia's flag
34 Former ruler of Russia
35 Raised, as steer
38 Long ____ (way back when)

73

Across

1 British Commonwealth member
6 Equal, in Marseilles
10 Civil rights org.
11 Chip's chum, in cartoons
12 O.K.
14 Mets and Marlins div.
15 "I Should've Known" singer Mann
16 Dadaist artists Jean and Hans
17 Celtic sea god
20 Cores
23 "Yo Gabba Gabba!" character
24 ____ Fugard, playwright who works include "Blood Knot"
25 Asian antelope
26 Criminal, to a cop: abbr.
27 To the center
28 Fed. support benefit
29 Pierre's evening
30 Trick intended to deceive: hyph.
32 Albanian currency
35 Mass of air surrounding the Earth
37 Area around the altar of a church
38 Insignificant, slangily
39 Online tech news resource
40 Milk dispensers

Down

1 ____ uproar: 2 wds.
2 Salt, in chemistry class
3 Small river fish
4 Cap material?
5 Dress
6 Some Dutch cheeses
7 "Welcome Back, Kotter" star Kaplan
8 Christian chant
9 Arlington owner
13 Great Plains home for an Indian: var.
16 Crooked
18 Mech. whiz
19 Path
20 Downtimes for toddlers
21 Versatile vehicles, briefly
22 Baptize
23 Bryn ____, college in Pennsylvania
25 Scrap
27 Promises to pay, initially
29 Brown fur
31 One-named supermodel
32 River through Yakutsk
33 Formerly, in olden days
34 Lock unlockers
35 First three of 26
36 "____ Haw"

74

Across

1 Thresher shark
7 "My gal" of song
10 Six-headed monster from the "Odyssey"
11 Accra money
12 Good news from a forecaster, often: 2 wds.
13 One of five Norwegian kings
14 ___ long way (last): 2 wds.
15 "___ Poppins"
16 "Battle Maximus" band
19 Guacamole or fondue
21 Mongolian monk
22 180-degree reversals: hyph.
26 Athlete who won four gold medals at the Berlin Olympics in 1936
28 Lost badly, in slang: 2 wds.
29 Glue alternatives
31 Author O'Brien
32 In good shape
33 Carrot, e.g.
34 De ___ (from the beginning)
37 Rocker Ocasek
39 Korea Bay feeder
40 Baking by-products
44 Abbr. at the end of a list: 2 wds.
45 Walk unsteadily
46 A Chaplin
47 Winter fisherman's tool: 2 wds.

Down

1 Common ID, initially
2 Earth-friendly prefix
3 Birthplace of Robert Burns
4 Basketball call: 2 wds.
5 Miscellany
6 Poetic paradise
7 Actress Ward
8 Hebrew month
9 Augustan historian
11 PC language: 2 wds.
16 Hardly haute cuisine
17 Brass instrument sound: hyph.
18 Home of the Cyclones
20 Tropical fan palm
23 Try, try again
24 Hombre, once
25 "ER" command
27 Tre + tre
30 Low-altitude clouds
34 Humorist Bill and comedian Louis
35 Like Cheerios
36 ___ the Impaler (Dracula prototype)
38 Camaro ___-Z
41 Rx prescribers
42 Near-Miss. state
43 Finalize, with "up"

75

Across

1 Metric weight, casually
5 Regions
10 Certain schs.
12 "___ bleu!"
13 Say over and over: 2 wds.
15 ___ Tafari (Haile Selassie)
16 Matchsticks game
17 ___ Swanson, "Parks and Recreation" boss
18 Sensitive subject, to some
19 Special effects used in "Avatar," e.g.
20 Airport-screening org.
21 Chill
23 Barely passing grades
24 Break down and identify the parts of speech of, as a sentence
26 Tree trunk
29 Smarts
33 Shrinks' org.
34 ___ Lingus (Irish carrier)
35 "Cool"
36 Mauna ___ (extinct volcano)
37 "Science Guy" Bill
38 Mediterranean isl.
39 Shoe with rollers: hyph., 2 wds.
42 Football Hall-of-Famer Greasy ___
43 Like a shoe
44 Common knee stain for kids
45 Trevino and Harper

Down

1 Alex ___, N.F.L. lineman and actor
2 Big chill: 2 wds.
3 Ran out
4 "___ to the West Wind" (Percy Bysshe Shelley)
5 "Me, too": 3 wds.
6 Dust remover
7 Game similar to euchre
8 Melodic
9 Flowering plants of the tropics
11 Holy places
14 Striped quartz used in jewelry: 2 wds.
22 Large, ungainly fellow
23 ___ gratia (by the grace of God)
25 Beat
26 Kind of soda
27 First act
28 Second smallest Teletubby: hyph.
30 Cash register key: 2 wds.
31 Narrow chin-tuft
32 Destroys, in a way
34 Queen ___ lace
40 French pronoun
41 ___ Nidre (Jewish prayer)

76

Across

1 Windshield adjunct
6 According to: 2 wds.
11 Corpulent plus
12 Seine feeder
13 Car dealer's offering
14 Mighty oak maker
15 Cooler
16 Big wine holder
18 Constricting snake
19 Bug-eyed bird
20 Before, to Burns
21 Rocket interceptor, briefly
22 Hog haven
24 Brand of honey: 2 wds.
26 Army rank
28 Buster of silent movie fame
30 Confederate soldier: abbr.
32 "___ be seein' ya!"
33 Not, to a Scot
35 Alliance that includes Ukr.
37 Baseball's Maglie
38 Last, for short
39 Flight coordinators, initially
40 Paces
42 ___ couture
44 Like a haunted house
45 Mary-Kate or Ashley of "Full House"
46 Clothesline alternative
47 Cordwood measure

Down

1 "The Bonfire of the Vanities" author
2 Support group?: hyph.
3 Cheapest seats in a theater, slangily: 2 wds.
4 Serpentine letter
5 "Superman" actor
6 Non-professional
7 Baglike structure
8 Evidence sufficient to warrant an arrest: 2 wds.
9 Attire
10 Handle differently?
17 Magazine
23 Nevertheless
25 Hair may hide it
27 Teetotaler, e.g.: hyph.
28 Touched with the lips
29 Skipjack beetle
31 Acrimonious
34 Character
36 Public row
41 Alternative to cake
43 Cockpit dial: abbr.

77

Across

1 Content fully
5 Flattened at the poles
11 Cookie often eaten with milk
12 Person who loves books
13 Economical
14 Beam
15 Beaver's structure
16 Kind of top
17 Took a mighty cut
19 Sneezy's colleague
22 Performing on stage
24 "I ___ you're happy!"
25 Dish created by Mexican restaurateur Cardini: 2 wds.
27 Put on the payroll
28 Emotionally unavailable type
29 Navy rank: abbr.
30 Habituate
31 Famous pirate Captain William ___
32 Solemn promise
35 Dwell
38 Calf-length skirt
39 Warming device
40 Bit of physics
41 Doctor's ___
42 Baseball field covering

Down

1 Auction cry
2 Community
3 Truckers
4 Many, many years
5 Certain street musicians: hyph.
6 Living thing
7 Caper
8 Elaborate
9 Drive's start
10 Drop the ball
16 Sandwich filler
18 Judicious
19 The sweet life, in Italy: 2 wds.
20 October birthstone
21 Formally surrender
22 Pain in the neck, maybe
23 It may be raised at a party
24 "Aquarius" musical
26 Missile moniker
30 Downy duck
31 Toy with a tail
33 Bouquet
34 Cowardly sort
35 Letter after pi
36 "...all that wealth ___ gave": Gray
37 Heart-wrenching
38 Tangle

78

Across

1 Pick out of a crowd
5 Shimon ___, Israel president
10 "Four Weddings and a Funeral" actor Grant
11 "Carmen," for one
12 Not logical or reasonable
14 Facade
15 Be-bopper
16 Act greedily, perhaps
20 German composer Johannes
23 Coin introduced on 1/1/99
24 W.W. II fliers
25 Clinton, e.g.: abbr.
26 Crusader's kingdom
28 Walk nonchalantly
31 Broadway brightener
32 "The ___ and the Pendulum"
33 Sucker
38 "___ Cowboy" Glen Campbell hit of 1975
40 Hindu social division
41 Boat hands
42 "The Cherry Orchard" playwright Chekhov
43 Dame of the piano

Down

1 Drop off at FedEx Office, perhaps
2 Burmese sound
3 Blackguard
4 Straw roof
5 Dots
6 Heroic poem
7 Go back
8 Cenozoic or Paleozoic
9 Actor Mineo of "Rebel Without a Cause"
13 Cooperative unit
17 Charge
18 Atlas stat
19 Like sardines that are not filleted
20 Breakfast staple
21 Ascot event
22 1960s hairdo
27 Beat the draft?
28 Ovoid organ close to the stomach
29 Bothers
30 Very funny person
34 Catch ___
35 Dermatologist's hole
36 Bills with George Washington on them
37 Church benches
38 Electronics brand, for short
39 "Star Wars" rogue

79

Across

1 State bordering Montana
6 Called balls and strikes
11 Off: 2 wds.
12 Couric of "Today"
13 Beyond the fringe
14 Heavenly prefix
15 National language of Bangladesh
17 "Or ___!"
18 Moves, in real estate jargon
21 What remains after deductions, British style
22 Really inelegant
24 Sporty cars, briefly
25 Dental org.
26 Inc., in Paris
27 Plump
29 Word repeated after "Que," in song
30 Night, in Napoli
31 French city near the English Channel
32 Brewers' needs: 2 wds.
34 No longer in
37 ___ Good Feelings: 2 wds.
39 ___ Kenyatta, Kenyan president
40 Former V.P. Agnew
41 Catch
42 ___ Domingo

Down

1 Rescuer of Odysseus, in myth
2 Two cards of a suit in a hand
3 Bears witness, in court: 2 wds.
4 Large social wasp
5 A thou, slangily: 2 wds.
6 Small guitar
7 Henner of "Taxi"
8 Class-conscious grp.
9 "Ich bin ___ Berliner"
10 "In excelsis ___"
16 2000s CBS show "Joan of ___"
17 MIT grad, perhaps
19 Not for the first time: 2 wds.
20 Vacation destination: 2 wds.
23 Give birth to a lamb, old-style
25 Paid (a debt): 2 wds.
28 Gives voice to
29 Shoe: It.
33 1940s first lady
34 French nobleman
35 U.S./Canadian sporting grp. since 1936
36 Your, in Roma
38 Egg ___ yung

80

Across

1 Blue-gray shade
6 Vigor
9 Popeye, e.g.
10 Gold container?
11 "Catch a ___" (Perry Como hit of 1957): 2 wds.
13 Ennoble
14 Altar area
15 ___ up (shredded)
16 Feels sorry for
18 "___ Given Sunday" (Al Pacino film)
19 Vocation
20 Trifled (with)
21 One thing after another
23 Chess pieces
26 Fertilizer
27 Deadly poison
28 Units of electrical resistance
29 Animal that's a symbol of China
30 Immensely powerful thermobaric bomb: hyph.
33 Elementary school class
34 Flower used in traditional medicine
35 Put in position, as bricks
36 Levees: var.

Down

1 Pay
2 Charles de Gaulle's birthplace
3 Got off, like a horse
4 Heavy weight
5 Bit of work
6 Savory dish: 2 wds.
7 Pencil end
8 Fathers, to Pierre
9 One who knew the Angles
11 Greek salad cheese
12 Completely filled
16 Check endorser
17 Bothers
19 Coconut fiber
20 Bridge support
21 1943 Bogart film
22 Ill will
23 "Praying" insect
24 Put a stop to
25 In the vicinity of
26 Like some jazz or folk songs
27 Clean
29 Hockey disk
31 Hebrew letter
32 "Hey!," e.g.

81

Across

1 Can't stomach
5 Assails
11 Soon, in a stanza
12 Short sock
13 Popular cocktail
15 Fall from grace
16 Respectful Turkish title
17 In-flight info, for short
18 Grazing expanse
19 Coffee order: abbr.
20 Diffident
21 Completes
23 Collector's goal
25 Hard to stir
27 Jitterbug, e.g.
31 Friend
33 Honeybunch
34 AAA offering
37 D.C. dealmaker
39 English river
40 Russell Cave Natl. Mon. locale
41 Freelancer's enc.
42 Datebook abbr.
43 Tremendous
46 Light wind
47 Bête noire
48 Edible mollusk
49 Downhill racer

Down

1 Troubles
2 Having existed for a very long time
3 Twister
4 Dir. opposite WSW
5 Some IDs
6 Fuming
7 Hit the slopes
8 Little people
9 Choppers, so to speak
10 Digress
14 Card game for two
22 Taste, as soup
24 Small amount
26 Flip
28 Roosevelt's program of reform: 2 wds.
29 Hot pepper
30 Put up
32 Casual shoe
34 Latin dance
35 Relating to a wing
36 Book parts
38 Hawaiian circle
44 Ball stopper
45 "JAG" network

82

Across

1 Actor Lew
6 Big name in brewing
11 High-pitched
12 Posture adopted in hatha yoga
13 Evaluations
15 Boom box abbr.
16 Chinese brew
17 Yellowfin, on Hawaiian menus
18 Sch. whose mascot is Cy the Cardinal
19 Hans Christian ___, pioneer of electromagnetism
21 Dribble
23 24 horas
24 Ages
26 Parentheses, e.g.
29 Sporting goods retailer
31 "Carmen Jones" song: "___ Love"
33 Hindu religious retreat sites
37 ___ Turner, slave rebellion leader from Virginia
38 Greek consonant
39 "My man!"
40 Actress Carrere
41 Loud and shrill: hyph.
44 Black ___ (winterberry)
45 Actress-singer Blakley
46 Horse, in poetry
47 A long time

Down

1 A Musketeer
2 Words of understanding: 3 wds.
3 Firefighter, at times
4 Dutch city
5 Marketer and distributor of foodservice products
6 Ancient city of central Palestine
7 Follower of Mao?
8 Rushed, as to attack: 2 wds.
9 ___ level (honest): 2 wds.
10 Jewish sectist
14 Abandon
20 Variety of quartz
22 Catherine who outlived Henry VIII
25 Puffin, e.g.
27 Bar, in Spain
28 He dyes for a living
30 2002 Literature Nobelist Kertész
32 Levels
33 Blocks
34 Commandment verb
35 Attila's crew
36 "My mistake"
42 Baseball Hall-of-Famer ___ Wee Reese
43 College in Cedar Rapids

83

Across

1 Equivalent of "lite": hyph.
6 Native Canadians
11 Coeur d'____
12 Funny Youngman
13 Battle
14 Deceived: 2 wds.
15 Longtime NBC show
16 Actor Tognazzi
18 Not safe, in baseball
19 Bradley and McMahon
20 Retro hip beer, initially
21 Alphabetic sequence
22 Letters identifying a combination of voices (music)
24 Covers with soil
26 Pig
28 ____-di-dah
29 Advance: 2 wds.
32 Wine: prefix
35 Bug, in a way
36 Laundry detergent brand
38 Marrakesh's nat.
39 "… ____ quit!": 2 wds.
40 A Chaplin
41 Dutch "uncle"
42 Carpe ____ (seize all): Lat.
44 "Haven't a clue!"
46 Rodents of South America
47 Big name in chips
48 Bonehead
49 India's first P.M.

Down

1 Scottish girls
2 Brazilian beach resort
3 Has problems with money: 3 wds.
4 "Brokeback Mountain" director Lee
5 Get ready to drive: 2 wds.
6 ____ hydrate (knockout drops)
7 Riddle-me-____ (rhyme)
8 When many people get paid: 4 wds.
9 Plenty
10 ARPs et al.
17 Brit. honor, initially
23 Offshoot of jazz
25 P.V. Narasimha ____, 1990s Indian P.M.
27 "You're probably right": 2 wds.
29 Bends Down
30 Airport area
31 Be nosy
33 Midday event
34 Brass that looks like gold
37 Supplemental computer software: hyph.
43 "____ a Man of Constant Sorrow": 2 wds.
45 A, in French

84

Across

1 Baseball arbiter, for short
4 Member of Cong.
7 Expected score, on a golf course
8 Scrape by
9 "Arlington Road" org.
12 Stayed longer in bed: 2 wds.
14 Night time, to Burns
15 Alleviate
16 Sparkle
18 Fine-tune
20 Advocate
21 Go astray
22 Previously
25 Goes quietly
27 Primes
29 "___ am I kidding?"
32 Bohemian
33 Country bumpkin
35 Bathroom fixture
38 Auction, e.g.
39 Shogun's capital
40 Small explosive device used as a signal
42 Cave
43 Break down, in a way
44 Big galoot
45 Hasten
46 Double agent, e.g.

Down

1 Distresses
2 African country with a namesake lake
3 Introduction
4 Animal in the family
5 1930s migrant
6 Camera part
9 Fairground attractions: 2 wds.
10 Ecru
11 Bury
13 Green legume
17 Cry softly
19 Visored cap
23 Devoured dinner
24 Having a red hue
26 Pastoral music
27 Given an X, say
28 Decrease, as popularity
30 Bring to a standstill: 2 wds.
31 Study of birds' eggs
34 Cleopatra biter
36 Mark permanently
37 3-D figures
41 Highball ingredient

85

Across

1 Bears: Lat.
5 Cutting into cubes
11 Bread in an Indian restaurant
12 Trading unit: 2 wds.
13 Like some airports: abbr.
14 Time away from prison
15 Eight, to Caesar
16 Fraternity letter
17 Mobutu ___ Seko
19 Mex. miss
23 Completely: 2 wds.
25 Waters, informally
26 Law, in Lyon
27 Eastern title
29 Bic filler
30 Victory: Ger.
32 Dress styles: hyph.
34 Extra: abbr.
35 D.C. ball team
36 Fashionable boot
38 Ford Galaxie 500s, for example
41 "___ in St. Louis" (1944 Garland film): 2 wds.
44 Peek
45 Be pleasing (to)
46 First James Bond movie: 2 wds.
47 Pays
48 "ER" actor Epps

Down

1 The "U" in B.U.: abbr.
2 "Doctor Who" villainess, with "the"
3 Pleased
4 Taking the place (of): 2 wds.
5 Ghostly doubles
6 Much may follow it
7 Red shade
8 1969 Peace Prize grp.
9 Cambodia's Lon ___
10 One-time phone company, initially
18 Hearst kidnap grp.
20 Heavy shower
21 Melody
22 Inquires
23 "Casablanca" heroine
24 Reason to be barred from a bar: 2 wds.
28 Birmingham's state: abbr.
31 Body sculptors' targets
33 "Take this: ___ you good": 2 wds.
37 Bus. school entrance exam
39 Lady of Lisbon
40 Hershey candy bar
41 Debussy piece, "La ___"
42 Hydrocarbon suffix
43 Harvard deg.

86

Across

1 Empty talk
5 Descended from the same male ancestor
11 Eastern nurse
12 Himalayan cedar
13 WKRP actress Anderson
14 Exercise in lanes: 2 wds.
15 Like some engines: hyph.
17 Pennsylvania county
18 Potter's materials
21 Astronomer Hubble
25 Where, in Latin
26 "Barely Lethal" studio, initially
27 Country, capital Nuku-alofa
30 Vestibule
32 Verdi aria sung by Renato
34 Epithet of Clark Kent's alter ego: 3 wds.
39 Mediterranean capital
40 Copter's cousin
41 Get tangled up
42 Disconnect
43 Rent payer
44 Tide type

Down

1 A little lower?
2 "Here ___, there..." ("Old MacDonald" lyric): 2 wds.
3 Half of Mork's sign-off, on "Mork & Mindy"
4 XXX in Roman numerals
5 Build on: 2 wds.
6 Name of six British kings
7 Commission-free: hyph.
8 Island of Alaska
9 Record, as a wedding
10 Sounds of hesitance
16 Bro's counterpart
18 Film director's cry
19 Action on Wall St.
20 Department of eastern France
22 Ironically funny
23 1950s political nickname
24 Neither fish ___ fowl
28 Types
29 Excite
30 Myers and Lauderdale, e.g.
31 Overpower in battle
33 "___ cap fits, wear it": 2 wds.
34 Word on the wall, in Daniel Chapter 5
35 Gets ready to fire
36 Mozart's "___ kleine Nachtmusik"
37 Mother of the Valkyries
38 Aerial maneuver
39 ___ canto (singing style)

87

Across

1 "Lord of the Rings" baddies
5 Downy juicy fruit
10 Artifice
11 Carpenter's machine
12 French Christmas
13 Take up residence: 2 wds.
14 Run wild
16 Some stingers
17 Difficult position
21 South American wood sorrel
23 Govt. property manager
25 Genetic messenger, briefly
26 Criticize harshly
27 Prefix for way or west
28 "Yadda, yadda, yadda"
29 Eyebrow shape
30 Not a "nay" vote
31 Cow comment
32 Bottom of the barrel
34 Unattractive-sounding fruit
36 Indefatigable
40 Stocks and such
43 Diva's delivery
44 Boutonniere's spot
45 "These are the times that try
    ___ souls" (Thomas Paine)
46 Short poem of rural life
47 Acts as the interlocutor

Down

1 Controls
2 Brilliant display, as of color
3 Department store event
4 One of Marge Simpson's sisters
5 Slog (through)
6 Icicle-forming spots
7 Enjoyed a buffet
8 "The Sweetheart of Sigma ___"
9 Cooped-up one
13 French men
15 Dwarf
18 Movies firsts
19 Knowledgeable of
20 Mexican sandwich
21 Birthstone of autumn
22 Give a hoot
24 "Haste makes waste," e.g.
33 Piano string material
35 Andean animal
37 "___ do for now"
38 Go to the bottom of the sea
39 Backtalk
40 "Sting like a bee" champion
41 Deplorable
42 Bug someone, e.g.

88

Across

1 Spanish model Sastre
5 Intrigue
11 Equine coloring
12 Biblical mountain
13 Massachusetts motto opener
14 Coercion
15 Reserved: 2 wds.
17 Barely gets, with "out"
18 Artist Chagall
22 Flows
25 Letters between M and Q
26 Blatant
27 Prefix meaning "likeness"
29 Texted three-letter acronym
30 Jeans magnate Levi
32 Badgers
34 Disabled
35 Repair shop inventory: 2 wds.
39 Classic Chevrolet
42 Eldest son of Adam and Eve
43 Charlotte ____, Virgin Islands
44 Indian tourist site
45 Ring-shaped bread rolls
46 Exude

Down

1 States of wrath
2 ____ of the above
3 It may have a roll on a Sunday: 2 wds.
4 Shoe for playing sports
5 Extreme cruelty
6 Unpleasant substance
7 Sheikh's bevy
8 Before, to Byron
9 Bell and Barker
10 Alien life forms, for short
16 Chairs
19 Cause ____ (arouse fierce anger): 2 wds.
20 Howard and Paul
21 Naval noncoms, initially
22 Any day now
23 Rating for "South Park," initially: hyph.
24 Flapjack topper: var.
28 Capital of Venezuela
31 Violent struggles
33 Bathroom item
36 Nutmeg's coat
37 Michelin product
38 Make noise with two fingers
39 One can be hailed
40 Simon and Garfunkel's "I ____ Rock": 2 wds.
41 Glossy publication, for short

89

Across

1 Most cautious
8 "As I see it," online
11 Spectacles
12 Zero, on the soccer pitch
13 Bar on "Three's Company" (with "The"): 2 wds.
15 Brings home
16 "The Jungle Book" wolfpack leader
17 No, to Nijinsky
18 Nourishing drink, especially barley water
19 Hanoi holiday
20 Spirited
21 Like Boston accents, as it were: hyph.
22 Comedienne Boosler
24 Seat, slangily
27 Goodyear's flying fleet
28 Acreage
29 Membranes in eggs of a reptile
30 Black cattle breed
31 High rollers: 2 wds.
33 Before, to Blake
34 Enduring
35 Patriotic org.
36 Flower-shaped decoration

Down

1 "You ___ kidding!"
2 Nocturnal lemur: hyph.
3 Wish undone
4 "___ to Hold Your Hand": 2 wds.
5 Congers
6 Rest time: abbr.
7 Formal exposition
8 Swallow
9 Female poet known to friends as "Vincent"
10 City on the Allegheny
14 "___ Before Dying": 2 wds.
18 Hammer parts
20 Old-time bug bait
21 "Groundhog Day" director
22 Mark Twain's New York hometown
23 Hang around
24 Pressing
25 French painter who developed pointillism (1859–91)
26 Bother
27 Innocent ones
28 Brooke's ex
30 Hydrocarbon suffixes
32 Command for D.D.E.

90

Across

1 Play the role of: 2 wds.
6 Bottler's offerings
11 Caterpillar, for one
12 "Ta-da!"
13 Simple: 4 wds.
15 N. ___, 39th state
16 Old White House inits.
17 Neighbor of Iran: abbr.
18 Graf rival
20 Dabbling ducks
23 Diploma word
27 One Saarinen
28 W.W. I biplane
29 "Raw Like Sushi" singer Cherry
31 Sail supports
32 He tested Job's faith
34 Legal letters
37 "Cool!": abbr.
38 "Big" burger
41 Tiara wearer
44 Advertising awards
45 Dissuade
46 Thick pieces
47 Courtroom statements

Down

1 "When I Was ___" ("H.M.S. Pinafore" song): 2 wds.
2 Hidalgo home
3 Long haul
4 Mrs. Sinatra, once
5 Waistbands
6 Georgia and Hawaii
7 Circus cries
8 Actor Johnny
9 "Jewel Song," for one
10 Go after
14 Big initials in fashion
18 Astringent fruit
19 "Goldengirl" Anton
20 Perfect score, often
21 A foot wide?
22 Prince Valiant's son
24 Brit. legislators
25 Tangle
26 Personals, e.g.
30 Pester
31 Got by (with): 2 wds.
33 Cap
34 Some movie theaters: inits.
35 Check
36 Flu source
38 Catcher's need
39 Banda ___ (Indonesian city)
40 Sonatas, e.g.
42 Weep
43 "Michael Collins" actor Stephen

91

Across

1 Check
4 Type of fly
7 Served lunch to, say
10 Grocery franchise letters
11 Beer
12 Grammar school basics, for short
13 U.S.A.F. decoration
14 Schedule C figure: 2 wds.
16 Japanese dish of chicken pieces grilled on a skewer
18 Tallahassee campus: inits.
19 Bypass
23 Prefix with graphic
25 Danish city
26 Benny Goodman's nickname (with "The"): 3 wds.
28 Accompany
29 QB's errors
30 Part of a La Scala opera
31 Suffix with inferior or infidel
32 Church curse
36 Muscle pain
39 Sound-related prefix
40 Two-time loser to DDE
41 ___ King, bearded giant or goblin of German myth
42 Eggs in water?
43 Lb. and mg, e.g.
44 Method: abbr.
45 ___-Caps (candy brand)

Down

1 Fastidious
2 Fuji competitor
3 Where gossip might be spread: 2 wds.
4 Xhosa's language group
5 Butter alternative
6 Groups of four
7 Curly coif, for short
8 Hesitant sounds
9 Medicos, for short
15 Tolerate: 2 wds.
17 Having equal angles
20 Getting ___ (elderly): 3 wds.
21 Ain't correct?
22 Colleges award them: abbr.
23 Eisenhower and others
24 Computer insert
25 Frequently, in poetry
27 Citrus fruits
31 Slanted type, casually
33 Breezy
34 Charged lepton
35 Mars: prefix
36 Animal's mouth
37 Even so
38 Foolish person

92

Across

1 Last Greek letter
6 Hiccup, for instance
11 Biological building blocks
12 Flower shop bouquet
13 "The Boy Who Cried Wolf" writer
14 Lid or lip application
15 Not mono
17 Whimper
18 Prefix with red
20 "___ Karenina"
23 Eastern headgear
27 Minimal
29 High nest: var.
30 Herman ___, Paul Reubens's creation: hyph.
32 Stallion, once
33 E'en if
35 Capital of West Germany between 1949 and 1990
38 Actress Bonham Carter
42 Came up, as a subject
44 Column style
45 Enjoy
46 Chart
47 Casual language
48 English exam finale, often

Down

1 Edible roots
2 Rendezvous
3 "Hand it over or ___!"
4 Star of the movie "Sadie Thompson" (1928): 2 wds.
5 Poplar variety
6 "Do the Right Thing" pizzeria owner
7 Red, blue, and green, e.g.: 2 wds.
8 Prime: hyph.
9 Merganser relative
10 Clay-sand mixture
16 Frequently, for short
19 Morgue, for one
20 Mont Blanc, e.g.
21 Born: Fr.
22 Dundee denial
24 "Dude!"
25 Be bedridden
26 After-tax amount
28 ___ el Amarna, Egypt
31 Archaic verb ending
34 Beat around the bush
35 Angler's quarry
36 ___ hygiene
37 Astronomer's sighting
39 Historic spans
40 Mangrove swamp palm
41 Hurting
43 A little work

93

Across

1 Hungry feeling
5 Blocks
9 Long-necked Indian lute
10 All over
11 Runway material
13 News magazine
14 What a "Wheel of Fortune" contestant might buy: 2 wds.
15 "We're sinking!" letters
17 Harebrained
18 "Yes, I'm looking at ___!"
19 Bill accompanier, initially
20 "All the Things You ___"
21 Trifling conversation: 2 wds.
24 All except the clergy
25 Futile
29 Boat mover
30 Conk out
31 Catchall abbr.
33 Disobeyed a zoo sign?
34 Grass patch
35 Demure
36 Bolt
38 Nine-day Catholic prayer
40 Exuberance
41 Become broader
42 Chip's chum, in cartoons
43 Can't live without

Down

1 Products with pedals
2 Courtyard
3 "Platoon" setting, for short
4 Prairies
5 Belfry creature
6 Moose, e.g.
7 Say
8 Stockholm resident
9 Hang around
12 Alliance of political parties
16 Take root: 2 wds.
22 Boxer in "The Rumble in the Jungle"
23 Yes, to a sailor
25 Saffron-flavored dish made of rice with shellfish
26 Big test
27 Leave
28 Pelted with rocks
29 Did in, mobster-style
32 Blue-green shade
37 Direction away from WSW
39 C'est la ___

94

Across

1 Farm soil
5 Summarized or abridged
11 Groundless
12 Commotion
13 Brook
14 Van Gogh painting, "The ___ Night"
15 It may follow systems
17 Beluga delicacy
18 Texas cook-off dish
22 Hard strikes
24 Church council
25 It's not me
26 Ballerina's prop
27 Bit of color
30 Arduous journeys
32 Finish with, as a high note: 2 wds.
33 Dinghy mover
34 Not moving
38 Dried grape
41 Skid around
42 Charge with a crime
43 Aromatherapist's substances
44 Nearsighted people
45 Fountain order

Down

1 Italian currency, before the euro
2 Father of Balder
3 Many sided: hyph.
4 Become less stressed, with "out"
5 Kitty
6 Fiber ___ (telecommunications technology)
7 Tastelessly showy
8 Craggy prominence
9 Audio receiver
10 Drought-stricken
16 Cry of success
19 Among other things: 2 wds.
20 Pointer's word
21 Mid-month date
22 Computer info quantity
23 A little lamb?
28 Person given to spreading rumors
29 Attract
30 Dress (with "up" or "out")
31 Money demanded by a kidnaper
35 Aardvark food
36 ___ and void
37 It's needed to make the grade
38 Cup part
39 Some quantity
40 "Indeed ___!": 2 wds.

95

Across

1 Jury members
6 Spot away from sunlight
11 Synthetic fiber
12 "The Farnsworth Invention" playwright Sorkin
13 Climber's respite
14 Persona non ___
15 Vain hopes: 2 wds.
17 Beginnings
18 ___ were: 2 wds.
20 Film director Vittorio
24 The 21st, e.g.: abbr.
25 Trading under the name of, initially
26 Head, slangily
27 Design on the skin
29 Not cooked very much, like a steak
30 Units of weight
32 Make waves: 3 wds.
36 ___ diem
37 Cow catcher
38 One making a choice
39 Old
40 Air Force installations
41 Antique guns

Down

1 Spider's sense organ
2 "… ___ saw Elba": 2 wds.
3 Terminus
4 Member of the governing body of a university
5 Coasters
6 Herbal drink: 2 wds.
7 Bother repeatedly
8 Biblical name for ancient Syria
9 Specks
10 Old Spanish queen
16 Singer Leon
18 Memorize lines and hit the stage
19 The Red or the Med
21 Agitated: 3 wds.
22 Either of two N.T. books
23 Lincoln, casually
25 Firemen, often
28 Removable locks
29 Find a new chair for
31 Three of spades and nine of clubs, e.g.
32 Spanish cape
33 Sculpting, painting, et al.
34 Coast-to-coast highway: 2 wds.
35 Physics units
36 Corn's home

96

Across

1 Parenting challenges
6 Some sports cars, for short
11 Irish nationalist leader Robert
12 1957 #1 song
13 Maudlin
14 How some music is sold: 2 wds.
15 Command to a dog
16 Generosity
18 Blissful
20 Shih-tzu, e.g.
21 "___ Men" (2010 movie)
22 Rogen of "The Guilt Trip"
24 Leaking
26 Considers
29 Bobby and Colton
31 "There's ___ in the air": 2 wds.
32 Massachusetts state tree
34 Sabotage carried out for ecological reasons
36 Checks: 2 wds.
38 One-time MTV afternoon show
39 Romantic flowers
40 Court proceeding
42 Balanced bridge bid, briefly: 2 wds.
43 Make ___ of (write down): 2 wds.
44 Grown dearer in price
45 Sectioned, as a window

Down

1 Mosaic piece
2 Sent with a click: hyph.
3 What politicians might give to get elected: 2 wds.
4 Fiber knot
5 Pens and needles
6 Trimmed
7 Cod cousin
8 Long-running CBS news show: 3 wds.
9 Subsequently: 2 wds.
10 Flip, in a way
17 "___ in apple": 2 wds.
19 "Bon ___"
23 Part of a cow's udder
25 Continue moving forward: 2 wds.
27 Change places
28 Read out letter by letter
30 "Nova" subj.
32 Computer's "I don't understand what you want"
33 Actress Téa
35 How some beer is served: 2 wds.
37 Hawaiian state bird
41 Genetic initials

97

Across

1 Large and hurried swallow
5 Building blocks
11 Blood (prefix)
12 Involve
13 Cybercafe patron
14 Dad's mom
15 George of "Star Trek"
17 Dietary, in ads
18 Harmless
19 Old Roman road
20 Blackbird
21 "Dragonwyck" author Seton
23 Summer hrs. in San Jose
24 Arlington owner
25 2100, in Roman numerals
28 Einstein home, circa 1904
29 Nonprofessional sports grp.
30 "Shave ___ haircut": 2 wds.
33 Pursues
35 Afrikaner
36 "Chicago Hope" Emmy winner
37 News office
39 Counting-out word
41 "Hold on!": abbr., 2 wds.
42 Catholic title, for short
43 "You shouldn't have done that": 2 wds.
44 Psychiatrist's appt.

Down

1 Egyptian god of light and air
2 Fashionable area of London: 2 wds.
3 "This is serious!": 3 wds.
4 "Children of the Sun" playwright
5 Success achieved by a novice: 2 wds.
6 Genre of popular music, initially
7 Florence's country, to natives
8 "Quieten down!": 2 wds.
9 Kunta ___ ("Roots" role)
10 More cunning
16 The same, in Sevres
18 Protestant denom.
22 Busybody
25 Toy dog
26 Ingredients
27 Boxing promoter D'Amato
28 Least covered
30 Head monk, at a monastery
31 People, places or things
32 John ___, "Ghosts Can't Do It" writer and director
34 Cries for attention
38 Loser to H.C.H.
40 Calendar spans: abbr.

98

Across

1 African capital
6 Cockeyed
11 Body snatcher
12 Barrier or boom preceder
13 Carries on
14 Less dangerous
15 Little creature who helps Santa
16 Eugene's state: abbr.
18 "___ fallen …"
19 Fish that's a general backwards
20 Mouse's cousin
21 Green, in a way
22 "Hogan's Heroes" setting
24 Blow off steam?
25 Alcoholic drink that's also a card game
26 Bunk
27 Pat baby on the back
29 Fondle
32 Genetic info. carrier
33 A long way away
34 Approximately
35 Giant of a Giant
36 Three-point line in basketball, for example
37 "___ alive!"
38 Bay window
40 Fess up, as to a crime
42 Subatomic particles
43 Animal catcher
44 Brains
45 Oregon's capital

Down

1 Goes along with
2 Alpine abode
3 Major destructive fire
4 Narrow groove
5 Election loser: hyph.
6 Black ink item
7 Bygone bird
8 Immeasurably small
9 Strainers
10 Grooved nails
17 Tabloid, perhaps
23 It's right under your nose, literally
24 Old TV knob, briefly
26 Dead body of an animal
27 Sweeping tools
28 Disloyal
29 Buick or BMW
30 Lampoon
31 Modus operandi
33 Bogus
39 Coast Guard rank: abbr.
41 Kind of test letters

99

Across

1 Flubs
6 As of
11 Elite military unit: hyph.
12 Dream stealer
13 Sine or cosine
14 B.B. King's musical genre
15 Liqueur with a yellowish green color
17 Trigger, for one
18 Accustomed
22 Bard's foot
25 Rubbernecker
26 Machine powered by electricity
27 Mazuma
28 Movie house
29 Black-and-white treats
31 Like some suits: hyph.
36 Allied
37 Like a beaver
38 Irk
39 Out
40 Puff ___ (hognose snake)
41 Crowded

Down

1 Russian-born French painter, ___ Chagall
2 A Four Corners state
3 Greek salad chunks
4 Carnival
5 Put out a fire, one way
6 ___-toothed tiger
7 Conjuring trick
8 Sicken
9 Largest Canadian tribe
10 Type widths
16 Bacillus shape
18 ___ roll
19 Glasgow denial
20 Sent a file to a central computer
21 Bring back
23 Apple pie baker
24 Car accessory
26 Didn't understand properly, as an article
28 Bill's partner in love
30 Council member, perhaps
31 Even, as a score
32 Dude
33 Opposed to, in dialect
34 New members of society
35 Lake near Niagara Falls
36 Splashy resort

100

Across

1 Someone ___ (not mine)
6 Alloy of copper and zinc
11 Had to do (with)
12 Rajah's wife
13 Medical picture-taker: 2 wds.
15 Asner and Bradley
16 Big load
17 ___ Ripken, Jr. (baseball great)
18 Both having hearts or diamonds, like a pair of cards
20 Back
23 Records
26 European capital
27 "Psycho" motel
28 Made ___ for it (escaped quickly): 2 wds.
29 Wild West movies
30 Cowboy's seat
32 "Krazy ___"
34 Be sick
35 Wall St. wheeler-dealer
38 Whiskey and cream drink: 2 wds.
41 Immune system lymphocyte: hyph.
42 Coal carters
43 Reid and Lipinski
44 Hindu dresses

Down

1 Slight advantage
2 Element removed from gasoline
3 Snead and Shepard
4 Common street name
5 Height
6 Migratory goose
7 Aries is one
8 Amusing tale
9 Hospital fluids
10 Make tight against leakage
14 Penny, nickel or dime
18 Medicinal plant
19 Make happy
20 What attys. join
21 To be, in Barcelona
22 More reliable
24 Berlin's country: abbr.
25 Leaky tire sound
27 Forms of elections
29 Lyrical
31 Roald and Arlene
32 "Santa Baby" singer
33 Ancient strongbox
35 On the horizon, perhaps
36 Do follow-up?: 2 wds.
37 Eleanor's successor
39 Patty Hearst kidnap grp.
40 ___ Angelico, Early Italian Renaissance painter

101

Across

1 Celebrity
5 "Green ___" sitcom with Eddie Albert and Eva Gabor
10 Christmas tune
11 Some "war paint"
12 Less than 90 degrees, as an angle
13 Calm Down
14 Commemorated
16 Jeff Buckley's "___ Wine"
17 Impudent stuff
20 Circus sites
24 Greek letter
25 That thing's
26 Future members of a species, in biology class
27 Breathing problem
29 All hands on deck
30 Breathlessness while sleeping
32 Schemes
37 Spurs
38 Tear to shreds: 2 wds.
39 Reaches the upper limit
40 Mournful poem
41 Group of three
42 Henna and others

Down

1 Confront
2 Jack-in-the-pulpit, e.g.
3 Roadside stops
4 Aromatic resin
5 They may be paid with interest
6 Bully
7 Be a monarch
8 Brit's cry of astonishment
9 Either of male or female
10 Automobile
15 Barefaced
17 Place to "take the waters"
18 Dunderhead
19 Obedience school lesson
21 Postal motto conjunction
22 Monopoly property, often: abbr.
23 Cut through
25 Stalemate
28 Go solid
29 In a crafty way
31 Kind of seal
32 Fly high
33 Curbside call
34 Sword used in Olympic competition
35 Hoodlums
36 007, for one
37 Clock standard letters

102

Across

1 City in southern King County, Washington
7 Mil. school
11 Minor ____ (part of a tarot deck)
12 "Smooth Operator" singer
13 Lion
14 Flat piece
15 Coffee brand
16 Org. whose members often strike
18 Political pawn González
21 Coal-rich German region
25 Higher, as a building
27 Moon material, supposedly: 2 wds.
29 Of the ankle
30 Spreadsheet material
31 "Buona ____"
32 Grazing area
33 Bayonet
37 Interest figure
40 Neighboring: 2 wds.
42 Latin trio center
43 Physicist Fermi
44 ____ souci
45 Justification

Down

1 Cutty ____
2 Ending for "switch" or "buck"
3 Open ____ of worms: 2 wds.
4 "Scarlett" setting
5 Chemistry suffix
6 Shag spiffer-upper: 2 wds.
7 Went after
8 "Silent" prez, familiarly
9 Boise's county
10 Cotillion V.I.P.
17 Boring
19 Caesar: "Iacta ____ est" ("The die is cast")
20 Birth place
21 ____ Hulka ("Stripes" role)
22 Galway Bay's ____ Islands
23 Prefix before space
24 Constantly in motion
26 "V for Vendetta" actor Stephen
28 Archibald of the N.B.A.
33 ____ Delano Roosevelt
34 Baseball's Speaker
35 Bobby Darin's label until 1963
36 Beneficial bestowal
37 Dorm overseers, for short
38 Doctors' org.
39 Acquire a bronze tone
41 Hydrocarbon suffix

103

Across

1 Close to closed
5 Slow tempo
11 Level, in London
12 Composed
13 Gremlins
14 Wooer
15 Deep
17 Bireme implement
18 "Back in the ___" (Beatles song)
22 Red shade
26 Garden pond swimmer
27 Miserable abode
28 Hangout
30 Flatter, in a way
31 Certain length
33 Half a matched set?
35 Stoplight color
36 Star on a page
41 Seafood dish
44 Fifty-fifty
45 Able to absorb fluids
46 "___ Smile" (Hall & Oates song)
47 Obliquely
48 Jacket fastener

Down

1 Diva's showstopper
2 Piece of door siding
3 Small cobras
4 Fix up
5 Cinch
6 Jupiter, e.g.
7 Goodbye, to the French
8 Channel through sandbanks
9 Four-time Japanese prime minister
10 Neath's opposite
16 Come from behind
19 Gull-like bird
20 ___ of Solomon
21 Ceremonial practice
22 Bygone royal
23 Deal with successfully
24 Affirm
25 Number in a trio
29 Deal with
32 Studio worker, perhaps
34 Island group near Tonga
37 Twirled
38 Lendl of the court
39 Word repeated after "Que," in a song
40 Word attached to "sack"
41 Hydromassage facility
42 Businesses: abbr.
43 Noah's boat

104

Across

1 "Self-Reliance" author's monogram
4 Utah metropolis, initially
7 "That's 2 funny!"
10 Bygone nuclear agcy.
11 Short, for short
12 Palindromic name
13 Furious: 4 wds.
16 Parisian soul
17 "___ small world": 2 wds.
18 Big book of stories
22 Juilliard deg.
23 180° from NNW
24 1983 comedy with Mr. T: 2 wds.
27 Computer magnate Perot: 2 wds.
31 It's not quite lge.
33 Cabinet dept.
34 Not recurring at regular intervals
37 Dies ___ (Requiem Mass part)
39 Age abbr.
40 Female superhero: 2 wds.
45 Contribute
46 French pronoun
47 Wife of Saturn
48 Cincinnati-to-Nashville dir.
49 "Son of," in Arabic names
50 Alphabet openers

Down

1 Brit. bombers
2 Chinese dynasty
3 Outer: prefix
4 Replay option, for short: hyph.
5 Puts down, in writing
6 French key
7 Parishioners, e.g.
8 Sugar suffixes
9 Russian car make
14 Papeete's island: abbr.
15 Princeton mascot
18 Semiconductor company: inits.
19 Grp. for Panthers and Cardinals
20 Tic-___-toe
21 City in western Kyrgyzstan
25 Pumped
26 Drone, e.g.
28 Bizarre
29 Due + quattro
30 NCO rank
32 Marinade alternative: 2 wds.
34 Root beer brand: 3 wds.
35 Footballers Heath or Hale
36 Spanish bear
37 "___ afraid of that!": 2 wds.
38 Farm measures
41 Crimson rival
42 Extinct bird
43 P.D. alert
44 Foreign policy gp.

105

Across

1 Like a horse or lion
6 It's a plus
11 Gland: prefix
12 ___ voce: softly
13 Straight
15 Communiqué segue: 2 wds.
16 Channel swimmer Gertrude
17 Hagen of Broadway
18 Grabbed a bite
19 Diarist Anaïs
20 Layer of skin
22 Flesh as food
23 Centerpins on which wheels revolve
25 Places for experiments
28 Punctual: 2 wds.
32 Baboon's big cousin
33 Landscaping stuff
34 Swamp
35 Rags
37 Verse's author
38 State of non-importance
40 Part of a play
41 More competent
42 Wounds
43 Final approval: hyph.

Down

1 Pillage and plunder
2 Carol opener
3 Sugary plant fuild
4 Course on insects, for short
5 "Where ___ begin?": 2 wds.

6 To the left or right
7 Loudness unit
8 "Tristram Shandy" author
9 List shortener: 2 wds.
10 Apartment window sign: 2 wds.
14 Sets free: 2 wds.
18 ___-en-Provence
21 Humanities degs.
22 Denver clock setting, initially
24 Cut off
25 At a somewhat advance hour

26 Quick glance
27 Carrier
29 "I wish!": 2 wds.
30 "I hate those ___ to pieces!" (Mr. Jinks, re Pixie and Dixie)
31 Prefix relating to the intestine
33 Tennis's Monica
36 E-mail client folder
37 Sunscreen ingredient, for short
39 "___ in Victor": 2 wds.

106

Across

1 Shocked reaction
5 ___ longue
11 Kind of exam
12 Manhattan cocktail made with Scotch whiskey: 2 wds.
13 Peruvian capital
14 Apprehension
15 Result of collapsed arches
17 Anchors in the soil
18 Bath bath
21 Augusta is its capital
23 Bird's claw
25 Hostile to
26 Like some decrees
27 Orderly pile
29 El Misti's locale
30 Cooped-up female
31 Game show host, e.g.
33 Dancers' wear
36 Inexpensive and low-quality
39 Artificial bait
40 Annoy
41 Blithe spirit
42 Current amount
43 No longer working: abbr.

Down

1 Game for Woods or Woosnam
2 Husk
3 Good one in the Bible
4 Free from physical desire
5 Condiment container
6 Truthful
7 Assist, in a way
8 "Rosemary's Baby" novelist Levin
9 "Send help!," initially
10 Providence feature on a $1 bill
16 Opponent
18 Old calculating tool: 2 wds.
19 Sit for a photo
20 Black-billed birds
21 Sitcom set in Uijeongbu, South Korea
22 First few chips, usually
24 Glassworker, at times
28 Certain hockey player
29 Make a scene?
32 Bond player, once
33 After the due date
34 "Darn!"
35 E-mail program button
36 Balancing pro letters
37 ___ and haw
38 Paranormal power letters

107

Across

1 Formerly, formerly
5 Boxing venue
10 Copycat's phrase: 2 wds.
12 Plump and comely
13 Brainy
14 Postgame summary
15 Balderdash
17 Shocked sounds
18 Opposite of post-
20 Great divide
22 "Hello, sailor!"
24 Chemical cousin
27 Clear up, as a cold windshield
29 Brownish gray
30 Mythological half-men, half-goats
32 Make a sweater, maybe
33 Bunk
35 ___ cream sundae
36 "___-Devil" (1989 Meryl Streep movie)
38 Zeno, notably
40 Lollygags
42 Grind, as teeth
45 March follower
46 Part filler
47 Small-minded
48 Egg producers

Down

1 Fat letters
2 Ad ___ (to the point)
3 Most recent stage of development: 4 wds.
4 Pressure unit
5 Alongside
6 Street: Fr.
7 Expel from a religious society
8 Ancient mariner
9 Intensifies, with "up"
11 Auricular
16 21st Greek letter
18 Paw parts
19 ___ Perlman (Carla Tortelli of "Cheers")
21 Good, long bath
23 Famous Ma
25 Grander than grand
26 Network of blood vessels or nerves
28 How some things are overstated
31 6–2 or 7–6, in tennis
34 Practice with a "lotus position"
36 Hit with an open hand
37 Bill Clinton's birthplace
39 Mark of a ruler
41 Appropriate
43 One of the Trinity
44 Mins. and mins.

108

Across

1 "Groundhog Day" director
6 Brainiac Simpson
10 "Woman with ___" soap opera: 2 wds.
11 "A Prayer for ___ Meany"
12 James Bond's drink: 2 wds.
14 Suffix for sugars, in chemistry
15 Jack and Jill's container
16 Afr. nation
17 Bawdy
21 Elevate: 2 wds.
25 USN cleric, for short
26 "A League of ___ Own"
27 Some noblemen
29 NHL's Tikkanen
30 Diatribes
32 Chronic drinkers
34 Boom box abbr.
35 High hair style
37 Narcotics watchdog, initially
40 Jim Morrison moniker, "The ___": 2 wds.
43 Tiger Woods's ex
44 "That ___ of the strangest things I've ever seen": 2 wds.
45 ___-Ball (arcade rolling game)
46 Doctor

Down

1 "Hair" co-author James
2 Busy times at the I.R.S.
3 Outfielder Lee ___ (1959–71)
4 Any doctrine
5 Office items
6 100 lisente in Lesotho
7 "White Album" ballad: 2 wds.
8 D.C. bigwig
9 Folkie DiFranco
13 Pasta sauce maker
16 Do-say link: 2 wds.
18 "Jane ___"
19 Fuse with a torch
20 Ersatz bed, to Brits
21 Hwy. abbrs.
22 Facetious "I see": 2 wds.
23 "___ my peas with honey…": 2 wds.
24 Regular
28 Old nuke org.
31 U.S.N. rank
33 Step in the Lindy Hop, ___-Q: var.
36 Piece of glass in a window
37 Promoter of the "New Look"
38 Feminine ending
39 Antiquing agent
40 "___ Liaisons Dangereuses"
41 Class
42 Wildcats of the Big 12 Conference, initially

109

Across

1 Church pre-wedding announcement
6 Line of cliffs
11 Bye that's bid
12 Computer programmer
13 Hourglass contents
14 Higher than
15 Gray, in a way
16 ___ and haw (stall for time)
18 Basketball game figure with a whistle, for short
19 On, as a lamp
20 Poe's "The ___ of the Perverse"
21 "Look ___ ye leap"
22 Christmas gifts, often
24 Check payee, maybe
26 Victor Vasarely's genre: 2 wds.
28 Livestock buildings
31 To be, to Tiberius
35 Famous mummy, for short
36 Particularly: abbr.
38 Chum
39 Crumb
40 Sailor's agreement
41 Labor group initials
42 Met expectations?
44 Tiny bit, as of food
46 Alloy of lead and tin
47 Motif
48 Ending for in or farm
49 "Wonderwall" band

Down

1 Igneous rock
2 Slow movement
3 Between eighty and one hundred
4 Dad of Rod and Todd Flanders
5 Sour, cold rice dish
6 Run quickly
7 Corn core
8 Worshiper
9 April 18, 1775 rider
10 Favor
17 Government outpost
23 La lead-in
25 Visited a restaurant, with "out"
27 Delighted
28 Worn furs
29 Tank top
30 Clothing
32 Church high points
33 Deli offering
34 Runs off (with)
37 Basil-based sauce
43 Santa ___, Calif.
45 When repeated, a Latin dance

110

Across

1 Frog sound
6 Bowling game
11 Main artery
12 Auto option
13 Yemen's capital
14 Take in again
15 Middle Easterner, often
16 Public speaker
17 Place for a father-to-be: abbr.
18 "___ you there?"
19 H.S. subj.
20 Star in Cygnus
22 Old knife
23 "Certainly not!": 2 wds.
25 Brother of Cain and Abel
27 "Crime and Punishment" heroine
29 Mozart's "L'___ del Cairo"
30 Actor Chaney, Jr.
31 "Independence Day" assailants, for short
33 Wicker material
35 "Portnoy's Complaint" author Philip
36 Enemies of the Iroquois
37 Girlfriend, to Luis Miguel
38 Mink cousin
39 Back
40 Distance races: 2 wds.
41 Jazz pianist Chick

Down

1 Houses, in Spain
2 Sounded like a lion
3 Decoration
4 Keep ___ on (watch): 2 wds.
5 Kipling snake
6 Ballet school handrail
7 Olive genus
8 View: 4 wds.
9 Cuisine style
10 Come to light
16 "Crying" singer
18 1950s election monogram
21 Form of Japanese drama
22 D.C. lawmaker
24 L. ___ Hubbard, writer of "Battlefield Earth"
25 Most painful or raw
26 Card game for two
28 Deck out
30 Endures
32 Journalist Alexander
34 Furniture wood
35 Old printing process: abbr.
37 White House advisory group, initially

111

Across

1 Stupid people, slangily
7 Foster and Kingsley
11 Iroquoian language
12 Building block
13 World class chess player
15 Drag something heavy
16 Moldovan monetary unit
17 Sony rival, initially
18 Plaintive poem
20 Hellenic
22 Pitta bread sandwich
23 Mozzarella or Muenster
24 Sharp, as pain
26 Hostage taker
29 Enormous
33 Come together
34 Passover supper
35 Wisecrack
36 Beer keg outlet
38 Letter that's a symbol of victory
39 Economic policy of the Soviet Union in the 1980s
42 Dark, in poems
43 Get-go
44 Sound from a diseased lung
45 Measuring devices

Down

1 Sharp bend in a route
2 Rambunctious
3 Unsubstantial
4 Coal holder
5 Unusually
6 Equivalent
7 City vehicle
8 It's what's for dinner
9 Family tree members
10 Continuous band of planking on a ship
14 Nada
19 Some mountain dwellers
21 Chaucer pilgrim
23 Mangy mutt
25 Prices
26 Tent tenant
27 Microscopic organism
28 Detachment used for security
30 Recommend
31 Inquirer
32 Deals with
34 Channel into a mold
37 Hanna-Barbera's heroic Ant
40 Toronto to Montreal dir.
41 Giant Hall- of-Famer

112

Across

1 Beret or beanie
4 Dowel
7 Blow away
8 Roman's roe
9 Sudden abrupt pull
12 Managed
13 Port city in Campania, Italy
15 Loses moisture
17 Bakery beckoner
18 Irish ___ (big dog)
20 Bed part
21 Effortlessness
22 Last word of an ultimatum
23 Hot dog holder
25 Bathroom installation
27 Barely make, with "out"
28 "___ the Groove" (Madonna hit)
30 Green feeling that's a cardinal sin
32 Bit of kindling
33 Flock related?
36 Board
38 Money of Freetown
39 "So soon?"
41 Comedic actress Gasteyer
42 Carry on, as a trade
43 Filling station filler
44 "Le ___" five-act French tragicomedy by Pierre Corneille
45 Mel who hit 511 home runs
46 The Crystals' "___ a Rebel"

Down

1 King of clubs and queen of diamonds, e.g.
2 Cognizant
3 An American can!
4 Haunt
5 Juan Peron's wife
6 Apple variety
9 Passenger bus with an electric motor: 2 wds.
10 Expose
11 Pointy beard
14 Old World language
16 Certain fraternity chapter
19 Chase away
23 JPEG alternative
24 Ill
26 Shrink
29 Eye
31 Be a contender
34 "Tomorrow" musical
35 Principal movie roles
37 Palm starch
40 "Can't Help Lovin' ___ Man" (song from "Show Boat")

113

Across

1 Scribbles (down)
5 Evergreen shrub
10 Rich tapestry
12 Flash the pearly whites
13 Capital of Argentina: 2 wds.
15 Flabbergast
16 Coolers, initially
17 Space rocks
21 ___ canto
22 "___ geht's?" (German "How are you?")
23 Goes after
26 Esau's father
30 Bit
32 Choo-choos: abbr.
33 Turns away
36 Suffix with Euclid
38 Greek war goddess
39 Los Angeles suburb: 2 wds.
44 Corp. official
45 Rosacea and vulgaris
46 Acts as an usher
47 Beer barrels

Down

1 Quick punch, to boxers
2 Tulsa sch. named for a televangelist
3 Railroad support
4 Health, in Paris
5 New Deal org.
6 Pal, to Pierre
7 Bygone coins
8 Actor Baldwin
9 Diminished by
11 Like some pickles
14 Winter whiteness
17 "Six-pack" on the stomach: abbr.
18 Behold
19 Sundial figure
20 ___ Arc, Ark.
24 Sorts: abbr.
25 Enjoyed the couch
27 French forest region
28 "Here we ___!"
29 Authors Lewis and Forester, initially
31 ___ Rabbit, Bear or Wolf
33 Prefix meaning "nine" that can precede -gon
34 "I" of "The King and I"
35 Inner suburb of New York City
36 Ballpark figs.
37 Rhine tributary
40 Blubber
41 Slalom segment
42 B.S., e.g.
43 C.I.A. forerunner

114

Across

1 Brawl
6 Greek abode of the dead
11 Have actual being
12 Hemorrhage
13 Total abstainers
15 Earth, in Berlin
16 Legendary Notre Dame coach Parseghian
17 Baby's seat
19 Pedal digits
23 Clueless: 3 wds.
27 Coastline feature
28 "Grumpier Old Men" actress Sophia
29 Church words
31 Back
32 As one: 2 wds.
34 Takes to task, legally
36 Med. land
37 Make "it," on the playground
39 Fed.: hyph.
43 Sanskrit epic of ancient India
47 Spinning
48 Discourage
49 Author Zora ____ Hurston
50 Completely clueless: 2 wds.

Down

1 Apportion, with "out"
2 Phys. activity
3 Pseudologized
4 1967 Oscar winner Parsons
5 D.D.E.'s command
6 I-beam relative: hyph.
7 Arabian moon goddess
8 Ruby of "The Stand"
9 Always, to Yeats
10 1960s protest grp.
14 Faucets
18 Choice: hyph.
20 Bank deposits
21 One, in Vienna
22 Manuscript encl.
23 "Sad to say …"
24 Flavor-absorbing food
25 "Vissi d'____" (aria from the opera "Tosca")
26 ____ Club (Costco rival)
30 Actress Ann-____
33 Approaching
35 Belletrist Madame de ____
38 Empowered
40 Gym floor covers
41 "That suits me to ____": 2 wds.
42 Former Japanese capital
43 Guy
44 "____ you sure?"
45 "Hath ____ sister?" (Shakespeare): 2 wds.
46 Palindromic heroine of "The Piano"

115

Across

1 Play, as bongo drums
5 Saddam Hussein, e.g.
11 City where the Taj Mahal is
12 Canada's capital
13 Baby sheep
14 Married
15 Bucolic poem
16 Blackout
17 Bird in the Harry Potter books
19 Racers' goal, sometimes
23 Looks up to
27 "___ & Order"
28 Legendary screen dancer: 2 wds.
30 Green
31 Artist
32 Look like a wolf
34 Crooked
35 Fleet member
37 Be an omen of
41 Popular numbers puzzle
44 "Do as I say"
45 Emphatic, in a way
46 Antiwar advocate
47 Debt indicator: 2 wds.
48 365 days, usually

Down

1 "___ Ha'i"
2 "Consarn it!"
3 General assembly?
4 Celebrity scandal source
5 Twenty dollar bill, slangily: 2 wds.
6 "Empedocles on ___" (Matthew Arnold poem)
7 Restrict
8 Reward, as a dog
9 Be down, in a way
10 Little bit
18 "That's a ___!"
20 Detrained, say
21 Reduce, as expenses
22 The America's Cup trophy, e.g.
23 ___-Caribbean music
24 Bring unwillingly
25 Cry like a baby
26 Ado
29 No one in particular
33 Bacteria discovered by Theodor Escherich
36 Like, with "to"
38 Instrument also called the "hautbois"
39 Hindu god
40 Peeping Tom, e.g.
41 Round Table address
42 All-purpose vehicle, briefly
43 Little League coach, often

116

Across

1 Piece of celery
6 Fountain locale
11 Similar: prefix
12 Four-star reviews
13 Construction site vehicles
15 Big record label initials
16 Light units: abbr.
17 "___ to worry"
18 ___ King Cole
19 Medicare minders, initially
20 Soldiers, for short
21 Take out ___ in the paper (publicize): 2 wds.
23 Lorelei, in legend
25 Classic Camaro: inits., hyph.
27 Celebrate
29 Lhasa ___ (dog)
33 Race, as a motor
34 A thou. mil.
36 Did a marathon
37 Widow in "Peer Gynt"
38 A, in Mexico
39 Mommy's threesome?
40 "Go along": 3 wds.
43 ___ a sudden: 2 wds.
44 "Get me ___ here!"
45 Last name that means "kings" in Spanish
46 More timid

Down

1 TV's "Queen of the Jungle"
2 Unanimously: 3 wds.
3 Drink of the Hindu gods
4 Affranchise
5 Department store retail chain
6 Lacking imagination
7 Washroom, briefly
8 Even the score
9 Direct onto a target: 2 wds.
10 Aides: abbr.
14 Italian dictator
22 Math operation: abbr.
24 Hip hop musician who founded Soul Temple Records
26 Snubs
27 Fix, as a pump
28 In a fair way
30 Attractive
31 Medieval silk fabric
32 GM brand
33 "M*A*S*H" company clerk
35 Chief city of Nigeria
41 Little piggy, maybe
42 "How's that again?"

117

Across

1 Mia of U.S. soccer
5 Sewing machine spindle
11 Water buffalo's cousin
12 Up ___, resisting hotly: 2 wds.
13 "What are the ___?"
14 Hollywood industry
15 Guinness Book suffix
17 Campus sports org.
18 250, to Nero
20 Manage to get, with "out"
22 Internet protocol, initially
24 Melodic pieces
26 "The X-Files" extras
27 Fictional character created by David Chase: 2 wds.
29 City near Padua
30 Building material
31 Abilene to San Antonio dir.
32 Alias
33 "If only ___ listened …"
34 Pint-size pest
36 Anat. or biol., for example
38 Fishing nets
40 Flat: hyph.
43 Chinese philosopher: hyph.
44 Attorney General Janet
45 Drink of the Hindu gods
46 Religious title: abbr.

Down

1 Vietnamese coin
2 "Then what?"
3 Homestyler's representation, sometimes: 2 wds.
4 Come together
5 Clic Stic maker
6 Cat ___ tails (kind of whip): 2 wds.
7 French bench
8 Loaf makers: 2 wds.
9 Innateness
10 Decryption org.
16 Hardy heroine
18 "Gremlins" actress Phoebe
19 Joist, for example
21 Newsstand
23 Hair net
25 "___ Como Va" (1971 Santana hit)
26 Steve Carell's "Despicable Me" character
28 Elhi orgs.
32 "This is ___" (radio line): 2 wds.
35 ABM part
37 Base of a crocus stem
38 Patty Hearst's kidnap grp.
39 Baltic or Aegean
41 Coll. major
42 Palme ___ (Cannes award)

118

Across

1 "Orphée" painter
6 Like cornstalks
11 "Luck Be ____ Tonight": 2 wds.
12 "32 Flavors" singer Davis
13 Catch a break?
14 3:50, vis-à-vis 4:00: 2 wds.
15 Seasonal candy treats: 2 wds.
17 "____ is human …": 2 wds.
18 "Que ____"
21 Words to a ship's captain: 2 wds.
25 Botanist Gray
26 Division of time
27 Aggravation
31 Be disrespectful to
32 Extra
34 Word in some law firm names
39 Foot-long stick, often
40 Dior creation: hyph.
41 Agreeing (with): 2 wds.
42 Dryer materials
43 Particles
44 Gawk

Down

1 Beer buy
2 Cooking pot
3 Actress Martha, et al.
4 One-named folk singer
5 Blood group: 2 wds.
6 Cafeteria
7 Porto ____, Brazil
8 "You ____?" (butler's query)
9 Doctors who check out head colds, for short
10 1957 Physics Nobelist Tsung-____ Lee
16 Actor Stephen of "V for Vendetta"
18 Faux-____
19 Barbados clock setting letters
20 Mediterranean isl.
22 Yellow, for one
23 Apr. addressee
24 Dorm staff, initially
28 Ancient Palestinian
29 Seeds
30 Bag
31 "____ With a Kiss" (Britney Spears' song): 2 wds.
33 Muscat money
34 Hyundai or Honda
35 Place on the schedule
36 Fey of "30 Rock"
37 ____'acte: intermission
38 Zaire's Mobutu ____ Seko
39 Battering ____

119

Across

1. Sir Walter ___, British author (1771–1832)
6. Hungarian leader Kadar
11. Counselor-___: hyph.
12. Apply, as pressure
13. Tired of going from place to place: hyph.
15. "Dies ___" (hymn)
16. Philosopher Lao-___
17. ___ Maria (liqueur)
20. "Here Is Your War" author Ernie
22. WWW addresses
24. Label again, as a computer file
28. Classic breakfast: 2 wds.
30. Summer cooler: 2 wds.
31. NYSE units
32. "Livin' la ___ Loca"
34. Enzyme ending
35. Santa ___, Calif.
38. Greek cheese
40. Changing places at the gym: 2 wds.
45. Buy-one-get-one-free item?
46. Jazz pianist Blake
47. Fountain orders
48. Some collars

Down

1. Convened
2. Cir. midpoint
3. Ending for pay or gran
4. Rikki-tikki-___
5. Pipsqueak
6. Covered with stones
7. Can
8. "Cool!"
9. Bobby and others
10. Eye ailment
14. Church figure: 2 wds.
17. Paraguayan people
18. Camaro ___-Z
19. Wings: Lat.
21. Chemical endings
23. "___ Network" (1980s comedy series)
25. Turkish title
26. Supervisors, briefly
27. Latin 101 verb
29. Herd members
33. "___ Grows in Brooklyn": 2 wds.
35. Hannibal's hurdle
36. ___ contendere
37. Battery fluid
39. August, to Auguste
41. Hawaii's other Mauna
42. Letters after the price of a used car
43. Not max.
44. French possessive

120

Across

1 Attention-getting cough
5 Vladimir Nabokov work
11 Data-entry acronym
12 Like some humor
13 Hot and dry
14 Cast lines
15 Providing opposition
17 Charges
18 Former federal agency for carriers: inits.
21 Allot
24 Get-out-of-jail money
25 Small part in a play
26 Caffè ___
27 Old expletive
28 Cash in
29 Medic, shortly
30 Dinner, lunch or brunch
31 Knickers: 2 wds.
36 Frightened, in dialect
38 Sheltered and secluded place
39 Rock that can be sculpted
40 Pastrami purveyor
41 Sped by, on the highway
42 Winter toy

Down

1 Culture medium
2 Add to the staff
3 Protection: var.
4 Altered in some way
5 Lend an ear
6 Killer whales
7 Desolate
8 Get going
9 Restaurant calculation
10 Take to the stage
16 Utah's state flower
19 Recognize as a source
20 Red Skelton's Kadiddlehopper
21 Breezed through
22 Kind of palm
23 Dollars, slangily
24 Barren plateau region of North and South Dakota and Nebraska
26 Bound
28 Thatched
30 First name in country music
32 Brings in, like a crook
33 "Mad Dogs and Englishmen" writer Coward
34 Enameled or lacquered metalware
35 Lose traction
36 Increase, with "up": abbr.
37 J.F.K. regulators

121

Across

1 Eccentric
8 "Casablanca" pianist
11 Conditionally released prisoner
12 Color chart component
13 "Merchant of Venice" moneylender
14 30-second spots on TV
15 Give the go-ahead
16 "E lucevan le stelle," for one
17 Vent, as a volcano
20 Blows one's top
22 "Robinson Crusoe" locale
23 Animal that carries the plague
24 Manhattan area, ____ Square
26 Sudden invasion
30 Big shot, initially
32 Adult female horse
33 Kind of wax
36 Many a tournament
37 "American ____" (TV show)
38 Fall back, as the tide
40 Modern: prefix
41 Makes an appearance
45 S. ____, 40th state
46 Break
47 Artfully subtle
48 Core

Down

1 Saturn's wife
2 Morse T
3 Arid
4 Moth caterpillar that destroys crops: 2 wds.
5 ____ vera (lotion ingredient)
6 Hannibal ____, character in "The Silence of the Lambs"
7 Albanian coin
8 Astute
9 Sit in on, as a class
10 Table mountains
16 Motor vehicle
17 Get benched
18 Greek letter after chi
19 "Nightmare" street
21 Brit. mil. heroes
25 Envy or gluttony, e.g.
27 Séance sound
28 Equal
29 Asian capital?
31 Heatherlike shrub
33 Fastens securely
34 Perfection embodiment
35 Eccentric
39 Male sibs
41 Big rd.
42 Delivery vehicle
43 And more, for short
44 Discern

122

Across

1 Chairman Zedong
4 Animal tranquilizing drug, initially
7 A.C. letters
10 Hudson Bay prov.
11 Not just him
12 Head lines, for short?
13 Another: 2 wds.
15 Big: abbr.
16 Unusual, in Caesar's day
17 Astound
19 A-list
21 Pate base
23 Wee, to Burns
25 Kay of "Rich Man, Poor Man"
26 52, in old Rome
29 Rx org.
31 Narc's org.
32 Some blowups: abbr.
34 Grandma: Ger.
36 Minute floating sea creature
38 "___ in Toyland"
42 Flubs
44 Violinist André
45 French possessive
46 Atlantic game fish
48 Ending for Sudan or Taiwan
49 Scratch (out)
50 "Mamma ___" (ABBA song)
51 Hallucinogen's initials
52 Fix, in a way
53 Hallow ending

Down

1 Demi or Dudley
2 Year's record
3 SNL last name
4 Saigon soup
5 Book publisher Bennett
6 Pearl green shampoo
7 Dear
8 Of the world
9 Fashionable boot brand
14 Dojo flooring
18 Black gold
20 Voltaic cell meas.
22 Head producer for the Wu-Tang Clan
24 Brouhaha
26 "___ Miserables"
27 All fouled up: 3 wds.
28 Treated cruelly: hyph.
30 Embassy head: abbr.
33 Letters on a sunscreen bottle
35 Golden ager's org.
37 Following
39 Ecological community
40 First word of a counting rhyme
41 Novelist Sontag
43 "The Open Window" writer
45 ___ Aviv (Israeli city)
47 "Andy Capp" cartoonist Smythe

123

Across

1 "By the Time I Get to Phoenix" singer Campbell
5 At a slant
11 Choir part
12 Truth
13 Old Chinese money
14 Prove, in court
15 Army recruit
17 "Mad Men" protagonist Draper
18 Part of a place setting
22 Altar locale
24 Carry around
25 Serf
27 Pago Pago is its capital
28 "I don't mind ___, Except as meals…" (Ogden Nash)
29 1 of 18 on a golf course
30 Cut Down
32 Cookbook abbr.
35 Organism that lives in or on a host
37 Aplenty
40 End of grace
41 Some dresses: hyph.
42 Astute
43 Express
44 Sports achievement award, initially

Down

1 Like residential areas can be
2 Open, grassy plain
3 Forever
4 Court plea, informally
5 Slender
6 Anti-flooding device
7 Light blue Monopoly avenue
8 ATM code
9 List catchall: abbr.
10 Blonde's secret, maybe
16 A deadly sin
19 Occasionally
20 Skating champion Midori
21 Award-winning "Miss Saigon" actress Salonga
23 Put off
25 "___ got high hopes …" (song lyric)
26 Common Mkt., once
27 Fizzy drink
29 Speaking against the church's beliefs
31 Ran swiftly
33 Prepare, as tea
34 Copper
36 "For Pete's ___!"
37 Accelerator pedal
38 Mont Blanc, say
39 It isn't the truth

124

Across

1 Bros, e.g.
5 Billy Davis Jr.'s singing partner Marilyn
10 Ulster, e.g.
11 Blubber
12 High: prefix
13 Alternative
14 Broadway's "___ Yankees"
15 Toot
16 Country album?
18 "And this pertains to me … how?"
21 Ted of "Cheers" and "Curb Your Enthusiasm"
23 Bundy and others
24 North Pole toymaker
25 Billboard blurbs
27 Scottish "no"
28 Ghost's cry
29 Fast food chain that sells square-pattied hamburgers
31 Ending for cloth or bombard
32 Approvals
33 Parmenides' home
35 Cleaning cloths
38 Realtime broadcasting: 2 wds.
40 Gen. Robt. ___: 2 wds.
41 Baby's garment
42 Munich's river
43 Discloses
44 Drop the gauntlet

Down

1 Edible fish
2 Kansas city on the Neosho River
3 1995 Val Kilmer movie: 2 wds.
4 Is frugal
5 Broods
6 Pigeon's home
7 Spicy Tex-Mex munchies: 3 wds.
8 Tic-tac-toe line
9 Suffix with lag or lamp
11 Make moves like a boxer: 3 wds.
17 Mauna ___
19 Hydrating cream brand
20 Suffix for abnormalities
21 Actress Mazar
22 Diaper cream ingredient
26 French pronoun
30 Moon of Neptune
32 Abominable Snowmen
34 "___-majesté"
36 Clockwork component
37 Bone-dry
38 High shot in tennis
39 ___ flash: 2 wds.

125

Across

1 Computer's storage ability: abbr.
4 "Hardly!"
7 Monetary unit of Romania
10 AOL, e.g.
11 Bother
12 Cabinet Dept.
13 Reel
15 Accelerator bit
16 SeaWorld star
17 Mayberry letters
19 Wall St. figure
21 Natives of Nigeria
24 Show presenter, initially
27 Material like an adhesive
29 Attack-trained military unit: 2 wds.
31 It's below the chest
32 Suffix meaning "recipients of an action"
33 Diva's big moment
34 Starchy food
36 Indianapolis to Chicago dir.
38 Poetic feet
42 Legal org.
44 Divert
46 Considerably
47 Devoured
48 100 lbs.
49 Coral reef
50 Ltr. addenda
51 Hawaiian forest tree

Down

1 Get wrong
2 Bk. of the Bible
3 Film rating org.
4 1930s Chicago Bears great, Bronko ____
5 Complimentary poem
6 Unit of pressure
7 Uncovered: 2 wds.
8 Freudian topic
9 Coffee holder
14 "Today" rival, briefly
18 Flaky pastry
20 Burly
22 "____ bitten…"
23 Holy Fr. women
24 Department of Transportation agcy.
25 Awaken
26 Everyday
28 ____ d'honneur (duels)
30 Persian Gulf nation
35 Chairman who was also a poet and calligrapher
37 Tin foil, e.g.
39 Slime
40 ____ Spirit (stealth bomber): 2 wds.
41 ____ new standard: 2 wds.
42 Historical US non-interventionist group, initially
43 Cote quote
45 Bug-eyed ones, maybe: inits.

126

Across

1 Dirt, so to speak
5 Heatherlike shrub
11 Hightail it
12 Spin
13 Ram, for one
14 Kind of cuisine
15 "Do the Right Thing" setting
16 Manuscript encl.
17 Bath powder
19 Sleazy newspapers
23 Soft & ____ deodorant
25 A Gershwin
27 "Titanic" name
28 Crash into on purpose
29 "Ed Wood" director Burton
30 Incidentally, in e-mail shorthand
31 Bass ____
32 Turning twos, in baseball: abbr.
33 Small batteries' letters
34 Grass strip beside a road
36 Coming ____ end (concluding): 2 wds.
38 Hawaii tuna
40 High flyer
43 Shoelaces alternative
46 Brand of pet food
47 Beehive State native
48 Genetic letters
49 Prevents
50 "It comes ____ surprise to me...": 2 wds.

Down

1 Schools of thought
2 Final Four gp.
3 One working for the whole day: hyph.
4 Black Sea port, new-style
5 Doctors' orders?
6 Brief scintilla
7 Cyberspace
8 Dashed
9 "Lord, is ____?" (Last Supper question): 2 wds.
10 Dry, as wine
18 English prof.'s deg.
20 Tirana residents
21 "____ move on!": 2 wds.
22 Farm females
23 Boring, colorwise
24 Crackling sound
26 "I ____ over this...": 2 wds.
35 Hairy-chested
37 Director Kurosawa
39 1960s militant Brown, familiarly: 2 wds.
41 Bad bill collector?: hyph.
42 Gas acronym
43 Saturn model
44 Aliens, for short
45 California's largest newspaper, for short

127

Across

1 Chinese gelatin
5 Common sense?
10 Arm part
11 Cutting edges
12 Enjoy, as benefits
13 Extended
14 Physicist's study
16 Firearm, slangily
17 Board material
19 Waltz, e.g.
23 Flight from justice
24 "A League of Their ___"
25 Poseur
28 Imitates a hot dog
30 The Soul ___, eight-piece New Orleans based brass ensemble
32 Not having guns
36 Told stories
37 Measurement before worm or meal
38 Bearish
39 Genesis twin
40 Work, as dough
41 Chapter 11 issue

Down

1 A saint or star may have one
2 Valley in Scotland
3 Object of loathing
4 Kind of sharp wit
5 Scheduled
6 "Om," e.g.
7 Advantage
8 Bad look
9 Hallucinogen's initials
11 Babysitter' bane
15 April follower
17 Dobby or Winky or Kreacher, in Harry Potter
18 Blemish
20 Baloney
21 100 lbs.
22 Neon has two of them
26 Astronomy Muse
27 Rely (on)
28 Confident solver's tool
29 Fighting alongside one another
31 Foreshadow
32 Alert
33 European language
34 Healing sign
35 Bolted
36 Hearty "ha, ha, ha"

128

Across

1 Family member
4 Cambridge U.
7 Bake sale org.
10 Dockworker's org.
11 ____ dare: 2 wds.
12 Smoked salmon
13 Wounds
15 Over or on: prefix
16 Coast-to-coast: abbr.
17 ____ Sanford (Louise of "The Jeffersons")
19 Out of sorts
21 Graduates
23 ____-dokey
27 Starter: abbr.
28 Mass. setting
30 Highlands negative
31 Two states: abbr.
33 Aisle escorts
35 Aligned: 3 wds.
37 Explosive solid used in detonators
40 Maori war god
43 Biblical suffix
44 Idealized person or thing
46 Old French coin
47 General on a Chinese menu
48 The Buckeyes, initially
49 "Boo-o-o!"
50 Little, in Leith
51 Ayr man's hat

Down

1 "Runaround Sue" singer
2 ____ Romeo (Italian car company)
3 "Get Lucky" band: 2 wds.
4 Back-to-work time: abbr.
5 Principle of independence
6 Café cup
7 Common man of ancient Rome
8 Drink like a fish
9 Angle between stem and branch
14 Gr. 1-6
18 Rumpus
20 Propyl suffix
21 A hand
22 N.Y.C. airport
24 Was well-educated: 3 wds.
25 Hearing organ
26 "I agree"
29 Early role-playing game co., initially
32 British title
34 ____ sapiens
36 Russian negatives
37 Golfer's bagful
38 List enders, briefly
39 As a result
41 Santa ____, California
42 "E pluribus ____"
45 ____ good turn: 2 wds.

129

Across

1 Dry, as wine
4 Cape ____
7 "This means ____!"
8 Serenade, e.g.
9 Red or Dead, e.g.
12 Shipping hazard
14 Modicum
15 Clarified butter in Indian cookery
16 Club-sandwich layer
18 Course
20 Near Eastern honorific
21 Native range horse
23 Evergreens
25 Cable material, initially
26 Criticize harshly
28 ____ tse-Tung
29 Broadcasts
31 Goes off-course
33 Long-jawed swimmer
34 Comparative word
35 Foolish
37 Place to be picked up?
40 Note after fa
41 Woman's ideal marriage partner: 2 wds.
43 "____ luck?"
44 "Tarzan" star Ron
45 Long time, to a geologist
46 English river
47 Genetic evidence, shortly

Down

1 Big sip
2 Per person
3 Unpleasant insect: hyph.
4 Bowl over
5 Wind from a 45º direction
6 Hopeless or forbidden: 2 wds.
9 Carefully controlled for effect: hyph.
10 Destroy gradually: 2 wds.
11 Excited activity
13 Boyfriend
17 Can
19 Medicinal amt.
21 Tax returns pro.
22 French town on the Rhone
24 "Mayday!"
27 Extreme
30 ____ Lanka (country)
32 Delhi princess
35 Canada's neighbor, for short
36 Certain merganser
38 Unit of perceived loudness
39 Highest active volcano in Europe
42 Alternative to white or wheat

130

Across

1 Entice
6 Union member
11 Honolulu hello
12 Bring up the rear
13 ___ Major
14 Kingdom
15 "Walking on Thin Ice" singer Yoko
16 "___ also serve who…"
18 Doctor
20 "___ to Liberty" by Shelley
23 ___ d'amore
25 Riot
27 Ringworm
29 Major Asian language
30 Warbles
32 Attention-getter
33 "Lord of the Rings" beast
34 Drop off
36 ___ bean (versatile legume)
37 Lush's sound
40 Hoopster
43 Dirt
45 "The Barber of Seville," e.g.
46 Popular fragrance
47 Sheba, today
48 Swelling

Down

1 ___ Bell (Mexican fast-food chain)
2 Distinctive flair
3 Flat, unvarying in pitch
4 Greek F
5 Spoonful, say
6 Elongate
7 3, in cards
8 Mini-battery letters
9 Kay Kyser's "___ Reveille"
10 Kind of beetle
17 Controls
19 Cinema can content
20 One who appreciates wine
21 Pedestal part
22 Broadcast
23 One of four Holy Roman emperors
24 Ethiopian money unit
26 Bar mitzvah, e.g.
28 Loser: hyph.
31 Cunning
35 Two under par, on a hole
36 Like leaves in late autumn
38 Prayer leader
39 Anatomical cavities
40 Coquettish
41 King Kong, for one
42 Diamond or ruby
44 Free from, with "of"

131

Across

1 Clubhouse drink
5 Drops off
11 Australian export
12 Stick or split
13 Celebration noisemaker
15 Big bang producer, for short
16 Plunder
17 Ltr. holder
18 Acceptances
20 Govt. agency founded in 1953, initially
21 Girl, in Scotland
23 ___ Aviv, Israel
24 Influences
27 Artery problems
29 Early night, in an ode
30 Canyon comeback
32 Back muscle, familiarly
33 Buffet
37 Before, either way
38 Order between "ready" and "fire"
39 Actor/bodybuilder Ferrigno
40 Type of breakfast
43 Adjusting (a piano)
44 "My Name Is ___"
45 ___ of Liberty
46 Celtic tongue

Down

1 Sentimental person, informally
2 Express
3 Game room activity, perhaps
4 Bubbly beverage
5 Down's opposite
6 Spill the beans
7 N.R.C. forerunner
8 Forms a fondness for: 2 wds.
9 50–50 wager: 2 wds.
10 Medium-sized African cats
14 Clothes line?
19 Astute
22 Big plan
24 Culls
25 Fatigue: 2 wds.
26 Feeler
28 Chop off
31 Shrink in fear
34 Aisle stop
35 Flies high
36 Gown fabric
38 Indigenous Japanese people
41 Palindromic bird
42 Born

132

Across

1 Letters on a Soyuz rocket
5 Powerful sharks
10 Gaza Strippers
12 Cleaned the floor
13 Like the "ng" sound
14 "Walk Away ___" (1966 hit)
15 ___-picking
16 Mont Blanc, for one
18 1975 AC/DC album
19 1995 Australian Open champ
21 Hems and haws
22 Well-pitched, in a way: hyph.
24 ___-Magnon man
25 Bel ___
27 Big name in pest control
29 Nonspecific amount
30 Singer Crawford
32 Big T-shirt size: abbr.
33 Jack-tar: 2 wds.
36 Fair-hiring inits.
37 W.W. II agcy. 1941–7
38 "Telephone Line" band, initially
39 Architect ___ Aalto
41 Harder to find
43 ___ anchor (be moored): 2 wds.
44 Head of a criminal org.: 2 wds.
45 Pale shades of beige
46 "Cagney & Lacey" actress ___ Daly

Down

1 Tropical plant with large foliage
2 Food writer Claiborne
3 Take a quick look: 4 wds.
4 Alley org.
5 Automobile ad letters
6 Astonish
7 Churchill Downs race: 2 wds.
8 Uncovered scan at some hospitals: 2 wds.
9 Cowboy's hat
11 Horror movie genre, slangily
17 52, to Caesar
20 Letters of distress
23 Gramophone needle holder: 2 wds.
25 Draft beer: 2 wds.
26 Saintly
28 Nutritionist's letters
31 "Antony and Cleopatra" prop
34 Liquid part of fat
35 Deep valley
37 Biscuit bits
40 Nonprofessional sports letters
42 "A jealous mistress": Emerson

133

Across

1 1990s Israeli P.M.
6 Model material
11 "Mefistofele" role
12 Noted Verdi aria: 2 wds.
13 Australian politico Sir Zelman
14 Canadian author Gallant
15 It comes before chi
16 Runs a hose on
17 Covered against loss or injury
20 Datebook abbr.
21 Those girls, to Juanita
22 Sincere
23 Scandinavian automobiles
25 "M*A*S*H" vehicles
26 Osculate
27 Indianapolis 500, for one
28 Soprano Sumac
29 Access to a sewer
32 Perfumed
34 Fix, as an outcome
35 Assume
36 On-the-rocks choice
38 Clumsy handler
39 Caught a glimpse of
40 Fifth-century pontiff: 2 wds.
41 Paper sections: hyph.

Down

1 Prefix meaning "straight"
2 What a bank may provide: 2 wds.
3 Show mental acuteness: 5 wds.
4 Chemistry suffix
5 Bread served with saag aloo
6 Hit the roof: 2 wds.
7 Smell ____ (be suspicious): 2 wds.
8 Motto of New Hampshire: 4 wds.
9 Rider's foothold
10 Natives of Melbourne, e.g.
16 Director Craven
18 Some computer ports
19 Dormitory heads, for short
22 Georgia ____, Altlanta university, familiarly
23 Airport porters
24 Targeted: 2 wds.
25 "The Brady Bunch" girl
27 Circle meas.
29 An "M" in M-G-M
30 Enjoyed
31 "Holy moly!"
33 Graf ____
36 Brandy letters
37 Facing: abbr.

134

Across

1 Bolted Down
4 Little devil
7 Dance, e.g.
10 Alternative to Rover
11 Drink in a pot
12 Baseball's Brock
13 Bumped into
14 Pop-ups, often
15 ____ of luxury
16 Lungful
17 Beyond tipsy
18 Burning sensation?
19 "CSI" sample
20 T.G.I.F. part
21 Come together
22 Ancient Greek gathering places
24 Pedestal part
25 Rampage: 2 wds.
27 Green gem
29 Like Chippendale furniture
32 Cummerbund cousin
33 Passing thing
34 Fleece
35 Portable firearm
36 First name in indie rock
37 Sign of infection
38 Fed. property manager
39 Ran in front
40 "Maid of Athens, ____ we part": Byron
41 Ballad's end?
42 Ed.'s request
43 Equine critter
44 Expressed matter-of-factly
45 Coast Guard officer: abbr.
46 ____ judicata

Down

1 Big fleet
2 ____ off (driving)
3 Weird
4 Language spoken in Siena
5 European sea
6 Histories
7 Avocado: 2 wds.
8 Bellowed
9 Mississippi city
23 "The Golden Girls" actress McClanahan
24 One of Snow White's buddies
26 Chemical salts
27 Ran for exercise
28 Exploitative type
30 Route
31 Haunt
33 Far from faithful

135

Across

1 ____ four
6 Molding at the base of a column
11 Circumvent
12 Alpine crest
13 Authorized
14 Physics lab device, for short
15 Thin canvas rug
17 Burnett or Channing
18 Clever tactic
21 One dozen
25 Suffix with mountain or musket
26 "We ____ to please"
27 Reddish-brown color
31 Edible roots
32 W.W. I soldier
34 Place for extra passengers in a small car: 2 wds.
39 Big house
40 Central, open areas
41 Dispatch boat
42 Musical "repeat" sign
43 Big name in oil
44 Moves briskly

Down

1 Ill-gotten gains
2 Diabolical
3 Food in a shell
4 Foolishness
5 "Four" at the fore
6 Fat used for making soap
7 Baltimore bird
8 1996 Tony-winning musical
9 2002 Winter Olympics locale
10 Dry, as wine
16 Computer monitor, for short
18 Podded plant
19 Moldovan monetary unit
20 Ball
22 Anita Brookner's "Hotel du ____"
23 ____ Appia
24 Bad ____, German resort
28 Highest
29 Manhattan cocktail made with Scotch whisky: 2 wds.
30 It's really nothing
31 Dismissal, expulsion
33 Minimal
34 1990s party
35 ____ cost
36 "Cogito, ____ sum"
37 Is not on the street?
38 Art colony of New Mexico
39 Glossy publication, for short

136

Across

1 Old-fashioned
8 "Miss Being Mrs." singer Lynn
9 FDR predecessor
12 Lower than low
13 Celestial altar
14 Bag of chips, maybe
15 "You're getting on my ___!"
17 "The Wind in the Willows" character
19 Suffix with dirt or draft
20 Code-breaking grp.
21 Core
24 Failed to include: 2 wds.
26 Government grant
28 "___ du lieber!"
31 Aoki of the PGA
32 Column foundation piece
34 Islamic leader
37 Deception
38 The Magic, on scoreboards
39 Encourage
41 Penn. neighbor
42 Decide mutually: 2 wds.
43 Sammy of baseball fame

Down

1 Support org. formed in 1951: hyph.
2 Machines resembling human beings
3 Fortune-tellers' needs: 2 wds.
4 Politically correct pronoun: 2 wds.
5 Cash cache letters
6 Make ___ adventure: 2 wds.
7 Racer Yarborough
9 "No idea": 3 wds.
10 Dimin.'s musical opposite
11 Undue speed
16 André ___, Dutch violinist and conductor
18 Mortgage adjustment, for short
22 Avg.
23 Some beans
25 Class for foreigners, for short
26 "The Goodbye Girl" writer
27 Charging too much interest
29 Humidor item
30 Strong types: hyph.
33 Not one's cup ___: 2 wds.
35 Literary olios
36 Science fiction's ___ Award
40 B.&O. et al.

137

Across

1 Broken-off branch
5 Conundrum
10 Dull hurt
11 In an ominous way
12 Pahlavi, e.g.
13 Ancient Roman magistrate
14 Dreadful
16 Fond du ___, Wisconsin
17 Joust weapon
21 Construction site sight
23 Ever ready
24 Blitzed
25 J.F.K. watchdog
26 Seaweed gelatins
29 Employs a stiletto
31 Excessive enthusiasm
32 Go public with
33 Take unawares
37 Small
40 Nonpareil: hyph.
41 Paid the penalty
42 Two-way
43 Euphemistic expletives
44 Catch a glimpse of

Down

1 Accessory for Miss America
2 Canyon effect
3 Flamboyant deceiver
4 1943 conference site
5 Rice dish made with saffron
6 Big test
7 Enjoy the Alps, perhaps
8 Connecting pipe
9 Monte Carlo ingredient
11 Apply gently
15 Dry ___ (it makes "smoke" in theater productions)
18 Wicked
19 Complain
20 Fraternity letters
21 Quahog or geoduck, e.g.
22 Baltic port
27 Getting up
28 Pan-fries
29 Dupe
30 Philippic
34 Valentine's Day color
35 Go ballistic
36 Hard to hold
37 Hip home
38 When a plane is due in, shortly
39 Freight weight

138

Across

1 Bonehead
6 Hourly pay
10 GMC pickup truck
12 IRS identifiers
13 Evil
14 Hit hard, slangily
15 Certain court hearings
17 Like some humor
18 Bread served with saag aloo
20 French annuity
22 Capitol Hill worker
24 Dog breed
27 Prettify oneself
29 Palindromic belief
30 Rubbernecking
32 He loved Lucy
33 Stravinsky and Sikorsky
35 "Wait a ___!": abbr.
36 Environmental prefix
38 Bleated
40 Prefix with phobic and lith
42 Sets of eight
45 Bidding site
46 Tattered along the edges
47 Thin (out)
48 Beasts of burden

Down

1 Away from NNE
2 Parisian pronoun
3 Not subject to limitations
4 Wasting time
5 High guy in Dubai: var.
6 One way to go: abbr.
7 Starts of Lents: 2 wds.
8 Watchdog's sound
9 Glimpse
11 Spot seller, for short: 2 wds.
16 Rotten little kid
18 Neighbor of 10-Across
19 Affectation
21 Follower of three- or pigeon-
23 Online issue
25 "___-majesté"
26 Suffix after "path" or "synth"
28 Difficulty: abbr.
31 ___ Empire (builders simulation game): 2 wds.
34 Pelvic bones
36 Big boss, for short
37 Island of the south central Philippines
39 Characters in "The Odyssey"
41 "Popeye" surname
43 Actor Billy ___ Williams
44 1960s campus grp.

139

Across

1 Ammonia derivative
6 Buds
10 Chief Justice after Marshall
11 Pope after John X: 2 wds.
12 "___ as I can see": 2 wds.
13 ABC sitcom
14 One way to get up a mountain: 2 wds.
16 Big: abbr.
17 100 yrs.
18 1997 U.S. Open champ
19 "___ on a Grecian Urn"
20 "Grazie ___!" (Italian for "Thank God!")
22 ___ blood (having murderous intentions): 2 wds.
24 Sawbuck: hyph.
26 "Turandot" and "Tosca"
28 "Eureka!" shouts
31 "___ Kapital" (Karl Marx)
32 E-mail ID, in short
34 Big music publisher, initially
35 "Either she goes, ___ go": 2 wds.
36 Put Down
38 Greek valley where games were held
40 See 37-Down
41 Zoo dart, for short
42 Ball game
43 1952 Winter Olympics city
44 Grab the wheel

Down

1 Lake ___, source of the Mississippi
2 Disguised
3 Immeasurably small
4 "Hud" Oscar winner
5 High nest: var.
6 ___ canto
7 Risky attempt to do something: 4 wds.
8 Exaggerate
9 Parton or Sinatra, e.g.
11 Eases: 2 wds.
15 One of the Bobbseys
21 "___ the fields we go"
23 Keats's "Ode ___ Nightingale": 2 wds.
25 Computerized system for trading in securities, initially
26 Tooth: prefix
27 Kitchen gadgets
29 Punish with an arbitrary penalty
30 Crablike mover
33 Snatches
37 With 40-Across, Tripping Daisy song of 1995: 2 wds.
39 "Achtung Baby" co-producer Brian

140

Across

1 Black bird
4 Shag rug made in Sweden
7 Clandestine
10 Mythical being, half man and half horse
12 Lao-tzu's "way"
13 Young offenders' institution of old
15 Overdo a scene
16 Confidence game
17 Bottomless pits
19 Comic's Muse
22 Occurs, poetically
24 Cyst
25 "Walk ___ Line"
27 Instinctive
28 Former GM make, shortly
30 Mean and cranky
32 Capital of the island of Hokkaido
34 1000 dirhams in Libya
35 Like some colonies
39 Hard to control
41 Scrape by (with "out")
42 Major news media
43 Frank McCourt memoir
44 Tolkien beast
45 Collector's goal

Down

1 Farm division
2 Indian tree
3 It's gathered by scouts
4 Baked dish
5 "Dee-lish!"
6 Keffiyeh wearers
7 Earliest known period of human culture: 2 wds.
8 Plant of the buttercup family
9 It comes easily to hand: hyph.
11 Full amount
14 Pshaw
18 Country bumpkin
19 Double standard?
20 Capital of Finland
21 Moderately slow musical movements
23 Dump
26 Unpredictable
29 Go a few rounds
31 Cactus related to the prickly pear
33 Place to see some Goya paintings
34 Health regimen
36 Nile bird
37 Nautical direction
38 Cozy retreat
40 Cadillac or Porsche

141

Across

1 Provider of top notes
8 Fleet runner: abbr.
11 1988 NFL MVP Boomer
12 Coastline feature
13 Inflatable sleeping surface: 2 wds.
15 Some tides
16 Big East team
17 Components of some PCs
18 1831 Poe poem
19 "-ish" alternative
20 Boredom
21 Mason-___ line, boundary between Maryland and Pennsylvania
22 Solitary man
24 Go after legally
27 Cinema films
28 Russian assembly
29 Angler's basket
30 Marla of "The Jeffersons"
31 Action of standing for election
33 After Sept.
34 On the fence
35 "Of course"
36 Covers up

Down

1 Rap session?
2 Some willows
3 Plagiarist
4 ___ up (accelerates)
5 Botanist Gray et al.
6 "___ a chance"
7 Punctually: 3 wds.
8 "___ Lonesome Tonight?": 2 wds.
9 Render harmless
10 Billiard shot
14 1998 Robert De Niro movie
18 Total stock of words in a language
20 Facebook format
21 Cut and ___ (clear)
22 Mann of education
23 Goings-on
24 Golf course location, perhaps
25 Darkest parts of shadows
26 Stands for painters
27 "Enterprise" medico
28 Same again
30 Indian bison
32 Animal house

142

Across

1 Intelligent
4 Enjoy the rink
9 Seize
11 Lavish bestowal
12 Damsel's rescuer
13 English landscape painter (1775–1851)
14 Pertinent
16 Square dancer, perhaps
17 Bothers
21 In addition
25 UN anti-child-labor agcy.
26 Cantilevered window
27 Once more
29 At some point in the past
30 Christmas Eve fuel: 2 wds.
32 Color quality
34 Garden pond swimmer
35 Loud and resonant, with a mournful tone
40 Talk of the town?
43 Arab bigwig
44 Emotionally unavailable type
45 Ancient alphabetic symbol
46 Computer expert, slangily
47 "Get the picture?"

Down

1 Turkish official
2 Make ready, informally
3 Baseball field covering
4 Closed
5 "M*A*S*H" setting
6 Barley bristle
7 Athletic supporter?
8 Act like a human
10 Dance energetically
11 Fence feature
15 "It hurts to say…"
18 Clock face
19 Mélange
20 CD track, often
21 Dinghy or dory
22 As a result
23 Suffix for man, ten or pen
24 Beauty shop
28 ____ counter, radiation measurer
31 Decree
33 Geological span
36 Blossom from a bulb
37 Birds on some ranches
38 Opening time, maybe
39 Elder, e.g.
40 Barbecue site
41 Great serve, in tennis
42 ____-tac-toe

143

Across

1 Some Olympians, nowadays
5 Ancient Peruvians
10 Auto option
11 Demi ___, actress
12 Place to which one is traveling
14 Make a copy of: abbr.
15 Unshorn sheep
16 Some fraternity men, initially
17 Before, for Burns
18 Die-rolling possibility
19 Hurricane heading, initially
20 Wall panels
22 Tout's forte
23 Data processor's data
25 Balladeer Ives
28 Capers
32 Cenozoic or Paleozoic
33 Downs' opposite
34 Do the deck
35 "Who ___?" (slangy query)
36 Ball stopper
37 Penultimate Greek letter
38 Question closely
41 Dolphins' home
42 Went white
43 Paid attention: 2 wds.
44 Wooden vehicle mounted on runners

Down

1 Membrane enveloping a lung
2 Uttered in a grating voice
3 Morsel
4 In love
5 Adult insect
6 "___ to worry"
7 Originated, as a phrase
8 In the vicinity
9 Sight, hearing, etc.
10 Did some math, maybe
13 Daily publication
21 "Texas tea"
22 Baseball's Master Melvin
24 Frees from obstruction
25 Darkens
26 Astronomy Muse
27 Drum sound: hyph.
29 Pierce, in a way
30 Estimated the price of
31 Caught a glimpse of
33 Break open
39 Bird that can't fly
40 Young woman (coll)

144

Across

1 Ad-supported online video service
5 "Li'l Abner" cartoonist: 2 wds.
11 Balin and Claire
12 Finds a new purpose for
13 Author of "The Martian Chronicles": 2 wds.
15 Skillful, competent
16 "What I think is…," initially
17 Grp. for Cardinals and Panthers
18 Deputized: 2 wds.
20 "How stupid of me!"
21 My, in Marseilles
22 Blood pigment
23 Cassettes
26 Felt concern or interest
27 Astronaut Shepard
28 Six, to Italians
29 ___ Tin Tin
30 Subterranean cell for prisoners
34 "Luck ___ Lady Tonight": 2 wds.
35 Room coolers, for short
36 ___-cone (fair cooler)
37 Not worried
40 Looked after: 2 wds.
41 ___ de soie (silk cloth)
42 Warming device
43 Small land masses: abbr.

Down

1 Takes on
2 Not fitting

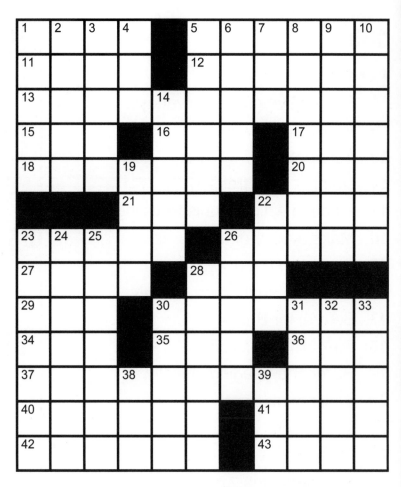

3 Bring a ship to rest: 2 wds.
4 Initially a mouse port
5 A Musketeer
6 ___ a wild goose chase: 2 wds.
7 Baby bear
8 In pieces
9 Scent
10 Excited
14 Carnival attractions
19 Foreboding sign
22 Reagan Secretary of State

23 Cap similar to a fez: var.
24 Property recipient
25 Nostrum
26 Odorize by burning
28 Assistance
30 "The Divine Comedy" writer
31 Old laborers
32 Actress Tatum
33 Knotty spot
38 Minn. neighbor
39 Oldest technological univ. in America

145

Across

1 One-____ (freak events)
5 Frozen spike
11 Bank deposit?
12 Lament
13 Deanna ____, Marina Sirtis's "Star Trek" role
14 ____ pentameter (kind of verse)
15 Strong black coffee
17 66, e.g.: abbr.
18 Appraises brazenly: 2 wds.
22 Accumulates, with "up"
24 Jackson 5 member
25 "____ Theme" ("Doctor Zhivago" song)
26 "The Faerie Queene" division
27 Lone Star State sch.
28 Narrow gorge with a stream running through it
29 "Let's Explore Diabetes with Owls" humorist David
31 Loafer designation
33 Automobile components: 2 wds.
35 Prompt
38 "So ____": 2 wds.
39 Leg wrap for soldiers
40 "Brokeback Mountain" heroine
41 More gloomy
42 Troughs for washing ores

Down

1 Blender brand
2 Ace: hyph.
3 Like some rabbits: hyph.
4 Cooking instruction
5 Wading birds
6 Knock off
7 Enduring
8 Corn core
9 "Love Story" composer Francis
10 Abbr. at the bottom of a letter
16 Antlered Alaskan animals
19 Complimentary close
20 When: 3 wds.
21 "____ bad!"
23 Power to learn
25 Light units: abbr.
26 Either horn of a crescent moon
28 Beam
30 Hindu queen
32 "Cómo ____?"
34 As blind as ____: 2 wds.
35 "World of Warcraft," e.g.
36 Part of E.U.: abbr.
37 1959 hit for The Kingston Trio

146

Across

1 Kind of pear
5 Catalog
11 Gp. against file-sharing
12 Finishing touches: hyph.
13 "Devil Inside" band
14 "Peter Pan" author
15 Dust Bowl denizen
16 Avail
17 Bad colds
19 A Muppet
23 Pakistani port
26 Ending for cloth or bombard
27 Conductor Seiji
28 "Little" girl of old comics
30 Harmful microorganism
31 Overpraise: 3 wds.
33 Part of a famous palindrome attributed to Napoleon: 2 wds.
35 Bound bundle
36 Rapper in the supergroup The Firm
38 Computer screens, briefly
41 Operate a plane
44 "East of Eden" character
45 Hold back, check: 2 wds.
46 ___ & the Gang ("Celebration" band)
47 Ball
48 Leave the theater

Down

1 Esprit
2 Pig's sound
3 Rock plant
4 Court precedent: 2 wds.
5 Waylay
6 Provided that: 2 wds.
7 Binge
8 Lord's Prayer starter
9 Coll. in Troy, N.Y.
10 Lao-___
18 West Coast sch.
20 It's in the catty corner?: 2 wds.
21 "From ___ You": Beatles: 2 wds.
22 North African port
23 Japanese port city
24 Cote d'___
25 ___ Ulyanov, Vladimir Lenin's father
29 Compressed linseed, etc., used as fodder
32 Gone
34 Counting everyone: 2 wds.
37 "It's ___!" ("Nobody wins!"): 2 wds.
39 "Star Trek" counselor, Deanna
40 Potato chip seasoning
41 iPhone program
42 Saturn ___, sport utility vehicle
43 In poor health

147

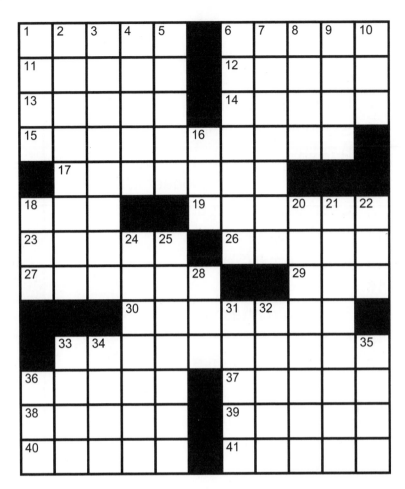

Across

1 Music industry assoc.
6 Spread, as lotion: 2 wds.
11 Lifted, so to speak
12 Port town on the coast of the Sea of Japan
13 Dog-____
14 Fender guitar model, briefly
15 "Healthy Aging" author: 2 wds.
17 Indiana, the ____ State
18 Pres. election mo.
19 Make brighter
23 Fop's footwear
26 Janitor's supply
27 TV watchdog
29 Sign for a packed theater, initially
30 50–50 wager: 2 wds.
33 Sacramento is its capital
36 First word of a counting rhyme
37 Florida city
38 Hightail it
39 Chipped in chips
40 Groups of actors
41 John ____ tractors

Down

1 Fishing, perhaps
2 Light open horse-drawn carriage
3 Pliable fine-grained leather
4 Old Oldsmobile
5 Footlike parts, zoologically
6 Scene of a mysterious crash in July 1947
7 Completely and without qualification
8 Adriatic port
9 Kind of hygiene
10 Filbert or cashew
16 Nintendo system
18 Presidential advisory gp.
20 Upper house of Congress: 2 wds.
21 Disney mouse
22 "Strange Magic" band letters
24 "Ash Wednesday" poet: 2 wds.
25 Americans' Cold War rivals
28 Gridiron official: abbr.
31 Desert wanderer
32 Pickling liquid
33 Anatomical cavities
34 Períodos de 52 semanas
35 Campaign staffer
36 Key in a corner, for short

148

Across

1 Rank below capt.
6 Stu's wife on "Rugrats"
10 Banish
11 Oral polio vaccine pioneer Albert
12 Court case standout: 2 wds.
14 "___ in alpha": 2 wds.
15 Away from WSW
16 ___U
17 Backboard attachment
18 Besmirches
20 Airline since 1948: 2 wds.
22 Act the masseuse
23 "She was ___ from the low country": old folk song lyric: 2 wds.
25 "Dear Sir or ___:"
27 Eric Cartwright's nickname on "Bonanza"
31 Popular Nintendo Game Boy game
33 Classic drama of Japan
34 Bard of boxing
35 Kind of dye
36 ___-Cat (winter vehicle)
37 Orson Welles's first feature film: 2 wds.
40 Mom's relative
41 Canadian physician Sir William ___
42 Part of R and R
43 Hard fats

Down

1 Lucrezia Borgia's brother
2 Beefy soup ingredient
3 Bad atmosphere
4 Middleman: abbr.
5 Marry again
6 "From ___ even to Beersheba": Judges
7 Airline to Madrid
8 Put down, slangily
9 R&D locales: abbr.
11 Backs of boats
13 Singer Cecil Campbell, familiarly: 2 wds.
19 "Entertainment Tonight" alum John
21 Bring on board
24 Class for expecting mothers
25 Illinois city
26 Curly-tailed dogs
28 Available for purchase: 2 wds.
29 Italian poem
30 Smiths
31 Harness racer
32 Desserts, to many dieters: hyph.
38 "The Addams Family" cousin
39 Wildcats of the Big 12 Conference, initially

149

Across

1 Turkish general
5 Wuss
10 Used
11 Clearly surprised
12 Of the blood
13 Arrive, as darkness: 2 wds.
14 Sad feelings of gloom and inadequacy
16 Arduous journeys
17 Austrian peaks
20 Son of Erebus and night
24 Gun, as an engine
25 Practice, as a trade
26 "America's Most Wanted" letters
27 Rogue
29 "Absolutely!"
30 Try to achieve, as a goal: 2 wds.
32 One who works his own land: 2 wds.
37 Charitable organization, e.g.
38 Spacious
39 Ellington and Wellington
40 High nest: var.
41 Clandestine meeting
42 Live wire, so to speak

Down

1 "Hard ___!" (captain's cry)
2 Hobbling gait
3 Playing card suit
4 "Inferiority complex" theorist
5 It opens many doors
6 Certain discriminator
7 Brussels-based alliance, initially
8 "Music for Life" magazine
9 Appetite
10 High degree, initially
15 Block up: 2 wds.
17 "Mustache Hat" artist Jean
18 Fragrant garland
19 Cable material, initially
21 "Green Eggs and ___"
22 Just make, with "out"
23 Bolted
25 Complain
28 Concurs
29 Rocky ravine
31 Propelled a boat
32 Forbidding
33 Black
34 "Encore!"
35 Arabic for "commander"
36 Bread for a pastrami sandwich
37 Environmental no-no, initially

150

Across

1 "Is that so!"
4 Guy
7 Armed services org.
10 Large percussion instruments
12 Ending for pistol or haban
13 Giving out
14 100 stotinki in Bulgaria
15 Elation
16 Sailor's agreement
17 "I Once Loved ____" (Scottish folk song): 2 wds.
20 Aired a second time
22 "Hawaii Five-0" actor, Daniel ____ Kim
23 Deutsch article
24 Empty boasting
30 Educ. institution
31 Big inits. in sports utility vehicles
32 Excite, as interest
35 Middle eastern currency unit
37 Big Ten inits.
38 ____ mater (brain membrane)
40 Outdoor sports chain
41 "King Lear," for one
45 A foot wide?
46 Administer, as laws
47 Prepared for the show to start
48 Barbados clock setting letters
49 N.C.A.A. football ranking system

Down

1 Volkswagen model
2 Ice: Ger.
3 German river
4 Posts
5 ____ of Cleves
6 Neighbor of Benin
7 Like some consonant sounds
8 Norse goddess of love
9 Made on a loom
11 Wrinkly dogs
17 Descriptive wd.
18 "____ note to follow soh…": 2 wds.
19 Old nuke org.
21 Med. specialty
23 Biblical suffix
25 Inst. in Nashville
26 Brewer's product: 2 wds.
27 Starter: abbr.
28 Grandma: Ger.
29 A.T.M. maker
32 Skin openings
33 "____ Dark Stranger" (1946 spy film): 3 wds.
34 "Shhh!"
35 Air current
36 Othello's betrayer
39 Caterer's collection
42 Tarzan creator's monogram
43 700, in Roman numerals
44 Positive reply

151

Across

1 "___ Adventures in Wonderland"
7 Bangkok native
11 Disperse: 2 wds.
12 Bribes
13 Rigid bracelet
14 Held back
15 Don't waste
16 "Save" shortcut on a PC: abbr., 2 wds.
17 Cedar Rapids college
19 Genetic letters
21 Former name of the cable network Versus, initially
22 Disentangle
26 Honorary law degree, initially
27 CAT scan relative
28 Make a move
29 Chinese religion
31 Measure of conductance
32 Top of the glass
34 Ability tested by Zener cards, initially
35 Clean up, in a way
38 Suppositions
40 "Free Willy" creature
41 Gourmet's sense
44 Come into view
45 Connect, as peripherals: hyph.
46 Clothing designer Taylor and TV newswoman Curry
47 Nerds

Down

1 Mil. jet locale
2 When doubled, a Teletubby
3 Insinuation
4 Gear parts
5 Noted blind mathematician
6 ___-Foy, Que.
7 Syllables of reproach: 2 wds.
8 Field worker
9 Freezer or blender, e.g.: abbr.
10 Adherents: suffix
16 "Would you allow me…?": 2 wds.
17 .45 maker
18 ___ podrida
20 1920s Olympics star from Finland
23 Junior, to Senior
24 Folk singer Phil
25 Car roof feature: hyph.
27 Amt. you don't expect to pay
30 Support group?: hyph.
33 Cat's cry
35 Gaucho's weapon
36 "Dianetics" author Hubbard: 2 wds.
37 Coll. major
39 A lot of ice
41 College prof.'s degree
42 Bath
43 Some dance records, for short

152

Across

1 Breaks for most of the players
6 Indigo-yielding shrubs
11 Oil can, maybe
12 Of certain ecological areas
13 "That's ___ nonsense!"
14 Dirt
15 "Aladdin" prince
16 Diamonds, to hoods
18 Old Tokyo
19 "Argo" director Affleck
20 Loire valley product
21 Beret or beanie
22 Crosspieces between the legs of a chair
24 Additionally
25 Chess pieces
26 "The Princess and the ___"
27 Alpine animal
29 Corps member
32 Hide-hair link
33 More, in Madrid
34 Sun follower?
35 ___ generis (unique)
36 Decide to leave, with "out"
37 Build (on)
38 Bring upon oneself
40 Permeate
42 Cornrow's place
43 Islamic teacher: var.
44 Like John Tyler, among presidents
45 Arab leader: var.

Down

1 Young pigeons
2 Bargain hunter's heaven
3 Mexican, e.g.: hyph.
4 State that "Portlandia" is filmed in: abbr.
5 Tried hard
6 Colorado ski resort, or a tree you might find there
7 Keanu Reeves's character in "The Matrix"
8 Insusceptible of reform
9 Martin of "Ed Wood"
10 Boats with one mast
17 Alliance that includes Russia, Tajikistan, Moldova, etc.
23 Annoy
24 The "p" in r.p.m.
26 Hobby
27 Put one's foot Down
28 ___ back (recover)
29 AAA offering
30 Tubercle
31 Make liked
33 Shift shape
39 Last, for short
41 Ornamental flower, for short

153

Across

1 Foreign Legion hat
5 Crops up
11 "___ (For You Baby)" (Ritchie family song): 4 wds.
13 Classic breakfast: 2 wds.
14 One laying down sticky stuff
15 Boundary: comb. form
16 ___-dink
20 Grammy category: abbr., 3 wds.
21 Chalon-sur-___, city SSW of Dijon
22 High-on-the-highway letters
23 Bleed
24 Indian state
27 Brad and William, e.g.
29 ___ music (compose a score for): 2 wds.
30 Tennis champ Arthur
31 Large soft hat of old
33 They're made on January 1st
38 Dish with lettuce, cheese and croutons: 2 wds.
39 Indifference
40 Half in front?

Down

1 Laotian money
2 "Hold on Tight" band, initially
3 Aristotle, for one
4 Bouncer's check: 2 wds.
5 Certain league: abbr.
6 Actress Winona and others
7 1968 James Michener novel
8 Circle pt.
9 Monogram of Mason mysteries' author
10 MA and PA
12 Laura Petrie's anguished cry: 2 wds.
15 Hole that an anchor rope passes through
17 End of the world?: 2 wds.
18 "All American" name
19 Aches (for)
20 Vitamin amts.
25 Not more than: 2 wds.
26 Simoleons
27 Agreements
28 Jeremiah preceder
32 Cover completely
33 "His Master's Voice" initials
34 Literary monogram
35 Bering, for one
36 "China Beach" setting, in short
37 "Star Wars" project of the 1980s

154

Across

1 Boone's nickname
5 Scottish portrait painter Allan
11 Epithet of Athena
12 Brazilian beach resort
13 Don't go
14 Crablike mover
15 Al of Dixieland
16 Suffix with cash
17 Booty
19 Actress Swenson
23 Cow chow
25 Port on the River Elbe, Germany
27 MOMA showing: 2 wds.
29 Containing element number 76
30 Opening for lubrication: 2 wds.
32 ___'s ice cream
33 ___ Alto
34 Danube feeder
36 1957 Physics Nobelist Tsung-___ Lee
38 Qatar's capital
41 Banner
44 Gigantic baby
45 Put in stitches?
46 Black-billed birds
47 Cheerless
48 Bookbinding leather

Down

1 100-meter, e.g.
2 High: prefix
3 Vast majority: 2 wds.
4 Apply with vigor: 2 wds.
5 Blue-green "Sesame Street" character
6 "I cannot tell ___": 2 wds.
7 Leaf bisectors
8 NBC sketch series
9 Cooler
10 Shostakovich's "Babi ___" Symphony
18 "___ be in England" (Browning): 2 wds.
20 Head honcho: 2 wds.
21 Map overlay
22 CIA pt.
23 Barrel band
24 Pacific capital
26 ___ Tavern ("The Simpsons" locale)
28 Element used in electroplating
31 Model train maker
35 Negative campaign feature: 2 wds.
37 Taj Mahal site
39 Early Chinese dynasty
40 Pt. of PGA
41 School grouping in some states, initially
42 Rapa ___, native Polynesians of Easter Island
43 OH and OK, e.g.

155

Across

1 Flood residues
5 Singer Guthrie and street skater Eisenberg
10 Intestinal parts
11 Marcos of the Philippines
12 Former Chargers/Patriots linebacker Junior
13 "I'm impressed!": 2 wds.
14 Boston basketballer
16 "Back in the ___"
17 Highway divider
19 Brit. honor, initially
21 Hot spot
25 3-D exam
26 "___ the fields …"
27 Suffix with Caesar
28 Crooner Frank
30 "60 Minutes" network
31 "Four Essays on Liberty" author Berlin
33 Stargazing, in college course books: abbr.
36 Sponsor of Ameritrade Park, Omaha: 2 wds.
39 Sentimental movie, to a Brit.
41 "Cogito, ___ sum": Descartes
42 Ancient: hyph.
43 Stravinsky ballet
44 Deadens
45 ___ Verde National Park

Down

1 Catchall abbr.
2 "___'s Gold" (1997 movie about a beekeeper)
3 New player's declaration: 3 wds.
4 Brown
5 "Yo te ___"
6 Adjust, in a way
7 Lawyers' degs.
8 Harem rooms
9 Baghdad's ___ City
11 Destroyed in a furnace
15 Numbskulls
18 Frightened
19 Baseball V.I.P.s
20 Man's nickname
22 Fill again, as energy in a battery
23 Apprehend
24 Come-___ (advertising ploys)
29 Cook corn, in a way: 2 wds.
32 At right angles to the keel
33 Lots, as of bills: 2 wds.
34 ___ Genesis (video game company)
35 Abound
37 Non-profit, voluntary citizens' groups, initially
38 Hawaiian coffee
40 French pronoun

156

Across

1 Stagehands
6 "Metamorphosis" protagonist Gregor
11 Checking account type: 2 wds.
12 Indo-European
13 Heretofore: 2 wds.
14 Airplane seat access
15 1990s Indian P.M.
16 African capital
18 New England sch., home of the Minutemen: 2 wds.
20 Teacher's deg.
23 Book of the Apocrypha
25 La ___ (fossil site)
26 "Me too!": 2 wds.
27 Cake part
28 Hosp. staffers
29 Inner part of a nut
30 Amphibious landing craft, initially
31 Foreword, for short
32 Flops, withers
34 Martin ___ Buren (8th president)
37 Celebrated Italian violin maker Nicolo
39 Opposition
41 Large house
42 It was ___ of the tongue: 2 wds.
43 Group of eight
44 Shocked with a device

Down

1 Snarl or growl
2 Santa ___, Calif.
3 "___ My Peaches (You'd Better Stop Shaking My Tree)" (Irving Berlin song): 4 wds.
4 "___-wee's Big Adventure"
5 Predetermined cost: 2 wds.
6 Swedish cars
7 "Tosca" tune
8 Detective fiction: 2 wds.
9 ___ soda
10 Chemical suffix
17 ___ Wednesday
19 Hr. divs.
21 "Groove Is in the Heart" singers ___-Lite
22 Clay-sand mixture
23 Actress Clayburgh
24 Ballpark figures
25 1990s Attorney General William
27 "Join me for a meal": 2 wds.
29 Chivalrous guy: abbr.
31 "But you said…!" response: 2 wds.
33 "___ Gift" (W. C. Fields movie): 2 wds.
35 Foreign pen pal
36 "___ Blue"
37 ___ , amas, amat
38 "Big" fast-food item
40 Code-cracking org.

157

Across

1 In ___ (mad): 2 wds.
6 Fairy-bluebird genus
11 Piece goods, perhaps
12 Taboos: hyph.
13 Municipal pound employees: 2 wds.
15 Balancing pro letters
16 "___-te-Ching"
17 ___ Tin Tin
18 Capacity of many a flash drive, informally: 2 wds.
20 Brit. gasolene
23 Barely beats
26 "Please have ___": 2 wds.
27 Hitlerites
28 Mia of U.S. soccer
29 Secretary of Transportation under Bush
30 Classic theater name
32 Affirmative vote
34 An N.Y.C. subway
35 Be worthwhile
38 Travel very fast: 2 wds.
41 1985 movie starring Kate Nelligan
42 Jay Silverheels role
43 "No mas!" boxer
44 Respected one

Down

1 Aussie hard-rock band
2 Food for pigs
3 Robe for Caesar
4 "Yadda, yadda, yadda"
5 Nondescript article
6 In disguise: abbr.
7 "Ruh-___!" (Scooby-Doo phrase)
8 Stimulate
9 Seaweed, in sushi bars
10 NBA part
14 Former Chinese monetary unit
18 Humorous ending meaning "big amount of"
19 Absurd
20 "Fiddlesticks!"
21 That, in Spanish
22 Modifying agent
24 Center of a peach
25 F.I.C.A. funds it
27 Wink: var.
29 Clay-sand mixture
31 ___ wait: 2 wds.
32 Sacked out
33 Korea Bay feeder
35 Lake's little cousin
36 ___ meridiem
37 "Son of Frankenstein" shepherd
39 Biochemistry abbr.
40 "Hilarious," to texters

158

Across

1 Speak foolishly
5 Deadly snake
10 Carry away
12 Burger topper
13 Fragrant oil
14 Backs, in anatomy
15 Article
16 C.E.O.'s degree, often
18 ___ Monte (Libby's rival)
19 Incursion
21 "And what have we here?"
22 Burn
24 ___ newton (cookie)
25 Decided
27 Mawkish
29 Bonehead
30 Old photo
32 Center of a peach
33 Boy sponsored at a baptism
36 Embitterment
37 Baseball great Brock or Gehrig
38 Ambulance chaser's exhortation
39 Lassitude
41 Thick rugs
43 Coral ridges
44 "___ Days a Week" (Beatles)
45 Razor sharpener
46 Guinea pigs, maybe

Down

1 "The Fiddler of Dooney" poet
2 Even if, briefly
3 Device that reduces mineral content: 2 wds.
4 Fund-raising grp.
5 Closing passage
6 "Walking on Thin Ice" singer Yoko
7 Avian migrant: 3 wds.
8 Fruit used to make tea and jelly
9 Comparison
11 Fine furs
17 Ask for alms
20 Old-fashioned contraction
23 Champion
25 Imitators
26 Restrainer worn on the head
28 Band-___ (scrape cover)
31 Bigheadedness
34 Should, with "to"
35 Bird houses
37 Slip of the tongue
40 Flying saucer, initially
42 Cool, man

159

Across

1 Hick
5 Less of a mess
11 Busy times at the I.R.S.
12 Kind of kick
13 Fighter of pirates, initially
14 Atomic trials of the past, for short: 2 wds.
15 Sharp-pointed
17 Honorary title holders
22 Conical tooth
26 Dept. of Labor arm
27 Asian palm
28 "A Doll's House" author
29 On the qui ___
30 Jostles
31 Simian
33 Impose (upon)
38 Fillet
42 River of Flanders
43 Beach atmosphere: 2 wds.
44 Nabokov heroine and others
45 Holly or Heidi of "The Hills"
46 "Promised Land" director Gus Van ___

Down

1 Singular, to Caesar
2 Gone ___ smoke (spoiled, wasted): 2 wds.
3 Act the blowhard
4 Grandson of Sarah
5 Lacking fame: hyph.
6 ___ nous
7 Enzyme suffix
8 "___ folly to be wise"
9 D.C. summer clock setting
10 ___ gestae
16 Olin of "Chocolat"
18 Former Virginia governor Chuck
19 "That ___ true!": 2 wds.
20 Strength
21 McEwan and Somerhalder
22 Spanish wine
23 "What ___" (that's robbery): 2 words
24 Actress Campbell
25 NATO member: abbr.
28 "Why should ___ you?": 2 wds.
30 "La Dolce Vita" actress
32 Aegean region
34 Hand-woven rugs
35 Letters seen in a butcher's case
36 College bigwig
37 Formerly, in olden days
38 Mil. award
39 Fair-hiring letters
40 Prohibit
41 ___ grass

160

Across

1 Cereal staple
5 Prevented from speaking out
11 Dab with absorbent paper
12 Burrowing rodent
13 "Field of Dreams" setting
14 Shade
15 Guard
17 "Absolutely!"
18 Deity with cow's horns
22 Compensate for
24 Classic color for stationery
25 Frog-dissecting class, for short
26 Pistol, slangily
27 Angled annexes
29 Church plates
32 Bind
33 From the beginning
34 Causing desire
38 Anatomical cavities
41 Canaanite deity
42 Domestic: 2 wds.
43 "___ for the poor"
44 Fishes with a dragnet
45 Delight

Down

1 Eastern ties
2 ___ vera (lotion ingredient)
3 Municipality dwellers
4 Condition
5 Large seabird
6 Bad fit?
7 Hands-on soccer player
8 Colt, e.g.
9 Abbr. after a comma
10 Backgammon cube
16 Anger
19 Wiggy
20 "Pumping ___"
21 Beer, casually
22 "Do as I say"
23 Flaky pastry
28 "Two for the ___," Gibson play
29 Flat stones
30 "Wheel of Fortune" buy: 2 wds.
31 It steeps in hot water: 2 wds.
35 Catch
36 "You can do better than that"
37 "… or ___!"
38 ___ Tuesday (Mardi Gras)
39 "___ Father"
40 "Fat" farm

161

Across

1 Homer Simpson's favorite beer
5 Army ranks, initially
9 "Hamlet" fop
11 Non-native, in Hawaii
13 Chortle
14 Cancel
15 Rene's "Okay"
16 Med. land
18 Modern-day storage medium, initially
19 Düsseldorf direction
20 ___ water (it's from the faucet)
21 Freudian topic
22 Compensates
24 Had a hankering
26 Tickler of the ivories
28 Compulsive thief: abbr.
30 Marine creature
33 Composer-conductor Calloway
34 Flight coordinators, initially
36 G.I.'s address
37 Diplomat: abbr.
38 "omg thats 2 funny"
39 "Shop ___ you drop"
40 Rich kid in "Nancy"
42 ___ curiae (friends of the court)
44 Sheep fats
45 Wined and dined, perhaps
46 Blog feeds, initially
47 Massachusetts motto opener

Down

1 Computer language iteration: 2 wds.
2 Olympics chant: 2 wds.
3 Breakfast brand since 1971: 2 wds.
4 Cookie fruit
5 Wrinkly-skinned dog: 2 wds.
6 Devotee
7 Denseness
8 Gunk
10 Voucher
12 Scott of "Men in Trees"
17 Decline: 3 wds.
23 Have a bit of, as brandy
25 D.C. advisory group
27 Clueless: 3 wds.
28 Some 1980s Chryslers: 2 wds.
29 Love interest of Crosby and Hope
31 High points
32 Large meteor that explodes
35 Cat's scratcher
41 Capt.'s inferiors
43 Broadway's "Five Guys Named ___"

162

Across

1 Airborne
6 Wine holder
9 Small lake near a larger one
11 ____ Bora (Afghan region)
12 Eastern hospice for travelers
13 24-hour bank features
14 Joint problem
15 ____ corpus (law)
17 "Four Weddings and a Funeral" actor Grant
18 Afternoon in Acapulco
19 Peach or beech
20 Catholic service book
21 Medieval stringed instrument
23 Spanish store selling wine
26 Acorn bearers
30 "Life is not ____, it is a gift": 2 wds.
31 Old-fashioned knife
32 Give the cold shoulder
34 "Zip-____-Doo-Dah"
35 Animal house?
36 Drinks with a loud sucking sound
38 Flat: hyph.
39 Double dealing
40 North Carolina capital: abbr.
41 Like "20 Questions" answers: 2 wds.

Down

1 Get off one's high horse?
2 "Last of the Breed" author Louis
3 Model railroad scale: hyph.
4 In order to get things straight: 3 wds.
5 Little piggy, maybe
6 Electorate
7 Big fleet
8 Decorative bunch of cords
10 To the ____ degree
11 McIlhenny Co. product: 2 wds.
16 Play to ____, draw: 2 wds.
20 C.E.O.'s degree, often
22 Bavarian river
23 Entruster of property
24 Princess Leia ____
25 Man in the lion's den
27 Spanish guitarist Segovia
28 Prevent from leaving: 2 wds.
29 Makes sure about: 2 wds.
33 Group of schools in one area, for short
37 Willy ____, "Exotic Zoology" author

163

Across

1 City bombed in the Gulf War
6 Houses, in Spain
11 "Rings ___ Fingers" (Henry Fonda film): 2 wds.
12 44th President
13 "A Confederacy of Dunces" author
14 Out: 2 wds.
15 Caribbean city: 2 wds.
17 Military camp (Fr.)
18 Appropriately named fruit
20 Foolishness
25 Nine, in Spanish
27 City and county in Texas
28 Be pleasing (to)
30 Cover the upper surface (a room)
31 Prefix with comic
33 "Poetry Man" singer
38 Good, in Guadalajara
39 Bread spread
40 Weekdays, initially
41 Filmdom's Mr. Chips
42 ___ the opinion (thought): 2 wds.
43 Relating to

Down

1 Not just one
2 Indonesian buffalo
3 Moved with a spade
4 Not absolute
5 "Gladiator" setting
6 Yield
7 Hunt's "___ Ben Adhem"
8 Letters identifying a combination of voices (music)
9 "___ Psycho" (song by Midwest rapper Tech N9ne): 3 wds.
10 ___ Clemente
16 Bee: prefix
18 One, in France
19 Portable firearm
21 Cut
22 Confrontational: hyph.
23 102, in Roman numerals
24 Big initials in fashion
26 Die down: 2 wds.
29 Battle of Atlanta soldier
32 ___ book (be literate): 2 wds.
33 "I ___ Spell on You" (Jay Hawkins song): 2 wds.
34 Chops
35 Knowledgeable of
36 Slave in "The Good Earth"
37 1984–88 skating gold medalist
38 German automaker known by three initials

164

Across

1 ABC rival
4 Round, green vegetable
7 In what way?
8 Account
9 "Understand?"
12 Showy flower
14 Father, to Huck Finn
15 Like helium
16 Close call
18 Things to pick
19 Face cream target
20 All prepared
21 Angelina Jolie, for example
24 Catered gatherings
26 Colors for an artist
28 Check
31 Go for
32 Serpent deity group, in Hinduism
33 Cockeyed
35 "Psycho" setting
36 Perfect score, sometimes
37 Form a mental image
39 Physics class unit
40 Magnum, for one, slangily
41 "___ to Liberty" by Shelley
42 Bleating belle
43 A Bobbsey twin

Down

1 Metal shackles
2 Gangsters ___ and Clyde

3 Flattering persuasively: hyph.
4 Connive
5 Many, many moons
6 "It's been ___!"
9 Salut 1 was the first of its kind: 2 wds.
10 Brings home
11 Fencing swords
13 "The Ghost and ___ Muir"
17 "The Alienist" author Caleb
21 Back at sea?

22 Animal that meows
23 Make equal, as the score
25 Club dues
26 Dish
27 Pointer
29 Something hidden, perhaps
30 Whalebone
32 Egg ___ (Christmas concoction)
34 Construction location
35 Defensive spray
38 Kitten's cry

165

Across

1 Sprayed in a way
6 Adjusts into an exact position
11 Greek poem composed of couplets
12 Man of Marseilles
13 Brit's service discharge
14 Fanatical
15 Diamond authority, for short
16 Like fans
18 Largest city in Washington
20 "Do the Right Thing" director Spike
21 Oakley and Leibovitz
22 "___ Island" (2008 movie starring Jodie Foster)
23 ___ and outs
24 "Arabian Nights" creature
25 Court helper: hyph.
27 Micromanager's concern
30 Actor McKellen
31 Salk Institute for Biological Studies site: 2 wds.
32 Great Plains tribe
34 Cassette successors, for short
35 Part of a healthy diet
36 Words on a desk box: 2 wds.
38 Reigned over
39 "Odyssey" enchantress
40 "___ of pottage" (what Esau sold his birthright for): 2 wds.
41 Broke off

Down

1 Snake-haired horror
2 Cave dwellers
3 Sociable
4 Tokyo, once
5 Argues
6 Pang
7 Crowd noise
8 Source of a fetus's food: 2 wds.
9 "8 Mile" actor
10 Marsh plants
17 Inventories of injured sports players, intially
19 Baby
22 Say ___ (turn down): 2 wds.
24 Celebrate
25 Nigerian civil war site, 1967–70
26 Element #56
27 "Camptown Races" syllable
28 Moniker for Mussolini: 2 wds.
29 Went the distance
31 Cooking fats
33 Shopping centers?
37 "Children of the Albatross" author

166

Across

1 Musical symbol: 2 wds.
6 Tool for bending metal
11 Laborare est ___ (Masonic motto)
12 Dragged, historically
13 Tiny time period
15 That, in Oaxaca
16 Break
17 1,002, in old Rome
18 It borders Fla.
19 Flat-screens, e.g.
20 Tooth-doctors' org.
21 Just so: 3 wds.
23 WWW addresses
24 Ford flop
26 P.I.s
29 Letter-shaped band on a shoe: hyph.
33 All-purpose truck, for short
34 Alliance that includes Russia, Tajikistan, Moldova, etc.
35 Mo. in which the Civil War began
36 "Monster" rock group
37 Gallic soul
38 Extinct bird
39 Sustainable source of power: 2 wds.
42 Inspector Appleby's creator Michael
43 Aussie shout
44 "Star Wars" droid Artoo-___
45 ___ Wiggin (protagonist of Orson Scott Card novels)

Down

1 Approach: 2 wds.
2 The Count of Monte ___
3 Random chorus syllables: 3 wds.
4 Schubert's "The ___-King"
5 Faked, as in boxing
6 Some guard dogs, for short
7 SPAR's counterpart
8 Baseball family name
9 Agreeable
10 Whirlpools
14 Uses a shortcut: 2 wds.
22 French possessive
23 Final: abbr.
25 Gist
26 Bombastic
27 Everlasting, to the bard
28 Building material
30 Musket accessory
31 High point
32 Message communicated to God
34 Playground retort: 2 wds.
40 Classified ad letters
41 Long period of time

167

Across

1 Lets go of
6 Closing act?
10 In the air
11 Bard
12 Flagship of Columbus: 2 wds.
14 Demolition ball alternative, initially
15 Best Musical of 1995–6
16 Away from the bow
17 "And don't forget…"
21 Darwin's interest
25 "But of course!"
26 Overhangs
27 Milk dispenser
29 "… ___ he drove out of sight"
30 Equipment of a horse for riding
32 Moist and cold
34 Electronics brand, for short
35 Chills and fever
37 Many a corp. hire
40 Arsonist
43 Thick reference book
44 Kind of power
45 Jewish month
46 Irregularly notched

Down

1 Play group
2 Flamboyance
3 Mom's warning
4 Little wriggler
5 Five-armed sea creature
6 Bridge measurement
7 Blood line
8 Hawaiian necklace
9 Pilot's announcement, for short
13 Distribute, with "out"
16 Air hero
18 Stow, as cargo
19 Bruce Springsteen's "___ the One"
20 Crew members
21 Caraway
22 Plane-jumping G.I.
23 All tied
24 Come to an end
28 ___ test ("Law & Order" evidence)
31 Cuckoo pint, e.g.
33 Fate
36 Migrant
37 Otis's movie partner
38 Meadow sounds
39 A lot of lot
40 Class-conscious grp.
41 Hebrew letter
42 "Neither a borrower ___ a lender be"

168

Across

1 Cold dessert
7 Here, in Le Havre
10 Group of three
11 ___ a good thing: 2 wds.
12 Charm
13 Cleave
14 Islamic weight
15 By the item
17 Early smartphone
18 Deserves it: 2 wds.
19 Bondman
20 Black key: 2 wds.
21 She hid the spies at Jericho
23 Generous
26 Absorbed
30 Adjust
31 Brightly colored fish
32 Blubber
34 "Dumb & Dumber" actress
35 Bounce
36 Building material
38 "___ Coming" (1969 hit)
39 Laugh lightly: hyph.
40 Ham, to Noah
41 Flip-chart homes

Down

1 Begins
2 At least: 2 wds.
3 Carpenter's tool
4 1791 legislation: 3 wds.
5 ___ out a living
6 "Be seein' ya": hyph.
7 "___ Doctor" (Dr. Dre/Eminem song): 3 wds.
8 Agree
9 Completely committed: 2 wds.
11 Dubliners may talk with them: 2 wds.
16 Galileo's birthplace
20 Bill amt.
22 ___ Domini
23 Coral ___, Fla.
24 Repetitive sounding Philippine city
25 Stringed instrument
27 Army helicopter
28 Kind of post
29 Violent struggles
33 Bone (prefix)
37 ___ Party Nation

169

Across

1 Alley animal
4 Atlas abbr.
7 Mediocre: 3 wds.
9 Gym set: abbr.
12 Progress
13 Sound of satisfaction
14 "Go, ___!"
15 Exploitative type
17 Deodorant place
19 D-Day target town: 2 wds.
20 Artistic frame
21 Cleaver nickname
22 Coral ridges: abbr.
23 Basketball net holder
25 1950s political monogram
26 Winston Churchill's "___ Country": 2 wds.
28 Peg Bundy portrayer ___ Sagal
30 Prefix with graph
31 Despite the fact that: 2 wds.
33 Having bony plates on the skin
35 Robt. E. Lee, e.g.
36 "Baseball Sluggers" commemorative stamp honoree
37 Founder of Lima
39 Codebreaking arm of govt.
40 Apples' mismatches
41 "The Racer's Edge," initially
42 Down units: abbr.

Down

1 ___ del Sol
2 Consequences: 2 wds.
3 Fish roe paste that's pink
4 "The ___ Squad" ABC TV series
5 Abuse: 3 wds.
6 Accident investigating org.
8 Easily-fooled folks
9 Useless effort: 2 wds.
10 1986 Chris de Burgh song that hit #3: 4 wds.
11 ___ Tuesday
16 ___ port (computer outlet), initially
18 Ending for beef or bump
22 Turns in to the cops: 2 wds.
24 Dallas cager, for short
27 Fam. member
29 Indie band ___ and Sara
32 Dental ___
34 Grand story
38 Blast

170

Across

1 Cause of septicemia: abbr.
6 ___ and blood (kin)
11 Life of ___
12 Really slow, on sheet music
13 A spoken curse
15 Bow
16 S. ___ (st. whose capital is Pierre)
17 Appear
20 Dance, music, etc.
22 Bearded bloomer
24 Language of southeastern India
28 Lower number in a vulgar fraction
30 Takes an oath
31 Farm building
32 "Aye" voters
34 "___ a Liar" (song by the Bee Gees)
35 Gangster's gun, for short
38 Creep
40 Overstated
45 Change, sci-fi style
46 Palatal pendant
47 Condescending one
48 Flexible

Down

1 ___ Lanka (country near India)
2 "Ed Wood" director Burton
3 Mont Blanc, e.g.
4 Exec's benefit
5 Animal known for its laugh
6 Make level

7 Release, with "out"
8 "Idylls of the King" lady
9 Ancient gathering place
10 Toot the horn
14 Steroid hormone
17 Assists
18 All hands on deck
19 Food sticker
21 Chunk or hunk
23 "General Hospital," e.g.
25 Its motto is "Industry"
26 Blood's partner

27 Caterer's collection
29 Perfect future husband: 2 wds.
33 Cancel
35 Beauties
36 Impulse transmitter
37 Member of the arum family
39 "___ a good one"
41 Agency providing printing for Congress, initially
42 252 wine gallons
43 Antiquity, once
44 86,400 seconds

171

Across

1 ____ grip (wrestling hold)

8 New Deal org.

11 Gush

12 New walker

13 "The Case of Charles Dexter Ward" author: 3 wds.

15 Flying high

16 Former unit of currency in Peru

17 "These are the times that try ____ souls" (Thomas Paine)

18 "Up" actor Ed

19 Airport abbr.

20 Cameraman's count: 2 wds.

22 Effervescent drink made from fermented cow's milk

23 Niacin or thiamine, e.g.

26 CD follower

29 Become unnavigable in winter: 2 wds.

30 Contradict

31 Crowd sound

32 Alert another car with a honk: 2 wds.

34 Journalist's scoop: 2 wds.

36 Fanciful story

37 Binds together: 2 wds.

38 Outer: prefix

39 Plastic component

Down

1 Big plan

2 Pill variety

3 Cuba or Jamaica

4 English variety

5 Prepare for a rainy day

6 Had too much, briefly

7 ____ center

8 Prefix meaning "tin"

9 Tone Down

10 Garb

14 Stair part

18 Comparable (to)

20 ____ worker (non-permanent staff): abbr.

21 Movie org. with a "100 Years..." series

22 Coniferous tree of New Zealand

23 Very manly

24 Classic, as an image

25 Cups, saucers, etc.: 2 wds.

26 Lounge

27 Jogging: 3 wds.

28 "Sorry, you're not ____" (classic rejection): 2 wds.

30 Block

32 Defeat

33 Athlete's award, initially

35 Skid row woe letters

172

Across

1 Eyeballs
5 Baby bouncers
10 French rake?
11 The ___ State (Connecticut nickname)
13 Magician's word
15 Money for the server
16 Party time, maybe
17 Order between "ready" and "fire"
18 Guarantee
20 Beluga yield
21 Break
23 Beer drinker's stomach
24 Steam bath
27 Became an issue
29 "King Kong" babe
30 Averse: var.
32 ___ Alamos, N.M.
33 Unemotional
37 Pride or wrath, e.g.
38 Mail place, initially
39 "Blastoff!" preceder
40 Artifact that belongs to another time
43 Scratches left by a glacier on rocks
44 Black and white cookie
45 Granite-colored
46 Dampens

Down

1 Be bombastic
2 Early bird
3 After-dinner sounds
4 Hemingway book "The Old Man and the ___"
5 Scoundrels
6 Art subject
7 H, to Homer
8 Trade stoppage
9 Grave
12 Reproductive cell
14 Some like it hot
19 Coffee maker
22 Arm art, maybe
24 Mexican restaurant condiments
25 Consecrates with oil
26 Disentangle
28 Character used in density
31 Fish hawk
34 France's longest river
35 Hawaii's location, in atlases
36 Audition tapes, briefly
38 Steps leading down to a river in Asia
41 "The Good Shepherd" org.
42 Immediately

173

Across

1 Angler's quarry
5 Gather on the surface, chemically
11 Astringent
12 Carrier
13 Political matriarch: 2 wds.
15 Copy, for short
16 Canadian pop duo ___ and Sara
17 Attempts
19 Hyperbolic sine
21 Honeydew-producing aphid: 2 wds.
25 Antiquity, in antiquity
26 180 degrees from WSW
27 South American wood sorrel
28 Giants' footballer Jennings
30 Gym floor covers
31 Dined at a diner, say: 2 wds.
33 256 in Ancient Rome
36 "Ad ___ per aspera" (Kansas' state motto)
39 Woman abducted by Paris in Greek myth: 3 wds.
41 Strange fact
42 Campbell of "Scream 3"
43 Shooting iron
44 Golf pegs

Down

1 "Roseanne" star
2 ___ vera
3 Postpones
4 U.S.S.R. counter-espionage org.
5 "Honest" president
6 Gum brand with the varieties "Fire" and "Ice"
7 Least crazy
8 Wash. neighbor
9 Hester's emblem: 2 wds.
10 ___ Mawr, Pa.
14 Sends to the canvas, briefly
18 "Biography" network: 3 wds.
19 Father's talk: abbr.
20 Dockworker's org.
22 Clothing stand: 2 wds.
23 After Sept.
24 "We ___ robbed!"
26 Gnaw away at: 2 wds.
29 "I ___ on good authority": 2 wds.
30 Contraction meaning "taboo"
32 Big brute
33 Hack
34 Accra money
35 Attys.' degrees
37 Amble
38 Navy replies
40 Olive ___ (Popeye's lady)

174

Across

1 "Paging Dr. ___" (CNN show)
6 Govt. security: hyph.
11 Up ___ (cornered): 2 wds.
12 Half of an old comedy duo
13 Clairvoyants
14 "Chaplin" actress Kelly
15 Disney movie with a 2010 sequel
17 Boat propellers
18 Average guy
20 Algae bed?
22 Gen. Robt. ___: 2 wds.
24 Occurring in spring
28 Afterwards
30 Drudges
31 Not uttered
33 "Two Years Before the Mast" writer
34 Extraordinary, in Scotland
36 All the rage
37 Spot on the air?: abbr., 2 wds.
40 Old Fords, sometimes
42 Gulf of Aqaba port
44 "___ Ben Jonson" (inscription on a tomb)
47 Arcade flubs
48 Ground
49 Early ___ (no night owl)
50 Comedian Wanda of "Curb Your Enthusiasm"

Down

1 Auto-tank filler
2 Adaptable truck, for short
3 9-to-12 set
4 Dakota, once: abbr.
5 B.C. fabulist
6 ___ Sawyer
7 Crimson: 2 wds.
8 Hip bones
9 Commuter rail company, initially
10 Cow's digs
16 11th of 12: abbr.
18 "___, Joy of Man's Desiring"
19 Lena in "Havana"
21 Fiber knot
23 Tailless
25 Biblical boat: 2 wds.
26 ___ mundi
27 Aspiring atty.'s exam
29 German one
32 650 in Roman numerals
35 Relatives of the Missouria
37 Four: prefix
38 Eight, to Nero
39 "___ fair in love and war"
41 Heavy cart
43 Early role-playing game co., initially
45 A1A, I65, or 66, e.g.
46 "Huh?" sounds

175

Across

1 Cold, hard money
5 Popular Nissan
11 Spanish cape
12 Gum tree dwellers
13 Jim-dandy
15 More bothersome
16 Conference badges: 2 wds.
21 "___ in Toyland"
24 Plinth supporting a column
25 "___ can you see": 2 wds.
26 ___ Galerie (Manhattan art museum)
27 Mountainous region north of the Himalayas
29 Broadcaster
30 In his day, the shortest player ever in the NBA (5' 7"): 2 wds.
32 Mrs. ___ cow (animal that caused the Great Chicago Fire)
36 Entrée served with crabmeat: 2 wds.
40 Offertory hall of a Shinto shrine
41 "Why did ___ him go?": 2 wds.
42 1998 winner of the Masters and British Open
43 ___ Linda, Calif.

Down

1 Letters on a Soyuz rocket
2 Alpine river
3 Fitness centers
4 Banal
5 Eddie's "Coming to America" role
6 "Casablanca" actor Peter and others
7 ___ Mahal
8 Pier gp.
9 "Big" burger
10 Exhibit curiosity
14 Korean autos
17 Singer of "Mickey" (1982)
18 Computer brand
19 Adhesive
20 Clairvoyant
21 Computerized video-game opponents
22 Have ___, try a drink: 2 wds.
23 Hindu Mr.
28 Double deal, slangily
29 In the hay
31 "Mefistofele" role
33 Hershey brand
34 Matter in the Big Bang theory
35 ___ good example: 2 wds.
36 HBO rival
37 President pro ___
38 Road reversal, familiarly
39 Rx org.

176

Across

1 Type measurements
6 Flippant
10 Mix socially
12 Bill of fare
13 Suggesting indirectly or obliquely
15 "Newsweek" writer Peyser
16 Common flower
19 "___ that funny?"
23 "The Sweetheart of Sigma ___"
24 Loathsome
26 Home, metaphorically
29 Baseball stat.
30 Beer barrel
31 Computer cookie, e.g.
32 Boito's Mefistofele, e.g.
34 Leave in a hurry, with "out"
36 Books that retail in large numbers
43 "Song of the Golden Calf," e.g.
44 Short garment
45 "Phooey!"
46 Earp at the O.K. Corral

Down

1 Beta preceder
2 "Am ___ the list?": 2 wds.
3 "CSI: Miami" network
4 "Princess Mononoke" genre
5 Echoic finder
6 Standard time, initially
7 Floral ring
8 Setting for TV's "Newhart"
9 Annoy persistently
11 FBI pt.
14 Base neutralizers
16 Desire analgesics, maybe
17 Dig discovery: var.
18 Beauty pageant wear
20 "Take a chair!"
21 Corners
22 Songs
24 "I get it now!" sounds
25 Kind of lily
27 "Bah!"
28 Ensnares
32 In steerage, say
33 Soothe, as fears
35 Common Market letters, once
36 Awful
37 Victorian, for one
38 "Certainly, ___!"
39 "The Joy Luck Club" author Amy
40 Pilot's announcement, briefly
41 The "R" in AARP
42 "Quiet on the ___!"

177

Across

1 New Age keyboardist John
5 Luster
10 "___ Me" (hit of 1931): 2 wds.
12 "Beyond Scared Straight" network: 3 wds.
13 One with a night job
15 Familia member
16 1968 hit for the Turtles
17 Driveway type
19 1,051, to Nero
20 Arizona city
21 Bottom of the ocean
23 Song of joy
25 Actually existing: 2 wds.
28 Hops kiln
32 Another name for the Sun
33 Korean carmaker
35 Ace
37 Address on the Web, initially
38 In a state of sulky dissatisfaction
40 Golfer Lorena
41 A first name in cosmetics
42 Champing at the bit
43 Blog feeds, initially

Down

1 Large metal gong: hyph.
2 Kay Thompson character
3 Boats with one mast
4 Sweetie-pie
5 Herbal drink: 2 wds.
6 Jessica or Otto
7 Seal in a sepulcher
8 1924 gold medal swimmer
9 Moon of Neptune
11 ___ market
14 Movie starring Blythe Danner: "___ in My Dreams": 3 wds.
18 Chance occurrences, old-style
22 In a bit, once
24 Smoker's need
25 Feminine-sounding man's name
26 Beginner
27 Actress Cuthbert
29 Former minors
30 Asian garments
31 Marks in Spanish class
34 Vase, in Vichy
36 "Yes, there is ___!" (believer's statement): 2 wds.
39 Dungeons & Dragons game co., initially

178

Across

1 Chain of hills
6 Milk: prefix
11 Early year: 2 wds.
12 Southernmost city of Israel
13 Checkerberry
15 Bullfight cheer
16 Long sweeping uppercut in boxing
17 Metered vehicles
20 Jerry Lewis's telethon org.
22 Chicken ___ King: 2 wds.
23 In an overly huge way
27 Yuletide tune: 2 wds.
29 Targeted: 2 wds.
30 "How Can ___ Sure?" (hit of 1967): 2 wds.
31 Application datum letters
32 "Back in the ___"
33 Dundee denizen
36 "___ Freischütz" (Weber opera)
38 Festive
43 Whisky ___, L.A. nightclub: 3 wds.
44 Actress Massey
45 Singer Cherry, whose albums include "Buffalo Stance"
46 Track set in a table for a router: hyph.

Down

1 Aisle
2 Kamoze of reggae
3 Cave
4 Spanish felines
5 Noble, in Essen
6 Gam
7 Center for military planes
8 1963 role for Liz
9 Old Chinese money
10 "My Heart Can't Take ___ More" (1960s hit for The Supremes): 2 wds.
14 Influential Dutch artist (1606–69)
17 Hombre's home
18 "Others" in a Latin phrase
19 Soothing ointment
21 Balance sheet item
23 Big ref. works, for short
24 Ivy League team
25 Law degrees, initially
26 1914 battle line
28 Trace
32 Europe-Asia divider
33 Look over quickly
34 Cr. transaction
35 Hebrew name for Uranus
37 Send forth
39 Fifth note in a musical scale
40 Another word for the Sun
41 ___ Balls (snack cakes)
42 China's Sun ___-sen

179

Across

1 Biology lab bacteria: 2 wds.
6 Sugar source
11 Make a dash toward: 2 wds.
12 Bull, of sorts
13 Queen's place: 3 wds.
15 "Song of the South" song syllables
16 Essen exclamation
17 "Empedocles on ___" (Matthew Arnold poem)
19 Community studies deg.
22 Agatha Christie detective
25 "I ___ Dark Stranger" (1946 movie): 2 wds.
26 Sudden feeling of fear: 2 wds.
28 Brake part
29 Ducts
30 Big ___
31 Agenda unit
32 Kamoze of reggae
33 Apple seeds
37 Coins often given away: 2 wds.
41 Flyer that extended its name in 1997
42 "Beat it!"
43 Explosive experiment: abbr., 2 wds.
44 "Who's there?" response: 3 wds.

Down

1 "Das Rheingold" goddess
2 Gave prompts to
3 A while ago
4 War of 1812 locale: 2 wds.
5 City in Japan
6 Big drawer?
7 Wife of Esau
8 Muslim saint or holy man
9 Calculator feature, initially
10 Aliens, for short
14 Wonderful
18 It has a lot of chapters, initially
19 Unable to hear
20 Denomination
21 ___ Fifth Avenue
22 Ltr. addenda
23 Hawaiian island
24 "___ out?" (poker query): 2 wds.
25 British Parliament outrage of 1765
27 First word, often
31 Dead to the world
32 Pupil's place
34 Calvary inscription: inits.
35 Major golf tourneys, initially
36 Hauler on the highway
37 Bright light
38 "Hey, you!"
39 Dental org.
40 Chinese philosopher Chu ___

180

Across

1 Medicinal plant
6 "___ cap fits, wear it": 2 wds.
11 Sing like Bing
12 Big name in Scotch whisky
13 Gymnastics apparatus
14 Blue-pencils
15 Be absent from
17 Real: Ger.
18 1950s talk-show pioneer
20 Wrap in waxed cloth
22 Engine part: abbr.
23 Gyrates
26 Timepiece that sounds like a bird: 2 wds.
28 Followers of a Chinese philosophy
29 Actress Myrna
30 1997 Peter Fonda role
31 Between assignments
32 "I get it," jokily: 2 wds.
34 Balance
36 Indian yogurt dish
38 "Delta of Venus" author ___ Nin
41 Reply to a playground insult: 2 wds.
42 Convinces
43 Simple question type: 2 wds.
44 Canned meat rival of Spam

Down

1 Coll., e.g.
2 Canyon or ranch ending
3 Famed proponent of nuclear disarmament: 2 wds.
4 Adamant refusal: 2 wds.
5 Hydrocarbon suffixes
6 Chemical ending
7 Kind of case
8 Hackneyed story: hyph., 2 wds.
9 "He that ___ a beard is more than a youth" (Shakespeare)
10 At first, once
16 Two-wheeled vehicle
18 Ancient Briton
19 The rain in Spain
21 List enders, briefly
23 Red, red flower
24 Biol. branch
25 ___ Terrier
27 Two million pounds
31 Tennis player John
32 "Knowledge can split ___ of light" (Dickens): 2 wds.
33 Curved part of a draft horse's collar
35 Toward sunrise
37 From ___ Z: 2 wds.
39 ___ de France
40 Retired flier's letters

181

Across

1 Beak
5 Ares, for one: 2 wds.
11 Hard on the eye
12 Any Smith grad.
13 "___ Grit" (1969 John Wayne film)
14 Austere
15 Lowly laborer
16 Barbie's guy
17 Geller feller
19 Thanksgiving dish
23 Implemented
27 Monetary unit of Romania
28 Ballpark figure, colloquially
30 Baseball number
31 Minnelli musical
32 Narcissist's love
34 Hallucinogen's initials
35 100 qintars
37 1996 also-ran
41 Game expedition
44 Bright thought
45 Surfing, perhaps
46 December drinks
47 Does salon work
48 Cave, to a poet

Down

1 Hard fruits
2 Beast
3 Bit of slander
4 Good looks
5 Precursors of cell phones: hyph.
6 Away from the wind
7 Semi-liquid
8 Clock std.
9 ___ in a million
10 Brown or Marino
18 Computer architecture, initially
20 Banned apple reddener
21 Deal (out)
22 Beef fat used in cooking
23 Countless years
24 Contaminant-free
25 Resound
26 "I call it!"
29 "Far From the ___ Crowd" (Hardy novel)
33 Swing wildly
36 Coastal flyer
38 Distinct smell
39 ___-mutton: hyph.
40 90 degrees
41 "Help!" letters
42 Tiny crawler
43 Birds do it

182

Across

1 Doesn't just sit there
5 Kind of wool
10 Greek muse of history
11 Making no value judgments
13 Infect
15 Biblical verb suffix
16 Caribbean or Mediterranean
17 By way of
18 Roughly built cabin
20 Amalgam
22 ___ record: 2 wds.
23 Elegant
24 Drilled into
26 Tart
29 Put on board, as cargo
33 Be theatrical
34 Of an ecological unit
35 Mar. follower
36 Cigarette pollutant
38 Its hdqtrs. is in Langley, VA
39 Substantial
42 Injury requiring emergency room treatment
43 White chip, often
44 "Come in!"
45 San Francisco and Monterey

Down

1 Admission
2 Cover
3 G.I.'s headgear, slangily: 2 wds.
4 Boozehound
5 Poor, as excuses go
6 Friendly
7 Calendar abbr.
8 Faces with courage
9 Glossy fabrics
12 Dull
14 Pose a question
19 Henry ___ Lodge
21 Cuplike spoon
23 Bawl
25 Erstwhile: hyph.
26 Minimum
27 "The ___ Strikes Back"
28 "The Shawshank Redemption" actor Freeman
30 Secret stuff
31 Lovely and delicate
32 Cheers
34 Hindu title
37 Way, way off
40 Cashew or almond
41 Truck section

183

Across

1 Natives of Nigeria
5 Breakfast order
11 Drone, e.g.
12 Son of William the Conqueror
13 "Girl With ___ Hat" (Vermeer): 2 wds.
14 Agreement
15 Place to buy rolls of tobacco: 2 wds.
17 Living dragon
18 24-hour endurance race locale: 2 wds.
21 Alaska's first governor
24 ___ belle étoile (in the open air): 2 wds.
25 "The Subject Was Roses" director Grosbard
26 Attention-getters
28 Heads
31 Family men
33 Fossilized marine animals
37 Haberdashery item: 2 wds.
38 "And here it is!": hyph.
39 Out of one's mind
40 Certain hosp. scans
41 Summarized or abridged
42 Doctors who check out head colds, for short

Down

1 Apple product
2 "Boss Lady" star Lynn
3 Cassini of fashion
4 Singer Neil
5 Divides
6 Odd-numbered page
7 Create a cryptogram
8 Discontinue a legislative session
9 Brontë's "Jane ___"
10 Old school comedian ___ Caesar
16 "A Beautiful Mind" director ___ Howard
18 ___ of luxury
19 1997 U.S. Open winner
20 Most old
22 1936 candidate Landon
23 Some fraternity men, initially
27 Cut with small quick strokes: 2 wds.
28 Copied gene for gene
29 New Test. book
30 Self-conscious question: 3 wds.
32 "Crazy" singer Patsy
33 Baseballer Martinez
34 Glacier-formed lake
35 Do magazine work
36 Be cheeky with
37 Service award

184

Across

1 Police rank: abbr.
5 How some music is sold: 2 wds.
10 Biting tool
12 "It's only ___!": 2 wds.
13 Data processor's data
14 Hartebeests
15 "___ where it hurts!": 2 wds.
17 Nighttime wear, for short
18 Thor Heyerdahl craft: 2 wds.
20 First-year cadet
22 Brief detail
24 Ready for slaughter
27 Acapulco assents: 2 wds.
29 Daughter of Ball and Arnaz
30 Like some cows
32 Certain cameras: inits.
33 ___ pocus
35 Comic's shriek
36 Letters after the price of a used car
38 African virus
40 C-E-G chord, e.g.
42 1991 Nicholson Baker book about his fascination with John Updike: 3 wds.
45 Greek goddess of chance
46 Wing (prefix)
47 Early year: 2 wds.
48 Eastern titles

Down

1 "Is ___?": 2 wds.
2 Sine qua ___
3 1982 movie starring Meryl Streep: 2 wds.
4 Spitting sound, in comics
5 Breakfast food
6 Aid group, often: initials.
7 Shag spiffer-upper: 2 wds.
8 Key of Bach's Brandenburg Concerto no. 5: abbr., 2 wds.
9 Meeting: abbr.
11 URL starter
16 "The Lord of the Rings" figure
18 Blog feeds, initially
19 Pacific capital
21 A/C stat.
23 Former nightclub owner
25 Cork's country
26 Carrel
28 Pulled out
31 Do a voice-over
34 Early course
36 "Beetle Bailey" barker
37 Welsh word in a Pennsylvania college name
39 Back muscles, for short
41 "Bingo!"
43 Soft & ___ (Gillette brand)
44 Greek island

185

Across

1 Bee product
4 Some sports cars, initially
7 Lincoln's state, for short
10 1972 treaty subj.
11 50–50, e.g.
12 It's mostly nitrogen
13 Investment option, initially
14 Kind of mark
16 "A" in the alphabet: 2 wds.
18 Family folk
19 "___ tu"
20 Head, in Rome
22 Lawful
25 "Infestation" rock group
26 "Que ___"
27 Like a nerd
29 Alvin of dance
30 Latin abbrs.
31 "Automatic for the People" band
32 Combined appliance: hyph.
37 Solar System's fourth-largest planet by diameter
38 Bigger than med.
39 Heckler's hoot
40 "Angels & Demons" author ___ Brown
41 "___ Heldenleben": R. Strauss
42 Colony crawler
43 German compass point
44 Govt. agency that has your number

Down

1 Dickensian child
2 Rock shelter at the base of a cliff
3 Treasure map phrase: 4 wds.
4 Active volcano in Sicily: abbr., 2 wds.
5 Demoiselle
6 Marine creature: 2 wds.
7 Measures of distance at sea: 2 wds.
8 Ireland, to the Irish
9 ___ Rabbit, Fox or Wolf
15 More banded
17 Wait it out: 2 wds.
20 Capote, to his friends
21 Suffix with Jacob
23 British verb ending
24 Longest river in Scotland
28 False start?
29 Passionate
32 Ladies sports org.
33 Long, long time
34 Genetic molecules, initially
35 Auspices: var.
36 Actress Sofer of soaps

186

Across

1 Bear, in a fairy tale
5 Wild and crazy
11 Individualists?
12 Botanical ring
13 Sore spots
14 Author Rushdie
15 Pakistani language
16 Big banger, initially
17 Marine flier
19 Out, in a way
23 Life's work
25 Bone-dry
26 Biblical craft
27 Medicinal amt.
29 Heavyweight boxer "Two ___" Tony Galento
30 Pseudologized
32 Slap the cuffs on
34 Christmas trio
35 Any of the Griffins on "Family Guy," e.g.
36 Big time
38 Laundry batch
41 One who has an effect
44 Similar to
45 Fitting measurement
46 Pennsylvanian city known as "The Gem City"
47 Livestock buildings
48 Split apart

Down

1 Andean nation
2 Jelly ingredient
3 Small barrel for explosives: 2 wds.
4 Give one's word
5 High-ranking naval officers: 3 wds.
6 Flaherty's "Man of ___"
7 River formations
8 Dot-___ (internet company)
9 Made like, in cookery: 2 wds.
10 Go for the gold?
18 Badminton barrier
20 Bane of one's existence: 2 wds.
21 "Aeneid" figure
22 1978 WSMVP, Bucky
23 Not all bent out of shape
24 "Mi chiamano Mimi," e.g.
28 Country club figure
31 Vin of movies
33 ___ coaster
37 Down-to-earth
39 Blood-related
40 Feat
41 Alliance that includes Kazakhstan, Kyrgyzstan, etc.
42 Aardvark's morsel
43 It's a free country, familiarly

187

Across

1 "Cool" amount of money
4 "Enemy of the State" org.
7 ___ blond
10 ___ de coeur
11 Sandwich, initially
12 Narc's org.
13 Spring outlook: 2 wds.
16 Cote de ___ (French entree)
17 Seat in stone for several persons
18 Debaucher
20 Wading birds
23 Letter-shaped construction piece: hyph.
27 Indonesian island
28 "___ sorry!" (apology): 3 wds.
29 Kitchen item: abbr.
30 Green
31 Japanese immigrant
33 Singer Twain
36 Supervisors, briefly
40 Kid's summertime employment: 2 wds.
42 Max Fleischer's Olive
43 "___ Largo"
44 Berne's river
45 Accelerator pedal
46 "Boo-o-o!"
47 Online feed, initially

Down

1 1205, to Nero
2 "Dies ___"
3 Singer McCann
4 Compass point, initially
5 Precipitates icily
6 Inability to co-ordinate voluntary movements
7 What Ritalin treats, for short
8 Ball handler?
9 ___-kiri
14 Italian dictator
15 Italian verse form: 2 wds.
19 Aviation prefix
20 "Give ___ try!": 2 wds.
21 Marcel Marceau character
22 Rascal
24 ASCAP rival
25 Nile nipper
26 Kind of deer
28 Chemical suffix
30 Conventions
32 Kitchen features
33 Bad air
34 Georgetown athlete
35 Punchers
37 "Battle Maximus" band
38 Cell messenger letters
39 Lat., Lith., and Ukr., once
41 River of France and Belgium

188

Across

1 Shin bone
6 "Zorba the Greek" author ____ Kazantzakis
11 French town
12 One of the official languages of India
13 Light ____ (floaty): 2 wds.
14 Fingers
15 Queeg's command
17 ____-One, stage name of Lawrence Parker
18 Arctic animal
20 Insurance giant
22 Ex ____ (out of nothing)
24 Paris airport
27 Packs tightly
28 Do ____ situation: 2 wds.
29 Evergreens
30 Detach with a hammer's claw
31 Aussie "bear"
33 Sample
34 Sack
36 Big Indian
38 Began
40 City on the Mohawk
43 "The Chronicles of Narnia" author C. S.
44 "Masters Without Slaves" author
45 Vernacular
46 "Fiddler on the Roof" role

Down

1 New Deal prog.
2 "____ for Iceberg": 2 wds.
3 2001 movie set in Somalia: 3 wds.
4 Hip bones
5 Overhead photos
6 Group of nine
7 Bank offering, initially
8 Wife of Kanye West: 2 wds.
9 ____ and terminer
10 Guff
16 Classic opener
18 Suffix with consist
19 Old money
21 Norse mythological being
23 "____ Excited" (Pointer Sisters hit): 2 wds.
25 53, to Caesar
26 Canine cry
28 Impaneled: 3 wds.
30 Suffix with form
32 "You ____ right!": 2 wds.
34 Fun time
35 "… ____ saw Elba": 2 wds.
37 Dip ____ in (test): 2 wds.
39 E-mail ID, in short
41 Kind of computer monitor, for short
42 Letters before a crook's name

189

Across

1 Some German cars, initially
5 Big name in pizza
11 Comedian Lew
12 Prevailed: 2 wds.
13 Some nest eggs, initially
14 Prefix with phosphate
15 1/100th div.
16 ____ polloi
17 "Call Me Maybe" singer Carly ____ Jepsen
18 "The Hermit" author Eugène
21 Aloof
22 Chorus voice
26 Destroys
27 Moves, in real estate jargon
28 A chorus line
29 Spicy condiment
30 Makes more orderly
32 Danger in Afghanistan, initially
35 Calypso kin
36 Capital of Ga.
38 Treeless plain
40 Plant with fleshy leaves
41 "____ Lonesome Tonight?": 2 wds.
42 Real estate ad abbr.
43 Clean, as a floor: 2 wds.
44 Low islands

Down

1 Radar image
2 Forgiving
3 "Does it matter?": 3 wds.
4 12th graders: abbr.
5 Rushing sound
6 Kind of acid
7 Director ____ Lee
8 Big laugh
9 ____ temperature: 2 wds.
10 Oklahoma tribe member
16 Dame Myra
19 Sheer, smooth fabric
20 Built round?
21 "____ et labora" (pray and work)
23 "M*A*S*H" actor: 2 wds.
24 Sorry tale: 2 wds.
25 F.I.C.A. benefit
27 Pro ____
29 Kind of call: 2 wds.
31 City in Finland
32 "____ what you did!": 2 wds.
33 Peut-____ (maybe, in Paris)
34 Bug repellent brand
37 Moon vehicles, initially
39 Poe's "The Narrative of Arthur Gordon ____"
40 "20/20" network

190

Across

1 Habituate: var.
6 Following
11 City in Kentucky
12 Dry Italian white wine
13 Goes off, as a timer
14 Seoul's home
15 Stings a little bit
17 Hall near the quad
18 Bar, legally
20 Big do
23 Medicinal plant
27 Architectural projection
29 Patterned fabric
30 Sawbuck
32 Secret language
33 Taste, touch or sight
35 LP player: hyph.
38 Reply
42 Building block
44 City on Honshu
45 Chap
46 Thesaurus compiler
47 Selfish person
48 Head lock

Down

1 Goes back, like the tide
2 Margosa tree
3 Common fertilizer ingredient
4 Deserving severe rebuke or censure
5 Bridge positions
6 Establish, as a price
7 Kitchen appliance: 2 wds.
8 Poi source
9 Anytime
10 500 sheets
16 Farm pen
19 Cracklin' ___ Bran
20 Computerized task performer
21 "Butterflies ___ Free"
22 Transgression
24 Brazil resort, familiarly
25 As ___ as the hills
26 Diminutive
28 Linda ___, Supergirl's alias
31 Genetic messenger material, briefly
34 Haughty response
35 Dagger grip
36 Cogitation creation
37 People
39 Hourly pay
40 Just makes, with "out"
41 "Gosh darn it!"
43 Attention, metaphorically

191

Across

1 Cove
4 Mineo of "Exodus"
7 "___-plunk"
10 Bibliophile's suffix
11 Mozart's "L'___ del Cairo"
12 Japanese capital, once
13 Mixed-breed dog
14 Big box of cigs: abbr.
15 Harvard deg.
16 Soil-exposing
18 "Lo's Diary" author ___ Pera
19 ___ Park, N.J.
20 Johnson's "Hellzapoppin'" costar
22 "The sign of extra service" sloganeer
23 Banded metamorphic rock
24 Small camping shelter: 2 wds.
26 Porto ___, Brazil
28 Gets ready to fire
31 Indian metropolis
32 Breathing problem
33 Currency unit of the U.S.: abbr.
34 Drive insane: 2 wds.
36 52, in Ancient Rome
37 Barley bristle
38 Cecil Campbell, a.k.a. ___ Kamoze
39 "… ___ Berliner"
40 ___-Bo (exercise system)
41 Former Serbian capital
42 Like a lot
43 It blinks and winks
44 Clinton, e.g.: abbr.

Down

1 Flower part
2 Gets used (to)
3 Executive producer of "The Love Boat": 2 wds.
4 Prefix with linguistics
5 End of "The Tempest": 2 wds.
6 Inside track: 2 wds.
7 Remembers: 4 wds.
8 Whirlpools
9 "Friends, ___, countrymen"
17 Jettison
21 Delaware Indian
23 AT&T competitor
25 Man, e.g.
26 Confused
27 Pope who crowned Charlemagne emperor of the Romans: 2 wds.
29 No-goodnik
30 Cruelty
32 Take ___ (run out the clock in football): 2 wds.
35 On vacation

192

Across

1 ____ breve
5 Associate
11 ____ & Chandon, champagne
12 Moonstruck: 2 wds.
13 Divided avenue: abbr.
14 Lose your temper: 2 wds.
15 Epithet of the mother of Romulus and Remus
16 Annoyance
17 Time in Illinois when it's noon in California: 2 wds.
19 Flat
21 Vex
24 Preschool attendee
25 "The Daughter of Time" writer Josephine
27 Bygone bird
28 Adept
29 Spirit raiser?
31 Italian town NW of Venice
32 Brass that looks like gold
36 Platte River tribe
39 One who wins by losing
40 Biggest city in the USA, initially: 2 wds.
41 Card game for two
42 Chaotic places
43 Put more bullets in
44 Boot out

Down

1 Prefix meaning "both"
2 Be lazy
3 Float in the air
4 Early in the morning: 2 wds.
5 Stressful: hyph.
6 11 hours ahead of the answer to 17-Across: 2 wds.
7 Diner orders, initially
8 ____ de plume (literary aliases)
9 ____ Office (president's place)
10 Eliot's "Adam ____"
18 Grain for horses
19 1968 hit "Harper Valley ____"
20 ____ cit.
21 Response to "This is what works for me": 3 wds.
22 Bird of myth
23 Actor Hakeem ____-Kazim of "24"
26 USN cleric, for short
30 Football coach Amos ____ Stagg
31 Prince Valiant's princess
32 Baltic feeder
33 Basmati, e.g.
34 A hearty one is square
35 Other, in Oaxaca
37 Lennon's in-laws
38 Method: abbr.

193

Across

1. Brief outline
7. "What are the ___?"
11. "The Picture of ___ Gray" (Oscar Wilde novel)
12. "___ #1!"
13. Somnambulist
15. Book part
16. Amaze
17. Where lessons take place
21. "___ Force One" (1997 Harrison Ford film)
22. Oarsmen
25. Follower of Aristotle
28. Kind of show: hyph.
29. "Down under" fowl
30. Spat out in small puffs
33. "The ___ and the Pendulum"
35. "Rules for Radicals" author Alinsky
36. Offer of reconciliation: 2 wds.
41. Former iPod model
42. One-dimensional
43. Book part
44. Funds

Down

1. "Inc." spots?
2. Campaign pro.
3. Bard's before
4. Cambodian coins
5. Accessories for vampires
6. Not justifiable
7. Barn bird
8. Metric unit of length
9. Attracted
10. All dried up
14. Like the game, to Holmes
17. Crime boss
18. Bank claim
19. Bringing to a standstill
20. "I ___ you one"
23. Icy coating
24. Soviet ballistic missile
26. Mischievous one
27. Temporary inactivity
31. 2006 Olympics host
32. African antelope
33. Ceremonial splendor
34. Pelvic bones
37. "C'est la ___!"
38. Logical lead-in
39. Crow's call
40. "48 ___"

194

Across

1 Bros, e.g.
5 Musically connected
11 Tech. product reviews
12 Real: 2 wds.
13 That's ___ concern: 2 wds.
14 Book after Nehemiah
15 Look back regretfully on
16 Difficult obligation
17 Furnish with a fund
19 Blot out
23 Bad thing to raise
24 Ten-cent coins
25 In-basket stamp: abbr.
27 ___ jockey
28 Opposing parties
30 "___ appetit!"
31 Fire starter
32 Days ___: 2 wds.
35 Dance and drama, for example
37 River to the Rhine
38 Stand-up comedian Carrington
41 Height, in combination
42 Actress Sissy of "Carrie"
43 One-named singer for the 1960s Velvet Underground
44 Tampa neighbor, briefly: 2 wds.
45 What Ritalin treats, for short

Down

1 Make a goal
2 Just for laughs: 2 wds.
3 Pope from 575–79: 2 wds.
4 Pou ___, basis of operation
5 Claim
6 Followed
7 Removes: 3 wds.
8 Cigar stuff
9 Literary inits.
10 Donne's "done"
16 Have debts
18 Authoritative order
20 Simple organic compound: 2 wds.
21 French possessive
22 PC bailout button
25 W.W. II fighter pilots' gp.
26 Certain photo order: abbr.
29 Highway
30 Actress Derek and singer Diddley
33 Tough, durable wood
34 Dickens's Edwin
36 Kid
38 Web letters in an orange button
39 Make a decision
40 Touch lightly on the water
41 Gasteyer of "Mean Girls"

195

Across

1 Tag ____ with
6 Certain fraction
11 Go through
12 Atlanta research university
13 Allude
14 Consume: 2 wds.
15 "____ luck?"
16 Common connector
18 QVC rival
19 G.I. entertainers
20 Light units: abbr.
21 Honshu city
22 DOT, alternatively
24 "The ____ Love": 2 wds.
25 Antique shop item
27 Looked for over the intercom
28 About, on a memo: 2 wds.
29 Embarrassing info, to the tabloids
30 General on a Chinese menu
31 Brief time, briefly
32 "____ Buttermilk Sky" (Hoagy Carmichael song)
35 Takeoff and landing overseers, initially
36 Common deciduous tree
37 Chat room initials
38 Senegal's capital
40 Smelly smoke
42 Cast out
43 Saharan sanctuary
44 Ancient Greeks' harps
45 Bridget Fonda, to Jane

Down

1 Pianist Claudio
2 Encumbrances
3 Nuts: 3 wds.
4 Nationals grp.
5 Talk show host Rivera
6 Demands
7 "____ little teapot…": 2 wds.
8 What a desperate person has: 3 wds.
9 Part of a board
10 Trance-like "state"
17 Macadamia or cashew
23 "Sprechen ____ deutsch?"
24 Dinghy propeller
25 Stronghold
26 Natural
27 Harasses: 2 wds.
29 Crime-busters' grp.
31 Puts into piles
33 Reasoned judgement
34 "Family Ties" mom
39 Enzyme ending
41 ____ chi (Chinese exercise)

196

Across

1 Near-sighted
7 Banquet
10 Eye site
11 Ltr. addenda
12 Cover for the center of a car wheel
13 Superlative suffix
14 Figures
16 From that time: 2 wds.
19 ___-mo cameras
20 Nocturnal Asian primate
22 "Raiders of the Lost Ark" producer George
26 Add color to
27 In need of scratch?
28 Betel palm
29 Congressman
30 Mouths, in zoology
32 Minor bones to pick
33 Join in: 3 wds.
37 Salt Lake City college team
38 Kay Thompson title imp
42 Café au ___
43 Renée of "The Big Parade"
44 Channel that reruns "Family Feud": inits.
45 Give out again, as cards

Down

1 Dash inits.
2 "___ rang?"
3 Gambling inits.
4 Oregon's western border: 2 wds.
5 Make ___ adventure: 2 wds.
6 Native Egyptians in the Roman period
7 Graf ___
8 Nation disbanded in 1991, briefly
9 Attention-getters
11 Eat everything in sight: 4 wds.
15 ___ Island National Monument
16 Sask. neighbor
17 Evening, in Paris
18 Alencon's department
21 Beatle Ringo
23 251 in Roman numerals
24 "Cat on ___ Tin Roof": 2 wds.
25 Dict. entries
31 "Don't shed ___": 2 wds.
33 Sofia's country: abbr.
34 Greek vowels
35 One end of a hammer head: var.
36 Shoppe sign word
39 Extreme soreness
40 Baltic or Irish
41 Elver's elder

197

Across

1 Sculptress Hepworth
8 Down Under bird
11 Not lubricated
12 ____ gestae
13 Grinling ____, sculptor (1648–1721)
14 Beer keg outlet
15 Grassy area
16 Naval rank: abbr.
17 Hamburg's river
20 Central point
23 Slap on
24 Before, in poetry
25 Band of eight
27 Certain sorority woman
31 Money in Moldova
33 Attractive device
34 Disastrous
36 Burrow
37 Boor
38 Bluejacket
40 Low noise
41 Tower on a mosque
45 Alicia of "Falcon Crest"
46 Characterized by strong feelings
47 Shot that moves across a landscape
48 Spoiled: 2 wds.

Down

1 Harmful microorganism
2 DiFranco of pop
3 Plunder
4 Areas where Protestant fundamentalism is widespread: 2 wds.
5 Cosmetic additive
6 File menu option
7 Pop-ups, often: abbr.
8 Romain de Tirtoff's, familiarly
9 Destined
10 Door-to-door service, initially
17 Nigerian language
18 Fond du ____, Wisc.
19 On the other hand
21 Make upset
22 Speed at which a population declines: 2 wds.
26 Afternoon break
28 Experienced
29 Chum
30 Mighty Joe Young, for one
32 Last month
34 Catalog of animals
35 He concocts campaigns
37 Bloke
39 Unsigned, as a poem
41 Ryan of "When Harry Met Sally"
42 "Spare" body part
43 Eddie's "Green Acres" costar
44 "Hazel" cartoonist Key

198

Across

1 Univ., sometimes
5 Got together
11 Check information
12 Treat badly: hyph.
13 And others, for short: 2 wds.
14 Score
15 Easily-irritated person
17 Hair-raising
18 Atlas page
21 Cover
23 Kind of change or talk
25 They come in a pack: abbr.
26 Chill
27 Page of some wall calendars
29 ____ donna
30 Dash widths
31 Of the eye
33 Hot pepper used in Mexican cooking
36 Breathing space in a line of verse
39 ____ and terminer
40 Keeps after
41 Act as usher
42 Trap: var.
43 Dangerous biters

Down

1 October 15, for example
2 Alliance acronym
3 Aries and Taurus, e.g.: 2 wds.
4 Put on
5 Kind of box
6 Irving Berlin classic
7 "Mush!" shouter's vehicle
8 Juliet, to Romeo
9 Approx.
10 "L.A. Law" actress Susan
16 Dupes
18 Transducers used to detect and measure light: 2 wds.
19 Graduate of a school, casually
20 "Not guilty," e.g.
21 Company patronized by Wile E. Coyote
22 Baum's was a coward
24 Plant with tulip-like flowers
28 Buys up
29 Elementary school group, for short
32 Shallow pool
33 May follower
34 Lowest high tide
35 Biscuit bits
36 Greek letter after phi
37 Proterozoic, for instance
38 Arithmetic result

199

Across

1 TV teaser: abbr.
6 Lab chemical dropper
11 Poker champ Stu
12 Arab leader: var.
13 Singer who played Hattie Pearl in "The Butler": 2 wds.
15 Widow in "Peer Gynt"
16 Riga denizen
17 One of the Spice Girls
18 Bill amt.
21 Extremely inflexible: hyph.
23 Asia's Trans ___ mountains
25 Dudley Do-Right's gp.
26 Mexican border language
30 Opposite of a ques.
31 "Give ___ further thought!": 2 wds.
32 "Tomb raider" Croft
33 Sleep attire, briefly
36 Having no awareness
40 Absorbed the cost of a contract, slangily: 2 wds.
41 Firth of Clyde island
42 Partner of wheres and whys
43 Church engagement announcement

Down

1 Mountain lion
2 Genetic strands, initially
3 Fairy-tale character
4 ___ tai (rum cocktail)
5 Word-of-mouth bettor
6 Jelly ingredient
7 "Where ___" (Eminem song): 2 wds.
8 ___ annum
9 Ample shoe width
10 "Don't give up!"
14 Bunch of bulls
17 Acquire
18 Function used in arrays
19 ___ and haw
20 Measure of an economy, initially
21 Lukas of "Rambling Rose"
22 About: 2 wds.
23 ___ rule: 2 wds.
24 Home care provider, initially
27 New York footballers
28 Posts: abbr.
29 Occupying a taxi: 3 wds.
32 Cut of meat
33 V-chips block it
34 Evita's hubby
35 Form 1040 IDs
36 Bob King's org.
37 ___ power
38 Bee follower
39 401(k) alternative

200

Across

1 Closes
6 ____ and aahs
10 Skater Harding
11 Does as instructed
13 Decoration for wounded soldiers: 2 wds.
15 Ethnic group of Vietnam
16 "Weekend Update" show, initially
17 Never, in Nuremberg
18 Crisp flat tortilla
20 Hair may hide it
21 ____'acte (break between two parts of a play)
22 Comedienne Boosler
24 With 26-Across: "Foundation's Edge" author
26 See 24-Across
29 ____ pit
33 Car tire abbr.
34 "Killing Me Softly with His Song" singer Flack
36 Mary of "Where Eagles Dare"
37 Bygone daily MTV series, informally
38 Boulogne-sur-____
39 Tiny time period
42 Accord, e.g.
43 Basil's "Captain Blood" costar
44 "You ____?"
45 Odes, sonnets, etc.

Down

1 Florida beach town, familiarly: 2 wds.
2 Sculptor Jean-Antoine ____
3 Civil ____ (riot conditions)
4 Newspaper worker: abbr.
5 Chip dip
6 "C'est magnifique!": hyph.
7 Honorary U.K. title, initially
8 "Death of a Naturalist" poet
9 Native of Damascus
12 Metric volume
14 Essays
19 Barber's job
23 #1 spot
25 Laundry job
26 Calla lilies
27 Comparatively quick
28 Marcos with a lot of shoes
30 At least: 2 wds.
31 Dictation experts, briefly
32 Not quite
35 Censor sound
40 Linked-computers acronym
41 ____ Magnon

201

Across

1 Benefits
6 They go with the flow
11 Bluebird genus
12 Leaning
13 Not so nice
14 Sealy competitor
15 Summit
16 League: abbr.
18 Chatter
19 Actor Wallach
20 Your, in Roma
21 Collection agcy.
22 Pro follower
24 ___ Van Huong, Vietnamese Prime Minister: 1965
26 Elite U.S. Navy squad
28 Money substitute
31 Skid around
33 Move, in real estate slang
34 Tooth-doctors' org.
36 IV units
38 Dot follower
39 Martial arts promo. co.
40 Modern F/X field
41 Eggs, in biology
42 Like Eric the Red
44 Waxed, old style
46 Corp. official
47 Actor Murphy of "Trading Places"
48 Small paving stones
49 They're rigged

Down

1 Related females
2 Ring of color
3 "This is just between you and me!": 4 wds.
4 Break off
5 Verb for thou
6 East Indian sailors
7 Absorbed, as a cost
8 Sir Richard Branson started it: 2 wds.
9 Church part
10 Random guesses
17 Away from the office
23 "Is that ___?"
25 Like a lot of the entries in this puzzle: abbr.
27 Triumph
29 "That was excellent!": 3 wds.
30 Hair salon stock
32 Arrhythmia detector, briefly
34 Some female relatives
35 Prior to, in dialect
37 Command to an attack dog: 2 wds.
43 Didn't straphang
45 Writer LeShan

Solutions

1

```
A P S E   ■ C A S I N O
P E A K   ■ O R A T O R
R A C E   ■ M O U S S E
E R R ■ S P U N ■ ■
S L I M E ■ S T O A T
■ L E E ■ E E R I E
E Y E S ■ ■ R A R E
M A G M A ■ H E N ■
S K E E T ■ E D G A R
■ R O A R ■ E R A
G E M I N I ■ B A I T
S E I Z E D ■ I D L E
A L T E R S ■ N E S S
```

2

```
R A P ■ E E L ■ A M P
A G E ■ M A Y ■ V I A
M E A S U R E M E N T
I N C H ■ ■ S A R E E
E T H I C S ■ D A R N
■ R O P Y ■ G A T
■ C A R R O U S E L ■
O R R ■ D I L L ■
C O R P ■ L E A S T S
T O A S T ■ C A R T
A N N I E O A K L E Y
V E G ■ S U N ■ P A L
E R E ■ T R Y ■ A T E
```

3

```
M A C E S ■ S P A T S
I R O N Y ■ C O B R A
D A R E S S A L A A M
A B A ■ T A R ■ S I P
I L L ■ O R E ■ E L L
R E S U L T ■ E S S E
■ L E O N E ■
P S S T ■ R E L I S H
R E M ■ T I E ■ N E O
E R A ■ W A D ■ T A U
F E R T I L I Z E R S
A N T E S ■ N O N C E
B E S E T ■ G O T H S
```

4

```
A C T V ■ S H I N T O
B A R I ■ N I N E O F
E R I E ■ O T T A W A
L E G W A R M E R S ■
■ ■ E S K E R ■
S H A D E S ■ N I C K
L I D ■ ■ T O E
A P E D ■ C I N E M A
■ A A L T O ■
■ H U D S O N H A W K
T A N G O S ■ E R E I
A T T U N E ■ L O A N
I S O M E R ■ P O N G
```

Solutions

5

```
M A C A O ▓ H A D E S
A G A R S ▓ A B O R T
T O N A L ▓ S A U N A
▓ A B O M B ▓ B E G ▓
B E D S ▓ P E A L ▓ ▓
U R I ▓ A G E L E S S
R I A L S ▓ N A C H O
G E N E S I S ▓ R O B
▓ B E A T ▓ T O P S ▓
O V A ▓ S O P H S ▓ ▓
P I C A S ▓ E A S E L
A I O L I ▓ E N E M Y
L I N E N ▓ P E R S E
```

6

```
B U L K S ▓ H A W S E
A P P A L ▓ O N E I S
M O N E Y O R D E R S
A N S ▓ E R R S ▓ ▓ ▓
▓ ▓ O S L O ▓ P S Y ▓
▓ I N T E R P O S E ▓
R U D D ▓ ▓ L E S H ▓
S A L E S R O O M ▓ ▓
A W E ▓ P O R T ▓ ▓ ▓
▓ ▓ T R U E ▓ O S I ▓
M I C H A E L J F O X
A S L A N ▓ S O A M I
A P I N G ▓ E N N E A
```

7

```
U N C ▓ P A S ▓ D A S
S A L ▓ T R I T O N E
D R A W E R L I N E R
T A M A R ▓ K E A T S
▓ ▓ P R O S I T ▓ ▓ ▓
G T E ▓ T E A B A G ▓
N O T Y O U R C A L L
P O T E E N ▓ N G O ▓
▓ ▓ N U T M E G ▓ ▓ ▓
M A D T V ▓ C L I M B
S Q U A R E D A N C E
R U S S E L L ▓ T C B
P I K ▓ S G T ▓ O V E
```

8

```
C O A L S ▓ M A M A S
A B B E Y ▓ A B O R T
T R A I L B L A Z E R
T I T ▓ P O T ▓ A N I
L E E ▓ H O E ▓ R A F
E N D S ▓ T S E T S E
▓ ▓ ▓ E L L E R ▓ ▓ ▓
C O W P E A ▓ G A S H
A N A ▓ A C T ▓ L E U
I L L ▓ D E W ▓ L I D
M I L L I S E C O N D
A N I O N ▓ R O W E L
N E S T S ▓ P O S S E
```

Solutions

9

T	A	B	O	R		O	F	F	A	L
A	W	A	R	E		A	R	O	M	A
T	E	N	E	T		T	A	X	I	S
		D	O	R	M		C	Y	S	T
L	E	A		O	U	S	T			
E	R	N	S		G	E	I	S	H	A
N	I	N	T	H		C	O	P	E	S
S	E	A	A	I	R		N	A	R	K
		M	E	A	T		C	B	S	
T	B	S	P		M	I	T	E		
H	O	L	E	D		D	O	M	E	D
E	L	I	D	E		A	L	A	R	Y
M	A	T	E	Y		L	U	N	G	E

10

C	A	R	B	O			T	O	S	S
A	T	E	A	M		D	I	R	T	Y
B	O	T	H	E	R	A	T	I	O	N
A	N	I		G	E	E		O	N	O
L	A	N		A	I	M		L	E	D
S	L	A	T		N	O	S	E	D	
	W	A	S	N	T					
S	N	O	U	T		Y	L	E	M	
S	E	A		P	A	D		A	Y	E
H	I	P		A	T	E		M	E	T
I	N	A	L	I	E	N	A	B	L	E
V	E	L	A	R		E	I	D	E	R
A	R	M	Y		B	L	A	T	S	

11

A	P	P	T		H	A	S	A	T
B	L	E	E	P		O	F	U	S	E
B	A	N	T	U		M	O	N	T	E
A	N	T		L	E	E	R	S	A	T
S	T	A	B	L	E	R		H	R	H
	G	A	U	S	S			I	T	E
T	R	O	M	P		I	N	N	E	D
R	O	N		S	O	M	M	E		
U	S	B		T	A	P	E	S	U	P
C	A	R	C	A	S	S		T	R	A
K	N	A	C	K		O	N	A	I	R
E	N	S	U	E		N	O	T	E	S
R	A	S	P	S		D	E	L	I	

12

G	A	M	E	Y		P	I	L	O	T
A	D	A	G	E		A	L	I	B	I
G	A	N	G	S		E	L	F	I	N
E	R	I	N		C	A	S	E		
	F	O	E	H	N		P	R	O	
G	E	E	G	E	E		R	A	P	
H	A	S		L	A	P		E	R	A
E	S	T		T	A	S	S	E	L	
E	T	A		E	E	R	I	E		
	T	S	A	R		E	R	R	S	
T	R	I	O	S		A	N	V	I	L
A	N	O	D	E		A	N	E	L	E
B	A	N	A	L		H	A	R	E	D

Solutions

13

```
A M A H . . I M A G E
R E L I C . B A N E S
A D I E U . I R O N S
B I G . R O S E T T E
S A N S E I . . H E N
. . P A L E . E E C
W H E A L . M E R L E
O A R . L O B E .
O V A . P A L A C E
D E S E R T S . S E A
M A U V E . S H I R R
A G R E E . Y O D E L
N O E N D . T E D S
```

14

```
P I P . C U R . E N E
O C A R I N A . P O L
T E L A V I V . O V A
. Y E T I . C A N
W O R S T . O O H E D
A R I . F L U .
R E D S Q U I R R E L
. R U N . Y O U
S E P I A . S L A N G
A V E . L A C E .
P E N . I S R A E L I
O R C . F E E D L O T
R Y E . Y A W . L S D
```

15

```
A L F A S . F I S T S
L E O N E . A S P I C
E E R I E . N A I R A
. S T O P S . I T E M
S H U N . M O A T .
C O N . S O P H I S M
A R E . Y O U . N E O
R E C A N T S . G N U
. O U C H . C I T E
S C O T . S W A M I
O A K U M . O R A N G
P R I M E . W A G E S
S P E N T . S T E L A
```

16

```
S W O P S . E L M S .
N A U R U . R E A C T
E N T E R T A I N E R
E T A . L O S . G N U
Z A G . Y O U . L E E
E D E N . T R E E S
. A S H E N .
N O N O S . D E S K
S A N . M O P . T A I
O P S . E M S . H U N
F A I R H E A R I N G
A L T H O . L O C A L
. M E O W . M E S S Y
```

Solutions

17

```
I C B M ■ ■ F A U N A
C O R A ■ D O L L E D
A D A R ■ R O U T E D
O A S T ■ E L M ■ ■
■ S E A S ■ N I S I
D O I N G S ■ A M P S
I V E ■ A C E ■ M E N
V E R B ■ I N S E C T
A R E A ■ R E E D ■
■ A R C ■ L I S P
S E R I A L ■ L A I R
A V E N G E ■ E T N A
W E D G E ■ R E S T
```

18

```
A N D E S ■ A D D T O
S I R E E ■ W O O E R
S T A R R ■ O C U L I
N E W ■ B O K ■ B E N
S R I ■ I L E ■ L O O
■ N C A A ■ D E S C
T A G O N ■ F A C T O
E R S T ■ N L E R ■
S I T ■ G E O ■ O A R
S S R ■ R O T ■ S S E
E T A P E ■ S A S H A
R O W D Y ■ A N E E D
A S S T S ■ M A S S E
```

19

```
S T A I D ■ S A R A
L I F E R ■ P T R A P
O R B A D ■ O R A M A
B O S T O N L E G A L
■ O N O N ■
J E R O M E ■ G L O P
N S E C ■ T A R O
R O T C ■ L A H O R E
■ L E E R ■
R E N U M B E R I N G
S T A D T ■ O T T E R
S T Y E S ■ L E O N I
S E A S ■ A S N A P
```

20

```
D U A D S ■ G E R M S
A Z U R E ■ O X E Y E
L I T U P ■ D E M O N
■ O B I S ■ S O P S
R A M ■ A I R ■ T E E
A W A Y ■ P O R E
F E T E S ■ B O C C E
■ I S L E ■ T O O L
S A C ■ Y A P ■ N O D
C R A B ■ T E S T
A G L O W ■ T O R S I
D O L L Y ■ A L O O F
S T Y L E ■ L O L L S
```

Solutions

21

S	T	O	A			H	E	A	R	S	E
I	O	N	S			Y	E	S	M	A	N
P	I	T	S			D	O	W	S	E	D
E	L	H	I		R	C	A				
		E	S	P	O			N	E	E	R
D	E	S	I	R	E	S		N	R	A	
I	D	I		O	L	E		D	E	T	
A	I	D		P	E	R	T	E	S	T	
N	E	E	T		C	E	R	A			
			E	D	T		A	V	I	S	
C	A	S	P	E	R		I	O	T	A	
M	E	D	I	C	I		T	R	O	I	
A	C	I	D	I	C		S	S	N	S	

22

A	S	P	I	C		W	A	N	D	S
T	I	L	D	E		I	C	E	U	P
E	X	A	L	T		D	E	R	M	A
		T	E	A	S	E		V	A	N
S	R	I		C	A	N	T	O		
C	A	N	O	E	D		H	U	M	P
U	V	U	L	A		D	O	S	E	S
D	E	M	I		T	R	U	S	T	S
		B	O	G	E	Y		Y	E	T
S	O	L		E	A	S	T	S		
A	B	O	V	E		H	O	T	E	L
S	O	N	E	S		O	M	E	G	A
H	E	D	G	E		D	E	M	O	B

23

R	E	C	A	P			E	M	M	E	R
A	M	O	U	R			T	I	A	R	A
M	U	N	G	O			A	D	D	O	N
		S	U	D	S		R	E	S	T	
B	O	E	R		E	D	I	T			
E	R	R		D	A	Y	B	O	O	K	
R	E	V		U	S	A		M	A	N	
G	O	A	H	E	A	D		E	K	E	
		T	E	L	L		P	A	Y	E	
O	D	O	R		T	H	I	S			
R	A	I	N	Y		E	Q	U	I	P	
C	U	R	I	A		F	U	R	O	R	
A	B	E	A	M		T	E	E	N	Y	

24

A	D	Z		A	B	C		A	N	T
I	R	E		P	R	O		D	O	E
M	A	R		T	O	X	E	M	I	A
E	P	O	S		K	A	K	I	S	
R	E	T	A	K	E		E	N	O	L
		O	D	I	N		D	I	M	E
H	A	L		T	H	Y		S	E	T
A	L	E	S		E	A	S	T		
S	A	R	I		A	M	O	R	A	L
		R	A	Z	O	R		B	A	L	I
A	M	N	E	S	T	Y		T	U	N
D	E	C		L	E	O		O	L	D
O	D	E		O	D	D		R	A	Y

Solutions

25

```
H I D E   ■   D O E S I N
A M E N   ■   E S S E N E
L E T O F F S T E A M
A T A   ■ L A I ■   S T E
L A T T I C E ■   A R S
■   E E E ■   Z W E I
H A M E R ■   L O S E S
A T A N ■   I E R
R I T ■   A R B I T E R
P S I ■ W E E ■ A N A
I S L E O F C A P R I
S U D O K U ■   G A O L
T E A S E L ■   S S N S
```

26

```
S P R A G ■   S A G O
T I A R A S ■ E L A N
A K I M B O ■ L O G E
Y E N ■ U N L E S S
■ D E B R I S ■
A B R E A S T ■ A F T
T R O L L ■ W A I L S
M A P ■ S T I R R U P
■ C A R T E L ■
S A L A M I ■ I M P
E S A U ■ B E A N I E
T H U S ■ E L D E S T
H Y D E ■ M O R E S
```

27

```
S A Y ■ B R O ■ S T Y
I C E ■ R E V ■ K O I
R E S T I T U T I O N
■ I C I L Y ■
S A F E K E E P I N G
C L A S S ■ S E D E R
A L I ■   I R E
L I N K S ■ S T O V E
A N T I C I P A T E D
■ T O N E R ■
A L T E R C A T I O N
P E A ■ C U R ■ T W O
T I N ■ H R S ■ S E T
```

28

```
M A S S ■ T R O P E S
P L A T ■ R A R E L Y
H A L O ■ E N T A I L
■ T R I A D ■ C O P
A L I E N S ■ E T H
P A N ■ G U T ■
E Y E ■ O R R ■ D A Y
■ T E A ■ I R E
S P A ■ C D R O M S
T A N ■ S H E E R
A U N T I E ■ M A L E
F L U I D S ■ I M A M
F I L L E T ■ T A B U
```

Solutions

29

M	I	C		O	S	O			
A	L	A	S	K	A	N		S	E	A
L	I	N	E	A	T	E		W	E	S
T	A	T	E		U	R	G	E	N	T
A	C	H	I	E	R		T	A	S	E
	E	N	I	D		S	T	I	R
D	C	C		N	A	M		B	E	S
E	L	O	I		Y	A	L	U	
R	A	M	S		N	A	I	L	E	D
M	U	E	S	L	I		M	L	L	E
A	D	D		U	G	L	I	E	S	T
L	E	Y		S	H	A	T	T	E	R
			H	T	C		S	S	E

30

W	A	U	G	H		T	A	P	E	S
A	P	N	E	A		S	W	O	R	E
S	P	I	L	L		P	L	U	M	P
T	A	N	D	E	M		S	N	I	T
E	L	F		Y	A	M		D	N	A
S	L	O	B		T	A	S	S	E	L
		R	A	T	A	T	A	T	
R	A	M	R	O	D		P	E	T	S
E	R	A		T	O	N		R	H	O
A	C	T	S		R	O	L	L	E	R
M	A	I	L	S		R	A	I	S	E
E	N	V	O	I		M	I	N	I	S
D	E	E	P	S		A	N	G	S	T

31

E	S	S	E	S		B	E	L	L	E
T	H	I	N	E		A	V	I	A	N
A	O	R	T	A		S	E	R	G	E
L	O	S	A	N	G	E	L	E	S	
		I	C	I	L	Y			
S	T	O	L	E	N		N	A	P	E
A	A	A					U	R	N	
T	O	R	S		M	A	S	K	E	D
		P	R	O	M	O			
	S	C	R	U	T	I	N	I	Z	E
S	P	O	I	L		D	A	V	I	D
P	I	S	T	E		S	T	A	N	D
A	N	T	E	D		T	A	N	G	Y

32

D	O	P	Y		O	W	N	E	R	S
A	B	L	E		L	O	A	T	H	E
B	O	O	S	T	E	R	S	H	O	T
O	L	D	M	A	I	D			
			U	N	E	A	R	T	H
W	H	I	R	R		D	A	N	I	O
I	A	M	A			H	A	N	S
S	M	U	R	F		A	S	S	T	S
E	M	P	E	R	O	R			
			I	H	A	V	E	I	T
T	U	R	K	E	Y	B	A	C	O	N
B	R	E	E	Z	E		S	C	U	T
S	N	O	R	E	S		T	E	S	S

Solutions

33

S	C	A	L	P	■	P	L	A	S	M
H	O	N	E	Y	■	H	E	N	C	E
E	N	T	E	R	T	A	I	N	E	R
I	C	E	■	E	A	R	■	A	N	I
K	E	N	S	■	T	A	B	L	E	T
H	A	N	K	■	S	O	L	■	■	■
S	L	A	I	N	■	H	I	R	E	D
■	■	■	R	O	B	■	N	O	N	E
S	T	A	T	U	E	■	G	U	L	P
P	A	L	■	R	A	T	■	S	I	R
I	M	A	G	I	N	A	T	I	V	E
T	I	M	E	S	■	M	A	N	E	S
S	L	O	T	H	■	S	I	G	N	S

34

B	A	C	H	■	H	A	R	A	S	S
A	S	H	Y	■	A	R	A	B	I	A
L	E	A	D	■	R	E	B	O	R	N
L	A	I	R	■	D	A	B	■	■	■
■	■	■	R	A	K	E	■	I	S	M	S
S	I	L	T	I	N	G	■	P	E	T
I	C	I	E	R	■	O	B	E	S	E
O	A	F	■	K	N	E	E	C	A	P
N	O	T	E	■	A	S	C	I	■	■
■	■	■	M	O	T	■	L	A	D	S
W	A	P	I	T	I	■	O	L	I	O
O	P	O	R	T	O	■	U	L	N	A
N	E	L	S	O	N	■	D	Y	E	R

35

B	O	O	■	R	D	S	■	A	B	A
O	E	N	■	E	E	E	■	S	O	A
R	I	N	■	E	N	T	■	S	L	R
A	L	O	H	A	S	T	A	T	E	■
■	■	■	B	R	E	E	D	■	■	■
A	P	R	O	N	■	R	A	R	E	R
P	A	M	■	■	■	■	■	C	O	B
E	S	S	E	S	■	S	P	A	N	S
■	■	■	A	L	A	N	A	■	■	■
■	P	I	N	A	C	O	L	A	D	A
A	I	S	■	V	A	R	■	B	A	N
R	E	T	■	E	R	E	■	A	D	S
C	D	S	■	S	I	S	■	B	E	E

36

P	O	P	P	A	■	A	S	H	E	R
A	R	I	E	L	■	S	P	A	R	E
N	E	E	D	L	E	P	O	I	N	T
S	O	D	A	■	V	E	I	L	E	D
■	■	■	G	N	A	R	L	■	■	■
S	A	L	O	O	N	■	■	S	A	T
P	R	O	G	R	E	S	S	I	V	E
A	C	T	■	S	E	T	T	E	E	■
■	■	■	P	A	C	E	R	■	■	■
S	E	S	A	M	E	■	E	T	N	A
T	R	E	P	I	D	A	T	I	O	N
A	I	R	E	S	■	S	C	E	N	E
B	E	A	R	S	■	S	H	R	E	W

Solutions

37

```
S E G N O ■ C O T E S
T A R O S ■ L O R E N
I R O N S ■ O H A R E
G N U ■ U S A ■ F I E
M E N ■ A U K ■ F E Z
A D D E R S ■ D I R E
■ C R Y P T I C ■ ■
F L O E ■ E R E C T S
R O N ■ D N A ■ I A N
A N T ■ O D D ■ R Y E
M E R C Y ■ U N C L E
E L O P E ■ C O L O R
D Y L A N ■ E W E R S
```

38

```
P A P A S ■ ■ E M S
A T R I U M ■ I M A C
S T E R N O ■ N O S H
T I L L ■ M A T T E L
A L A I ■ D E E R E
S A W N ■ H A R D U P
■ ■ ■ E W E R S ■
A L E P H S ■ E G E R
R A D I O ■ C A V E
I M E L D A ■ T M E N
O E N O ■ F R I E N D
S N I T ■ L A O T S E
O T C ■ ■ O N E O R
```

39

```
A R A B ■ T E A S E S
K O B E ■ I M B E A T
I T A L ■ R I S Q U E
O E N O ■ A L E ■
■ D W A N ■ N C A R
E R O ■ L A S C A L A
L A N A I ■ A E S I R
S V E L T E R ■ S E E
A I D E ■ M A Y A ■
■ R P I ■ E N T R
H O R T O N ■ A D E E
S T E E L E ■ T R A M
I C E D A M ■ S A K S
```

40

```
B O L E ■ S M O T E
A M E N ■ E A G E R
B E S T S E L L E R
U N S E T T L E
■ N I H ■ S T E P
S T E T T E D ■ H I E
A Z T E C ■ I N U R E
F A N ■ H A L O G E N
E R A S ■ P A N
■ C L O T U R E S
G A R A G E S A L E
A G A V E ■ E L B E
T E P E E ■ R E A D
```

Solutions

41

```
W S J . C G I . . . . .
E E O . C R O . P E C .
E T H I C A L . E N L .
P O N D . P A T R I A .
E F F A C E . E S A S .
R F K . O S T R I C H .
. . E M P O R I A . . .
S A N T A F E . N H A .
H A N G . W E D G E S .
O N E E A R . R U I N .
A D D . A A M I L N E .
T E Y . A T E . F E W .
. . . A H H . . . . . .
```

42

```
C A D . . D R A P E S .
A X I S . E N T I R E .
M E M O . C A M E R A .
P S E U D O . . . . . .
. S L I M S . E N E .
B A T . S P A . N O R .
E G O . U R N . J A G .
E A R . S E E . O H S .
P R E . E S S A Y . . .
. . . . S T R A T A .
S A F A R I . T B A R .
A D A G I O . S L I M .
G O N E O N . . E L Y .
```

43

```
E B B S . M I A S M .
G O A T . B O O B O O .
O S L O . A R D E N T .
S H A N G H A I . . .
. L E A . S N A R F .
S C A D S . S E N O R .
A L I . . . . T E A .
Y I K E S . E G E S T .
S P A N K . L A N . .
. . S A C K R A C E .
F A J I T A . A T O P .
A M U L E T . G A P E .
A P S E S . E L S E .
```

44

```
R E B U S . U S A G E .
A M I N E . F U S E D .
F U N C T I O N I N G .
. . . L A N . B A T E .
D O S E . V I E . . .
E D O . B E R A T E D .
M I R R O R I M A G E .
I N T E R N S . K I N .
. . T E E . F A S T .
O F F S . S O L . . .
P L A I N S P O K E N .
T O N N E . A R E N A .
S W E A T . H A N D Y .
```

Solutions

45

D	E	B	S		A	B	A	C	U	S
O	R	E	L		E	T	E	R	N	E
O	M	N	I	P	R	E	S	E	N	T
W	I	D	G	E	O	N		W	A	H
O	N	E	O	R		S	E	I	S	
P	E	D		I	N	F	U	L	L	
			N	O	W	A	R			
	I	C	E	D	A	M		M	S	N
D	S	O	S			I	P	A	N	A
I	S	A		A	L	S	O	R	A	N
P	U	R	P	L	E	H	E	A	R	T
S	E	S	T	E	T		M	U	L	E
O	D	E	S	S	A		E	D	Y	S

46

K	A	P	U	T		S	T	R	E	W
N	O	R	M	A		T	H	E	T	A
I	N	E	P	T		R	E	P	A	Y
T	E	C		T	R	U	E	R		
		I	S	L	E	T		O	A	T
E	L	O	P	E	D		D	A	N	E
P	O	U	R	S		C	O	C	O	A
E	A	S	Y		A	L	O	H	A	S
E	N	S		S	C	A	R	F		
		T	O	T	E	M		U	S	A
A	B	O	V	E		O	R	L	O	N
C	A	N	E	R		R	E	L	I	T
T	H	E	R	E		S	T	Y	L	E

47

C	R	T		T	U	P		H	A	D
L	I	E		R	N	A		O	N	E
A	L	L		A	D	S		T	N	T
W	E	E	N	I	E	S		H	A	H
		G	E	N	R	E		E	R	R
S	P	R	E	E	S		A	B	O	
A	L	A		E	T	A		D	O	N
N	A	P			A	M	P	E	R	E
N	T	H		S	N	O	O	D		
Y	O	W		A	D	R	E	N	A	L
A	N	I		R	I	O		E	R	A
S	I	R		E	N	S		S	I	N
I	C	E		E	G	O		S	A	D

48

E	R	E		T	W	A				
R	E	X		H	I	S		I	S	M
A	C	T		E	N	H	A	N	C	E
S	E	R	E	N	E		I	D	E	A
E	D	A	M			F	L	I	N	T
R	E	S	I	D	U	E		R	E	S
		P	R	O	R	A	T	A		
A	C	E		E	N	R	A	G	E	S
R	A	C	E	R			L	A	K	E
I	R	I	S		O	P	E	N	E	D
S	T	A	T	O	R	S		D	O	G
E	E	L		H	E	S		H	U	E
				M	O	T		I	T	S

Solutions

49

```
O R E S . . P A S H A
R O T E . L A R I A T
F A C T . O R A N G E
F R E T . R E B . . .
. T O D D . L I F E .
R H E S U S . E M I R
O U R . O P T . P R O
B R A T . R E C E S S
E L S E . A D A R . .
. S T Y . T I P I . .
S W A T H E . T O A D
P O S E U R . L U L L
A P S E S . E S P Y .
```

50

```
A M M O . . L A U D .
S E A R S . A N N E X
S A C R A . C A I N E
E L K . G A T . T U N
T I E . E R E . E D O
S E R A . S A D D E N
. E C H E L O N . . .
S U L T A N . C A T S
H R S . B I B . T H E
R A H . I C E . I R E
U N A P T . S L O O P
B U R S A . T O N N E
. S K I T . U S E D .
```

51

```
B A R . S A C . . . .
I P A . E G O . L A A
O P I A T E S . L A B
. S I S S . G O R E .
A D E L A . S T Y E S
A D A . S T A I D . .
A E F . I A L . B A A
. A N D R E . E A N .
A I M E E . S I N E S
B R I C . C R I T . .
B A L . T A O I S T S
R E Y . A N O . E A P
. . B A M . N S A . .
```

52

```
M E Z E . F R I G H T
E R I N . L I M I E R
L I M A . A D A G I O
D E B T . M E M O R Y
. . A I R E R . . . .
B O B C A T . . M A O
Y A W . T H Y . A D D
E R E . R A M R O D .
. . T O P A Z . . . .
N A R R O W . T I P I
E Q U I N E . U P O N
S U M M E R . R A N K
T A P E R S . E N D S
```

Solutions

53

```
U P R I S E S ▓ G M A
P R O M I S E ▓ R A T
D O U B L E A G E N T
A S S E T S ▓ E T U I
T E E D ▓ O N E A L
E S D ▓ G O R I L L A
▓ C O L I C ▓
E R E L O N G ▓ B A T
A I D A N ▓ J A D E
R C M P ▓ O B I T E R
W H O S T H E B O S S
A I N ▓ E N T E N T E
X E D ▓ L O E S S E R
```

54

```
D E P ▓ A D S ▓ S N A
I L E ▓ D E N ▓ T E N
S A R A L E E ▓ R E G
S I F T ▓ S E C E D E
E N E M Y ▓ H E L L
D E C ▓ S P R I T E S
▓ T H E R E S A
A S P E R S E ▓ D C C
S H I M ▓ F E D O R
E A T E R S ▓ C R U E
A F C ▓ E A S T E N D
N T H ▓ A R A ▓ S T O
D I D ▓ S S S
```

55

```
C A B ▓ A G E ▓ T A P
U S A ▓ F A N ▓ E V E
T S H I R T S ▓ M A N
▓ N O E L ▓ P I N
P A N T S ▓ A P T L Y
U S E R ▓ O V A
S H O U L D E R P A D
▓ D A D ▓ T I D Y
A S S E T ▓ S W E D E
T H E ▓ I D E A
L A P C A L Y P S O
A N I ▓ E L M ▓ A P P
S K A ▓ S E A ▓ P A T
```

56

```
H A N G A R ▓ A R T
A P O L L O ▓ S P A R
S T R O P S ▓ U P T O
▓ C H A M B R A Y
P O L K A ▓ I T O ▓
A L O E S ▓ D E V A S
S I G N ▓ R I L E
T O R S I ▓ E R N S T
▓ O P T ▓ L A G O S
T A L I S M A N ▓
A B L E ▓ A T E A S E
R E E L ▓ L E A N O N
O D D ▓ A D N A T E
```

Solutions

57

R	S	V	P		A	L	G	A	E	
A	L	E	E		S	A	L	L	Y	
L	A	R	G	E	S	C	A	L	E	
E	S	S		S	E	E	D			
S	H	O	O	T	S		E	A	S	E
		L	E	S	S		B	O	W	
T	R	A	D	E		A	B	A	T	E
S	O	L		M	A	M	A			
P	E	E	R		C	O	R	P	S	E
		O	P	U	S		A	I	R	
A	U	T	O	M	A	T	I	O	N	
D	R	O	N	E		O	N	U	S	
S	I	R	E	N		N	E	X	T	

58

C	L	A	D		P	E	G	L	E	G
H	I	V	E		A	U	R	O	R	A
O	M	I	T		W	R	O	N	G	S
C	O	V	E	R	N	O	T	E	S	
			C	H	E	S	T			
T	I	P	T	O	E		O	P	A	L
A	C	E						O	V	A
B	E	A	R		S	A	L	T	E	D
		A	P	P	L	E				
	I	N	T	E	R	E	S	T	E	D
P	O	E	T	R	Y		S	A	R	I
A	T	E	A	S	E		E	R	I	N
D	A	R	T	E	R		R	O	E	S

59

P	L	A	S	M	A		P	E	P	
R	I	C	H	E	S		S	L	U	E
O	P	E	R	A	S		T	A	R	E
		E	L	E	V	A	T	O	R	
	O	L	D	S	T	E	R			
G	N	U		S	A	V	A	N	T	
A	T	L	A	S		L	E	M	O	N
D	O	U	B	T	S		O	P	T	
		B	E	C	A	U	S	E		
F	O	R	E	W	A	R	N			
I	R	I	S		R	E	C	I	P	E
L	E	N	S		E	N	A	M	O	R
L	O	G		D	A	P	P	L	E	

60

T	O	P	O	S		S	T	O	A	
A	W	A	S	H		G	H	O	U	L
X	E	N	I	A		A	R	O	S	E
I	N	T	E	R	S	T	A	T	E	
		R	I	P	E	N				
A	G	E	S		O	A	K	L	E	Y
S	A	W		G	N	U		E	R	E
S	P	E	A	R	S		P	E	A	T
		N	A	O	M	I				
C	O	N	T	R	O	L	L	E	D	
D	U	B	A	I		C	L	O	S	E
A	R	I	L	S		H	A	U	S	A
B	E	T	S		A	R	D	E	N	

Solutions

61

S	A	B	R	A				A	S	Y	E
A	G	E	O	L	D			H	T	M	L
W	A	S	A	B	I			A	A	H	S
			I	D	E	A	S		N	A	E
P	A	D			E	L	C	I	D		
U	S	E	E			S	A	L	I	N	E
T	H	O	N	G			N	Y	N	E	X
S	E	N	O	R	S			A	G	R	O
			E	L	E	N	A		G	O	D
A	D	S			G	I	N	S	U		
G	E	E	K			P	O	T	A	S	H
H	A	L	E			E	D	E	R	L	E
A	R	F	S				E	N	D	O	W

62

M	I	R	A			A	B	A	T	E	
O	N	E	S			L	I	G	E	R	
T	U	R	P	E	N	T	I	N	E		
I	R	A			Y	I	E	L	D		
F	E	N	N	E	C			E	R	A	S
			B	L	O	C			I	L	O
F	O	R	C	E			H	U	L	A	S
E	V	A		T	S	A	R				
Y	A	W	S			O	R	N	A	T	E
			D	E	A	L	T		D	E	L
	T	E	N	N	I	S	B	A	L	L	
	E	A	S	E	D			U	G	L	I
	C	L	E	W	S			M	E	S	S

63

A	T	A	L	O	S	S					
L	U	N	A	T	I	C			B	E	G
P	L	A	N	T	A	R			A	R	E
H	I	T			M	A	C	R	O	N	
A	P	H	I	D		P	A	R	S	E	
	S	E	B	U	M		B	E	E	S	
		M	I	N	I	M	A	L			
S	P	A	S		D	O	N	O	R		
N	O	T	E	D		B	A	R	E	D	
A	R	I	S	E	N			G	N	U	
F	E	Z		C	O	P	L	A	N	D	
U	S	E		A	L	I	E	N	E	E	
			L	O	C	U	S	T	S		

64

S	A	B	R	E			S	N	A	P	S
I	L	L	E	R			T	O	B	I	T
P	L	A	T	A			E	L	E	N	A
E	A	S	Y	S	T	R	E	E	T		
			P	E	O	N	S				
T	O	R	E	R	O			S	E	E	A
S	A	D		S	T	L		S	E	A	
R	S	S	S			S	E	T	T	E	E
		W	A	I	T	E					
	S	P	A	R	E	P	A	R	T	S	
B	E	A	N	O		A	R	I	A	L	
I	V	I	E	S		S	A	C	R	A	
D	E	D	E	E		S	T	O	N	Y	

Solutions

65

N	I	T	T	I		E	G	G	E	D
E	V	I	A	N		D	U	A	N	E
Z	O	R	R	O		O	N	L	O	W
		E	N	U	F		G	A	L	S
L	E	S		R	A	M	A			
A	V	O	W		S	E	D	A	T	E
G	A	M	E	R		N	I	V	E	N
O	N	E	S	E	C		N	E	R	D
			T	E	A	K		M	N	O
R	O	H	E		D	I	D	A		
O	L	O	R	D		T	O	R	O	S
M	E	R	L	E		T	R	I	E	S
E	A	S	Y	A		Y	E	A	R	S

66

O	B	I		D	O	N				
C	O	N	F	I	N	E		P	A	R
A	T	T	I	R	E	D		R	C	A
		E	V	E	N		B	E	R	G
S	A	L	E		I	R	I	S	E	S
A	I	L		A	G	A	T	E		
E	R	E		T	H	Y		N	A	B
		C	L	O	T	S		T	I	E
S	E	T	U	P	S		D	A	M	E
C	R	U	X		T	O	O	T		
A	N	A		M	A	R	T	I	A	L
B	E	L		O	N	S	H	O	R	E
			A	D	O		N	E	T	

67

S	T	O	I	C		A	C	E	R	B
T	E	R	R	A		L	O	V	E	R
O	S	I	E	R		D	R	A	P	E
U	T	E		A	L	E		C	O	W
P	A	L	A	V	E	R		U	S	E
			L	A	C		D	E	E	D
	C	O	U	N	T	R	I	E	S	
C	A	L	M		E	A	R			
O	D	D		B	R	I	T	I	S	H
H	E	M		I	N	N		D	O	E
E	N	A	T	E		B	A	L	L	S
I	C	I	E	R		O	G	E	E	S
R	E	D	E	S		W	O	R	S	E

68

W	O	R	K	S			B	A	I	L
A	D	I	E	U	S		A	N	N	A
R	E	P	A	C	K	A	G	I	N	G
			T	R	I	G				
A	M	U	S	E		A	P	E	X	
S	O	N		T	I	E	R	E	D	
K	I	T	C	H	E	N	W	A	R	E
S	L	I	P	O	N		T	O	W	
	S	L	A	Y		E	P	O	X	Y
		L	E	G	O					
W	I	N	T	E	R	G	R	E	E	N
I	C	O	N		G	A	T	E	A	U
N	E	W	T		R	E	C	U	T	

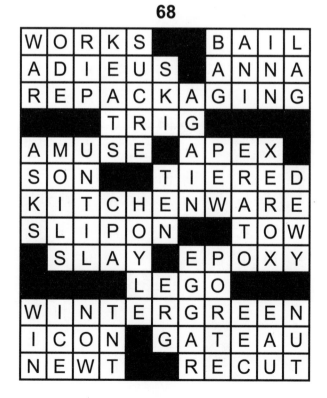

Solutions

69

B	L	A	S	T	S			R	B	S
R	E	S	T	O	N		P	E	A	T
A	G	O	R	A	E		E	S	T	E
N	I	N	O			E	S	T	A	T	E
D	O	I	N			E	E	L	E	R
S	N	A	G		P	A	R	E	R	S
		B	A	I	L	S				
S	N	A	R	L	S		E	S	A	S
K	O	R	E	A		L	O	O	T
O	R	I	E	N	T	L	I	R	E
A	T	O	Z		O	M	E	R	T	A
L	O	S	E		R	E	R	E	A	D
S	N	O		A	S	S	E	S	S

70

A	T	P	L	A	Y		C	W	T	S
N	E	R	O	L	I		L	E	S	H
D	R	O	W	S	E		R	A	G	A
R	E	C		O	L	D		R	A	L
E	S	E	S		D	E	N	I	R	O
W	A	S	H	Y		T	E	N	P	M
		S	E	E		A	R	G	
N	I	S	A	N		T	O	A	S	T
A	V	E	R	T	S		S	S	T	S
M	A	R		A	N	D		M	E	T
E	N	V	Y		A	R	T	I	E	R
I	K	E	A		P	A	E	L	L	A
T	A	R	R		S	T	R	E	E	P

71

A	N	D		I	M	P		R	C	A
R	E	A	C	T	O	R		A	R	C
E	X	T	R	A	D	I	T	I	O	N
S	T	E	A	L		M	A	N	S	E
		T	I	P	O	F	F	S	
U	N	S	E	A	L		T	A	E	L
P	A	P		N	A	P		L	Y	E
S	U	E	T		N	U	C	L	E	I
	S	C	O	O	T	E	R	
S	E	T	O	N		R	E	P	O	T
P	A	R	T	I	C	I	P	A	T	E
E	T	A		C	O	L	E	T	T	E
D	E	L		E	W	E		H	O	D

72

M	I	D		B	R	A		
O	B	I		E	E	R		W	A	N
R	E	S	E	R	V	E		A	D	O
O	R	I	N	G		A	G	L	O	W
S	I	N	E			O	K	R	A
E	A	T		D	E	S	T	I	N	Y
		E	L	A	T	I	O	N	
P	A	G	O	D	A	S		G	A	S
E	C	R	U			R	S	V	P
S	T	A	R	T		B	E	T	E	L
T	O	T		S	A	R	D	I	N	E
O	R	E		A	G	E		C	U	E
		R	O	D		K	E	N

Solutions

73

I	N	D	I	A		E	G	A	L	
N	A	A	C	P		D	A	L	E	
A	C	C	E	P	T	A	B	L	E	
N	L	E		A	I	M	E	E		
		A	R	P	S		L	E	R	
N	U	C	L	E	I		M	U	N	O
A	T	H	O	L		S	A	I	G	A
P	E	R	P		I	N	W	A	R	D
S	S	I		S	O	I	R			
		S	E	T	U	P		L	E	K
	A	T	M	O	S	P	H	E	R	E
	B	E	M	A		E	E	N	S	Y
	C	N	E	T		T	E	A	T	S

74

S	E	A	F	O	X			S	A	L
S	C	Y	L	L	A		C	E	D	I
N	O	R	A	I	N		O	L	A	V
		G	O	A		M	A	R	Y	
G	W	A	R		D	I	P			
L	A	M	A		U	T	U	R	N	S
O	W	E	N	S		A	T	E	I	T
P	A	S	T	E	S		E	D	N	A
		F	I	T		R	O	O	T	
N	O	V	O		R	I	C			
Y	A	L	U		A	R	O	M	A	S
E	T	A	L		T	O	D	D	L	E
S	Y	D			I	C	E	S	A	W

75

K	I	L	O		A	R	E	A	S
A	C	A	D	S		S	A	C	R	E
R	E	P	E	A	T	A	G	A	I	N
R	A	S		N	I	M		R	O	N
A	G	E		C	G	I		T	S	A
S	E	D	A	T	E		D	E	E	S
		P	A	R	S	E				
B	O	L	E		S	T	I	N	G	S
A	P	A		A	E	R		O	O	H
K	E	A		N	Y	E		S	A	R
I	N	L	I	N	E	S	K	A	T	E
N	E	A	L	E		S	O	L	E	D
G	R	A	S	S			L	E	E	S

76

W	I	P	E	R		A	S	P	E	R
O	B	E	S	E		M	A	R	N	E
L	E	A	S	E		A	C	O	R	N
F	A	N		V	A	T		B	O	A
E	M	U		E	R	E		A	B	M
	S	T	Y		S	U	E	B	E	E
		G	E	N	E	R	A	L		
K	E	A	T	O	N		R	E	B	
I	L	L		N	A	E		C	I	S
S	A	L		U	L	T		A	T	C
S	T	E	P	S		H	A	U	T	E
E	E	R	I	E		O	L	S	E	N
D	R	Y	E	R		S	T	E	R	E

Solutions

77

S	A	T	E		O	B	L	A	T	E
O	R	E	O		R	E	A	D	E	R
L	E	A	N		G	I	R	D	E	R
D	A	M		T	A	N	K			
		S	W	U	N	G		D	O	C
A	C	T	I	N	G		H	O	P	E
C	A	E	S	A	R	S	A	L	A	D
H	I	R	E		I	C	I	C	L	E
E	N	S		E	N	U	R	E		
		K	I	D	D		V	O	W	
R	E	S	I	D	E		M	I	D	I
H	E	A	T	E	R		A	T	O	M
O	R	D	E	R	S		T	A	R	P

78

S	P	O	T		P	E	R	E	S	
H	U	G	H		O	P	E	R	A	
I	R	R	A	T	I	O	N	A	L	
P	R	E	T	E	N	S	E			
		C	A	T		G	R	A	B	
B	R	A	H	M	S		E	U	R	O
R	A	F				S	E	N		
A	C	R	E		S	A	S	H	A	Y
N	E	O	N		P	I	T			
		L	O	L	L	I	P	O	P	
R	H	I	N	E	S	T	O	N	E	
C	A	S	T	E		C	R	E	W	
A	N	T	O	N		H	E	S	S	

79

I	D	A	H	O		U	M	P	E	D
N	O	T	O	N		K	A	T	I	E
O	U	T	R	E		U	R	A	N	O
	B	E	N	G	A	L	I			
E	L	S	E		R	E	L	O	S	
N	E	T	T		C	L	U	N	K	Y
G	T	S		A	A	E		C	I	E
R	O	T	U	N	D		S	E	R	A
	N	O	T	T	I		C	A	E	N
		T	E	A	B	A	G	S		
D	A	T	E	D		E	R	A	O	F
U	H	U	R	U		S	P	I	R	O
C	L	A	S	P		S	A	N	T	O

80

		S	L	A	T	E		P	E	P
	S	A	I	L	O	R		O	R	E
F	A	L	L	I	N	G	S	T	A	R
E	X	A	L	T			A	P	S	E
T	O	R	E		P	I	T	I	E	S
A	N	Y		C	A	R	E	E	R	
			T	O	Y	E	D			
	S	E	R	I	E	S		M	E	N
M	A	N	U	R	E		B	A	N	E
O	H	M	S		P	A	N	D	A	
D	A	I	S	Y	C	U	T	T	E	R
A	R	T		O	R	C	H	I	D	
L	A	Y		D	Y	K	E	S		

Solutions

81

```
H A T E ■ B E S E T S
A N O N ■ A N K L E T
S C R E W D R I V E R
S I N ■ A G A ■ E T A
L E A ■ R E G ■ S H Y
E N D S ■ S E T ■ ■ ■
S T O I C ■ D A N C E
■ ■ P A L ■ D E A R
M A P ■ P O L ■ W Y E
A L A ■ S A E ■ D E C
M A G N I F I C E N T
B R E E Z E ■ B A N E
O Y S T E R ■ S L E D
```

82

```
A Y R E S ■ S T R O H
R E E D Y ■ A S A N A
A S S E S S M E N T S
M I C ■ C H A ■ A H I
I S U ■ O E R S T E D
S E E P ■ D I A ■ ■ ■
■ E R A S ■ A R C S
■ R E I ■ D A T S
A S H R A M S ■ N A T
R H O ■ B R O ■ T I A
E A R P I E R C I N G
A L D E R ■ R O N E E
S T E E D ■ Y E A R S
```

83

```
L O F A T ■ C R E E S
A L E N E ■ H E N N Y
S I E G E ■ L E D O N
S N L ■ U G O ■ O U T
E D S ■ P B R ■ F G H
S A T B ■ E A R T H S
■ H O G ■ L A H
S T E P U P ■ O E N O
T A P ■ E R A ■ M O R
O R I ■ S Y D ■ O O M
O M N I S ■ D U N N O
P A C A S ■ I N T E L
S C H M O ■ N E H R U
```

84

```
U M P ■ P O L ■ ■ ■
P A R ■ E K E ■ F B I
S L E P T I N ■ E E N
E A S E ■ E S P R I T
T W E A K ■ U R G E
S I N ■ E A R L I E R
■ T I P T O E S ■
R E A D I E S ■ W H O
A R T Y ■ Y A H O O
T O I L E T ■ S E L L
E D O ■ T O R P E D O
D E N ■ C R Y ■ L U G
■ H I E ■ S P Y
```

Solutions

85

U	R	S	I		D	I	C	I	N	G
N	A	A	N		O	N	E	L	O	T
I	N	T	L		P	A	R	O	L	E
V	I	I	I		P	S	I			
	S	E	S	E		S	R	T	A	
I	N	F	U	L	L		E	A	U	S
L	O	I		A	G	A		I	N	K
S	I	E	G		A	L	I	N	E	S
A	D	D	L		N	A	T	S		
		U	G	G		L	T	D	S	
M	E	E	T	M	E		L	O	O	K
E	N	D	E	A	R		D	R	N	O
R	E	M	I	T	S		O	M	A	R

86

C	A	N	T		A	G	N	A	T	E
A	M	A	H		D	E	O	D	A	R
L	O	N	I		D	O	L	A	P	S
F	O	U	R	S	T	R	O	K	E	
			T	I	O	G	A			
C	L	A	Y	S		E	D	W	I	N
U	B	I					R	K	O	
T	O	N	G	A		F	O	Y	E	R
		E	R	I	T	U				
	M	A	N	O	F	S	T	E	E	L
B	E	I	R	U	T		G	I	R	O
E	N	M	E	S	H		U	N	D	O
L	E	S	S	E	E		N	E	A	P

87

O	R	C	S		P	E	A	C	H
W	I	L	E		L	A	T	H	E
N	O	E	L		M	O	V	E	I	N
S	T	A	M	P	E	D	E		
	R	A	Y	S		S	P	O	T
O	C	A		G	S	A		R	N	A
P	A	N		M	I	D		E	T	C
A	R	C		Y	E	A		M	O	O
L	E	E	S		U	G	L	I	
	T	I	R	E	L	E	S	S	
A	S	S	E	T	S		A	R	I	A
L	A	P	E	L		M	E	N	S
I	D	Y	L	L		A	S	K	S

88

I	N	E	S		S	C	H	E	M	E
R	O	A	N		A	R	A	R	A	T
E	N	S	E		D	U	R	E	S	S
S	E	T	A	S	I	D	E		
	E	K	E	S		M	A	R	C
S	T	R	E	A	M	S		N	O	P
O	V	E	R	T		I	C	O	N	O
O	M	G		S	T	R	A	U	S	S
N	A	G	S		H	U	R	T	
	C	A	R	P	A	R	T	S	
C	A	M	A	R	O		C	A	I	N
A	M	A	L	I	E		A	G	R	A
B	A	G	E	L	S		S	E	E	P

Solutions

89

W	A	R	I	E	S	T	■	I	M	O
E	Y	E	W	E	A	R	■	N	I	L
R	E	G	A	L	B	E	A	G	L	E
E	A	R	N	S	■	A	K	E	L	A
N	Y	E	T	■	P	T	I	S	A	N
T	E	T	■	F	E	I	S	T	Y	■
■	■	R	L	E	S	S	■	■	■	■
■	E	L	A	Y	N	E	■	U	S	H
B	L	I	M	P	S	■	A	R	E	A
A	M	N	I	A	■	A	N	G	U	S
B	I	G	S	P	E	N	D	E	R	S
E	R	E	■	E	T	E	R	N	A	L
S	A	R	■	R	O	S	E	T	T	E

90

A	C	T	A	S	■	S	O	D	A	S
L	A	R	V	A	■	T	H	E	R	E
A	S	E	A	S	Y	A	S	P	I	E
D	A	K	■	H	S	T	■	P	A	K
■	■	■	S	E	L	E	S	■	■	■
T	E	A	L	S	■	S	U	M	M	A
E	E	R	O	■	■	■	S	P	A	D
N	E	N	E	H	■	M	A	S	T	S
■	■	■	S	A	T	A	N	■	■	■
A	B	A	■	R	A	D	■	M	A	C
M	I	S	S	A	M	E	R	I	C	A
C	L	I	O	S	■	D	E	T	E	R
S	L	A	B	S	■	O	A	T	H	S

91

T	A	B	■	B	O	T	■	F	E	D
I	G	A	■	A	L	E	■	R	R	R
D	F	C	■	N	E	T	L	O	S	S
Y	A	K	I	T	O	R	I	■	■	■
■	■	F	S	U	■	A	V	O	I	D
I	D	E	O	■	O	D	E	N	S	E
K	I	N	G	O	F	S	W	I	N	G
E	S	C	O	R	T	■	I	N	T	S
S	C	E	N	A	■	I	T	Y	■	■
■	■	A	N	A	T	H	E	M	A	■
M	Y	A	L	G	I	A	■	A	U	R
A	E	S	■	E	R	L	■	R	O	E
W	T	S	■	S	Y	S	■	S	N	O

92

O	M	E	G	A	■	S	P	A	S	M
C	E	L	L	S	■	A	R	O	M	A
A	E	S	O	P	■	L	I	N	E	R
S	T	E	R	E	O	■	M	E	W	L
■	■	■	I	N	F	R	A	■	■	■
A	N	N	A	■	T	U	R	B	A	N
L	E	A	S	T	■	E	Y	R	I	E
P	E	E	W	E	E	■	C	O	L	T
■	■	■	A	L	T	H	O	■	■	■
B	O	N	N	■	H	E	L	E	N	A
A	R	O	S	E	■	D	O	R	I	C
S	A	V	O	R	■	G	R	A	P	H
S	L	A	N	G	■	E	S	S	A	Y

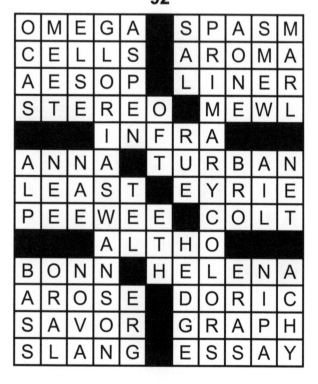

Solutions

93

	P	A	N	G			B	A	R	S
S	I	T	A	R			A	N	E	W	
T	A	R	M	A	C		T	I	M	E	
A	N	I		S	O	S		M	A	D	
Y	O	U		S	A	E		A	R	E	
	S	M	A	L	L	T	A	L	K		
		L	A	I	T	Y				
	P	O	I	N	T	L	E	S	S		
O	A	R		D	I	E		E	T	C	
F	E	D		S	O	D		C	O	Y	
F	L	E	E		N	O	V	E	N	A	
E	L	A	N		W	I	D	E	N	
D	A	L	E		N	E	E	D		

94

L	O	A	M		P	O	T	T	E	D
I	D	L	E		U	P	R	O	A	R
R	I	L	L		S	T	A	R	R	Y
A	N	A	L	Y	S	I	S			
	R	O	E		C	H	I	L	I	
B	L	O	W	S		S	Y	N	O	D
Y	O	U					T	O	E	
T	I	N	G	E		T	R	E	K	S
E	N	D	O	N		O	A	R		
		S	T	A	G	N	A	N	T	
R	A	I	S	I	N		S	L	U	E
I	N	D	I	C	T		O	I	L	S
M	Y	O	P	E	S		M	A	L	T

95

P	E	E	R	S		S	H	A	D	E
A	R	N	E	L		A	A	R	O	N
L	E	D	G	E		G	R	A	T	A
P	I	P	E	D	R	E	A	M	S	
		O	N	S	E	T	S			
A	S	I	T		D	E	S	I	C	A
C	E	N		D	B	A		N	O	B
T	A	T	T	O	O		R	A	R	E
		O	U	N	C	E	S			
	C	A	U	S	E	A	S	T	I	R
C	A	R	P	E		R	E	A	T	A
O	P	T	E	R		D	A	T	E	D
B	A	S	E	S		S	T	E	N	S

96

T	E	E	N	S		A	L	F	A	S
E	M	M	E	T		D	I	A	N	A
S	A	P	P	Y		O	N	C	D	S
S	I	T		L	A	R	G	E	S	S
E	L	Y	S	I	A	N		T	O	Y
R	E	P	O		S	E	T	H		
A	D	R	I	P		D	E	E	M	S
		O	R	R	S		A	N	I	P
E	L	M		E	C	O	T	A	G	E
R	E	I	N	S	I	N		T	R	L
R	O	S	E	S		T	R	I	A	L
O	N	E	N	O		A	N	O	T	E
R	I	S	E	N		P	A	N	E	D

Solutions

97

```
S W I G ■ B R I C K S
H E M O ■ E N T A I L
U S E R ■ G R A N N Y
■ T A K E I ■ L I T E
B E N I G N ■ I T E R
A N I ■ A N Y A ■ ■
P D T ■ L E E ■ M M C
■ B E R N ■ A A U
A N D A ■ S T A L K S
B O E R ■ L A H T I ■
B U R E A U ■ E E N Y
O N E S E C ■ M S G R
T S K T S K ■ S E S S
```

98

```
A C C R A ■ A M I S S
G H O U L ■ S O N I C
R A N T S ■ S A F E R
E L F ■ O R E ■ I V E
E E L ■ R A T ■ N E W
S T A L A G ■ H I S S
■ G I N ■ C O T ■
B U R P ■ C A R E S S
R N A ■ F A R ■ S A Y
O T T ■ A R C ■ I T S
O R I E L ■ A D M I T
M U O N S ■ S N A R E
S E N S E ■ S A L E M
```

99

```
M U F F S ■ S I N C E
A T E A M ■ A L A R M
R A T I O ■ B L U E S
C H A R T R E U S E ■
■ ■ H O R S E ■
E N U R E D ■ I A M B
G A P E R ■ M O T O R
G E L T ■ C I N E M A
■ O R E O S ■
T A I L O R M A D E
S I D E D ■ E A G E R
P E E V E ■ A L I B I
A D D E R ■ D E N S E
```

100

```
E L S E S ■ B R A S S
D E A L T ■ R A N E E
G A M M A C A M E R A
E D S ■ T O N ■ C A L
■ S U I T E D ■
A S T E R N ■ L O G S
B E R N E ■ B A T E S
A R U N ■ O A T E R S
■ S A D D L E ■
K A T ■ A I L ■ A R B
I R I S H C O F F E E
T C E L L ■ T R A M S
T A R A S ■ S A R I S
```

Solutions

101

```
F A M E . A C R E S
C A R O L . R O U G E
A C U T E . R E L A X
R E M E M B E R E D .
. . L I L A C . . . .
S A S S . A R E N A S
P S I . I T S . O V A
A S T H M A . C R E W
. . A P N E A . . . .
. S T R A T A G E M S
G O A D S . R I P U P
M A X E S . E L E G Y
T R I N E . D Y E S .
```

102

```
S E A T A C . A C A D
A R C A N A . S A D E
R O A R E R . S L A B
K O N A . P B A . . .
. . . . E L I A N . .
S A A R . T A L L E R
G R E E N C H E E S E
T A R S A L . D A T A
. N O T T E . . . . .
. . . L E A . S T A B
R A T E . N E A R T O
A M A S . E N R I C O
S A N S . R E A S O N
```

103

```
A J A R . A D A G I O
R A S E . S E D A T E
I M P S . S U I T O R
A B S T R U S E . . .
. . O A R . U S S R .
S C A R L E T . K O I
H O V E L . H A U N T
A P E . Y A R D A G E
H E R S . R E D . . .
. . A S T E R I S K .
S C A M P I . E V E N
P O R O U S . S A R A
A S K A N T . S N A P
```

104

```
R W E . S L C . L O L
A E C . L I L . A S A
F I T T O B E T I E D
. . A M E . I T S A .
A N T H O L O G Y . .
M F A . S S E . . . .
D C C A B . H R O S S
. M E D . D E F . . .
A P E R I O D I C . .
I R A E . Y R S . . .
W O N D E R W O M A N
A D D . L U I . O P S
S S W . I B N . A B C
```

Solutions

105

M	A	N	E	D		A	S	S	E	T
A	D	E	N	O		S	O	T	T	O
R	E	C	T	I	L	I	N	E	A	R
A	S	T	O		E	D	E	R	L	E
U	T	A		A	T	E		N	I	N
D	E	R	M	I	S		M	E	A	T
		A	X	L	E	S				
L	A	B	S		O	N	T	I	M	E
A	P	E		S	O	D		F	E	N
T	E	A	S	E	S		P	O	E	T
I	R	R	E	L	E	V	A	N	C	E
S	C	E	N	E		A	B	L	E	R
H	U	R	T	S		S	A	Y	S	O

106

G	A	S	P		C	H	A	I	S	E
O	R	A	L		R	O	B	R	O	Y
L	I	M	A		U	N	E	A	S	E
F	L	A	T	F	E	E	T			
	R	O	O	T	S		S	P	A	
M	A	I	N	E		T	A	L	O	N
A	N	T	I				N	I	S	I
S	T	A	C	K		A	N	D	E	S
H	E	N		E	M	C	E	E		
		L	E	O	T	A	R	D	S	
C	H	E	A	P	O		L	U	R	E
P	E	S	T	E	R		E	L	A	N
A	M	P	E	R	E		R	E	T	D

107

E	R	S	T		A	R	E	N	A
M	E	T	O	O		B	U	X	O	M
S	M	A	R	T		R	E	C	A	P
		T	R	I	P	E		O	H	S
P	R	E		C	H	A	S	M		
A	H	O	Y		I	S	O	M	E	R
D	E	F	O	G		T	A	U	P	E
S	A	T	Y	R	S		K	N	I	T
		H	O	O	E	Y		I	C	E
S	H	E		S	T	O	I	C		
L	O	A	F	S		G	N	A	S	H
A	P	R	I	L		A	C	T	O	R
P	E	T	T	Y		H	E	N	S	

108

R	A	M	I	S		L	I	S	A
A	P	A	S	T		O	W	E	N
D	R	Y	M	A	R	T	I	N	I
O	S	E		P	A	I	L		
		A	L	G		L	E	W	D
R	A	I	S	E	U	P		Y	E	O
T	H	E	I	R		E	A	R	L	S
E	S	A		S	C	R	E	E	D	S
S	O	T	S		M	I	C		
		U	P	D	O		D	E	A
L	I	Z	A	R	D	K	I	N	G
E	L	I	N		I	S	O	N	E
S	K	E	E		C	U	R	E	R

Solutions

109

B	A	N	N	S			S	C	A	R	P
A	D	I	E	U			C	O	D	E	R
S	A	N	D	S			A	B	O	V	E
A	G	E			H	E	M		R	E	F
L	I	T			I	M	P		E	R	E
T	O	Y	S		B	E	A	R	E	R	
			O	P	A	R	T				
S	T	A	L	L	S		E	S	S	E	
T	U	T		E	S	P		P	A	L	
O	R	T		A	Y	E		I	L	O	
A	R	I	A	S		S	C	R	A	P	
T	E	R	N	E		T	H	E	M	E	
S	T	E	A	D		O	A	S	I	S	

110

C	R	O	A	K			B	O	C	C	E
A	O	R	T	A			A	L	A	R	M
S	A	N	A	A			R	E	S	E	E
A	R	A	B			O	R	A	T	O	R
S	E	M			A	R	E		A	L	G
	D	E	N	E	B			S	N	E	E
		N	O	S	I	R	E	E			
S	E	T	H		S	O	N	Y	A		
O	C	A		L	O	N		E	T	S	
R	A	T	T	A	N		R	O	T	H	
E	R	I	E	S		N	O	V	I	A	
S	T	O	A	T		S	T	E	R	N	
T	E	N	K	S		C	O	R	E	A	

111

D	U	M	B	O	S			B	E	N	S
O	N	E	I	D	A			U	N	I	T
G	R	A	N	D	M	A	S	T	E	R	
L	U	G			L	E	U		R	C	A
E	L	E	G	Y		G	R	E	E	K	
G	Y	R	O		C	H	E	E	S	E	
			A	C	U	T	E				
C	A	P	T	O	R			V	A	S	T
A	M	A	S	S		S	E	D	E	R	
M	O	T		T	A	P		V	E	E	
P	E	R	E	S	T	R	O	I	K	A	
E	B	O	N		O	U	T	S	E	T	
R	A	L	E		M	E	T	E	R	S	

112

C	A	P		P	E	G					
A	W	E		O	V	A			T	U	G
R	A	N		S	A	L	E	R	N	O	
D	R	I	E	S		A	R	O	M	A	
S	E	T	T	E	R		S	L	A	T	
		E	A	S	E		E	L	S	E	
B	U	N		S	P	A		E	K	E	
I	N	T	O		E	N	V	Y			
T	W	I	G		L	A	I	C	A	L	
M	E	A	L	S		L	E	O	N	E	
A	L	R	E	A	D	Y		A	N	A	
P	L	Y		G	A	S		C	I	D	
				O	T	T		H	E	S	

Solutions

113

J	O	T	S	■	■	S	A	L	A	L
A	R	R	A	S	■	S	M	I	L	E
B	U	E	N	O	S	A	I	R	E	S
■	S	T	U	N	■	■	A	C	S	■
A	S	T	E	R	O	I	D	S	■	■
B	E	L	■	■	W	I	E	■	■	■
S	E	E	K	S	■	I	S	A	A	C
■	■	D	A	B	■	■	R	R	S	■
■	■	E	S	T	R	A	N	G	E	S
E	A	N	■	E	N	Y	O	■	■	■
S	A	N	F	E	R	N	A	N	D	O
T	R	E	A	S	■	A	C	N	E	S
S	E	A	T	S	■	■	K	E	G	S

114

M	E	L	E	E	■	H	A	D	E	S
E	X	I	S	T	■	B	L	E	E	D
T	E	E	T	O	T	A	L	E	R	S
E	R	D	E	■	A	R	A	■	■	■
■	■	L	A	P	■	■	T	O	E	S
A	T	A	L	O	S	S	■	R	I	A
L	O	R	E	N	■	A	M	E	N	S
A	F	T	■	E	N	M	A	S	S	E
S	U	E	S	■	I	S	R	■	■	■
■	■	T	A	G	■	G	M	A	N	■
M	A	H	A	B	H	A	R	A	T	A
A	R	E	E	L	■	D	E	T	E	R
N	E	A	L	E	■	A	T	S	E	A

115

B	E	A	T	■	D	E	S	P	O	T
A	G	R	A	■	O	T	T	A	W	A
L	A	M	B	■	U	N	I	T	E	D
I	D	Y	L	■	B	A	N	■	■	■
■	■	O	W	L	■	T	A	P	E	■
A	D	M	I	R	E	S	■	L	A	W
F	R	E	D	A	S	T	A	I	R	E
R	A	W	■	P	A	I	N	T	E	R
O	G	L	E	■	W	R	Y	■	■	■
■	■	C	A	B	■	B	O	D	E	■
S	U	D	O	K	U	■	O	B	E	Y
I	T	A	L	I	C	■	D	O	V	E
R	E	D	I	N	K	■	Y	E	A	R

116

S	T	A	L	K	■	P	L	A	Z	A
H	O	M	E	O	■	R	A	V	E	S
E	A	R	T	H	M	O	V	E	R	S
E	M	I	■	L	U	S	■	N	O	T
N	A	T	■	S	S	A	■	G	I	S
A	N	A	D	■	S	I	R	E	N	■
■	■	I	R	O	C	Z	■	■	■	■
■	R	E	V	E	L	■	A	P	S	O
R	E	V	■	B	I	L	■	R	A	N
A	S	E	■	U	N	A	■	E	M	S
D	O	N	T	F	I	G	H	T	I	T
A	L	L	O	F	■	O	U	T	T	A
R	E	Y	E	S	■	S	H	Y	E	R

Solutions

117

H	A	M	M			B	O	B	B	I	N
A	N	O	A			I	N	A	R	M	S
O	D	D	S			C	I	N	E	M	A
		E	S	T		N	C	A	A		
C	C	L		E	K	E		D	N	S	
A	R	I	O	S	I		G	M	E	N	
T	O	N	Y	S	O	P	R	A	N	O	
E	S	T	E		S	T	U	C	C	O	
S	S	E		A	K	A		H	E	D	
	B	R	A	T		S	C	I			
S	E	I	N	E	S		O	N	E	D	
L	A	O	T	S	E		R	E	N	O	
A	M	R	I	T	A		M	S	G	R	

118

C	O	R	O	T		E	A	R	E	D	
A	L	A	D	Y		A	L	A	N	A	
S	L	E	E	P		T	E	N	T	O	
E	A	S	T	E	R	E	G	G	S		
			T	O	E	R	R				
P	A	S	A		A	Y	E	S	I	R	
A	S	A						E	R	A	
S	T	R	E	S	S		S	A	S	S	
			S	P	A	R	E				
	A	S	S	O	C	I	A	T	E	S	
R	U	L	E	R		A	L	I	N	E	
A	T	O	N	E		L	I	N	T	S	
M	O	T	E	S		S	T	A	R	E	

119

S	C	O	T	T		J	A	N	O	S	
A	T	L	A	W		E	X	E	R	T	
T	R	A	V	E	L	W	E	A	R	Y	
		I	R	A	E		T	S	E		
T	I	A		P	Y	L	E				
U	R	L	S		R	E	N	A	M	E	
P	O	A	C	H	E	D	E	G	G	S	
I	C	E	T	E	A		S	H	R	S	
		V	I	D	A		A	S	E		
A	N	A		F	E	T	A				
L	O	C	K	E	R	R	O	O	M	S	
P	L	I	E	R		E	U	B	I	E	
S	O	D	A	S		E	T	O	N	S	

120

A	H	E	M		L	O	L	I	T	A	
G	I	G	O		I	R	O	N	I	C	
A	R	I	D		S	C	R	I	P	T	
R	E	S	I	S	T	A	N	T			
			F	E	E	S		I	C	C	
A	S	S	I	G	N		B	A	I	L	
C	A	M	E	O		L	A	T	T	E	
E	G	A	D		R	E	D	E	E	M	
D	O	C		M	E	A	L				
	K	N	E	E	P	A	N	T	S		
A	F	E	A	R	D		N	O	O	K	
M	A	R	B	L	E		D	E	L	I	
P	A	S	S	E	D		S	L	E	D	

Solutions

121

O	D	D	B	A	L	L	■	S	A	M
P	A	R	O	L	E	E	■	H	U	E
S	H	Y	L	O	C	K	■	A	D	S
■	■	■	L	E	T	■	A	R	I	A
S	P	E	W	■	E	R	U	P	T	S
I	S	L	E	■	R	A	T	■	■	■
T	I	M	E	S	■	F	O	R	A	Y
■	■	V	I	P	■	M	A	R	E	■
B	I	K	I	N	I	■	O	P	E	N
I	D	O	L	■	E	B	B	■	■	■
N	E	O	■	A	R	R	I	V	E	S
D	A	K	■	V	I	O	L	A	T	E
S	L	Y	■	E	S	S	E	N	C	E

122

M	A	O	■	P	C	P	■	B	T	U
O	N	T	■	H	E	R	■	E	E	G
O	N	E	M	O	R	E	■	L	R	G
R	A	R	A	■	F	L	O	O	R	■
E	L	I	T	E	■	L	I	V	E	R
■	■	S	M	A	■	L	E	N	Z	■
L	I	I	■	F	D	A	■	D	E	A
E	N	L	S	■	O	M	A	■	■	■
S	A	L	P	A	■	B	A	B	E	S
■	M	U	F	F	S	■	R	I	E	U
T	E	S	■	T	A	R	P	O	N	S
E	S	E	■	E	K	E	■	M	I	A
L	S	D	■	R	I	G	■	E	E	N

123

G	L	E	N	■	S	L	O	P	E	D
A	L	T	O	■	V	E	R	I	T	Y
T	A	E	L	■	E	V	I	N	C	E
E	N	R	O	L	L	E	E	■	■	■
D	O	N	■	U	T	E	N	S	I	L
■	■	A	P	S	E	■	T	O	T	E
H	E	L	O	T	■	S	A	M	O	A
E	E	L	S	■	H	O	L	E	■	■
S	C	Y	T	H	E	D	■	T	S	P
■	■	P	A	R	A	S	I	T	E	■
G	A	L	O	R	E	■	A	M	E	N
A	L	I	N	E	S	■	K	E	E	N
S	P	E	E	D	Y	■	E	S	P	Y

124

S	I	B	S	■	M	C	C	O	O
C	O	A	T	■	B	O	O	H	O	O
A	L	T	I	■	O	P	T	I	O	N
D	A	M	N	■	B	E	E	P	■	
■	■	A	T	L	A	S	■	S	O	O
D	A	N	S	O	N	■	A	L	S	
E	L	F	■	A	D	S	■	N	A	E
B	O	O	■	W	E	N	D	Y	S	
I	E	R	■	Y	E	S	E	S	■	
■	■	E	L	E	A	■	R	A	G	S
L	I	V	E	T	V	■	E	L	E	E
O	N	E	S	I	E	■	I	S	A	R
B	A	R	E	S	■	D	A	R	E	

Solutions

125

M	E	M		N	O	T		L	E	U
I	S	P		A	D	O		A	G	R
S	T	A	G	G	E	R		I	O	N
S	H	A	M	U		R	F	D		
		A	R	B		I	B	O	S	
U	S	O		S	E	A	L	A	N	T
S	T	R	I	K	E	F	O	R	C	E
M	I	D	R	I	F	F		E	E	S
A	R	I	A		Y	A	M			
	N	N	W		I	A	M	B	S	
A	B	A		R	E	R	O	U	T	E
F	A	R		A	T	E		C	W	T
C	A	Y		P	S	S		K	O	A

126

I	N	F	O		P	I	E	R	I	S
S	C	U	D		R	O	T	A	T	E
M	A	L	E		E	T	H	N	I	C
S	A	L	S		S	A	E			
		T	A	L	C		R	A	G	S
D	R	I		I	R	A		L	E	O
R	A	M		T	I	M		B	T	W
A	L	E		D	P	S		A	A	S
B	E	R	M		T	O	A	N		
		A	H	I		K	I	T	E	
V	E	L	C	R	O		I	A	M	S
U	T	A	H	A	N		R	N	A	S
E	S	T	O	P	S		A	S	N	O

127

A	G	A	R			S	M	E	L	L
U	L	N	A		B	L	A	D	E	S
R	E	A	P		R	A	N	G	E	D
A	N	T	I	M	A	T	T	E	R	
		H	E	A	T	E	R			
E	M	E	R	Y		D	A	N	C	E
L	A	M						O	W	N
F	R	A	U	D		P	A	N	T	S
		R	E	B	E	L	S			
	W	E	A	P	O	N	L	E	S	S
Y	A	R	N	E	D		I	N	C	H
U	R	S	I	N	E		E	S	A	U
K	N	E	A	D			D	E	B	T

128

D	A	D		M	I	T		P	T	A
I	L	A		O	N	A		L	O	X
O	F	F	E	N	D	S		E	P	I
N	A	T	L		I	S	A	B	E	L
		P	E	E	V	E	D			
A	L	U	M	N	I		O	K	E	Y
I	G	N		E	D	T		N	A	E
D	A	K	S		U	S	H	E	R	S
		I	N	A	R	O	W			
T	E	T	R	Y	L		M	A	R	U
E	T	H		E	I	D	O	L	O	N
E	C	U		T	S	O		O	S	U
S	S	S		S	M	A		T	A	M

Solutions

129

S	E	C		A	N	N		
W	A	R		W	O	O		S	E	A
I	C	E	B	E	R	G		T	A	D
G	H	E	E		T	O	M	A	T	O
		P	A	T	H		A	G	A	
C	A	Y	U	S	E		Y	E	W	S
P	V	C		P	A	N		M	A	O
A	I	R	S		S	T	R	A	Y	S
	G	A	R		T	H	A	N	
U	N	W	I	S	E		N	A	P	E
S	O	L		M	R	R	I	G	H	T
A	N	Y		E	L	Y		E	O	N
		W	Y	E		D	N	A	

130

T	E	M	P	T		S	T	A	T	E
A	L	O	H	A		T	R	A	I	L
C	A	N	I	S		R	E	A	L	M
O	N	O		T	H	E	Y			
	T	R	E	A	T		O	D	E	
O	B	O	E		S	C	R	E	A	M
T	I	N	E	A		H	I	N	D	I
T	R	I	L	L	S		T	O	O	T
O	R	C		S	L	E	E	P		
	S	O	Y	A		H	I	C	
C	A	G	E	R		G	R	I	M	E
O	P	E	R	A		L	I	L	A	C
Y	E	M	E	N		E	D	E	M	A

131

S	O	D	A		A	B	A	T	E	S
O	P	A	L		C	L	E	A	V	E
F	I	R	E	C	R	A	C	K	E	R
T	N	T		R	O	B		E	N	V
Y	E	S	S	E	S		S	B	A	
		L	A	S	S		T	E	L	
S	W	A	Y	S		C	L	O	T	S
E	E	N		E	C	H	O		
L	A	T		R	E	P	A	S	T	
E	R	E		A	I	M		L	O	U
C	O	N	T	I	N	E	N	T	A	L
T	U	N	I	N	G		E	A	R	L
S	T	A	T	U	E		E	R	S	E

132

C	C	C	P		M	A	K	O	S
A	R	A	B	S		S	W	E	P	T
N	A	S	A	L		R	E	N	E	E
N	I	T		A	L	P		T	N	T
A	G	A	S	S	I		U	M	S	
	N	O	H	I	T		C	R	O	
P	A	E	S	E		O	R	K	I	N
A	N	Y		R	A	N	D	Y		
L	G	E		S	E	A	D	O	G	
E	E	O		O	P	A		E	L	O
A	L	V	A	R		R	A	R	E	R
L	I	E	A	T		M	R	B	I	G
E	C	R	U	S		T	Y	N	E	

Solutions

133

R	A	B	I	N	█	B	A	L	S	A
E	L	E	N	A	█	E	R	I	T	U
C	O	W	E	N	█	M	A	V	I	S
T	A	I	█	W	A	T	E	R	S	█
I	N	S	U	R	E	D	█	F	R	I
█	E	S	A	S	█	T	R	U	E	█
S	A	A	B	S	█	J	E	E	P	S
K	I	S	S	█	R	A	C	E	█	█
Y	M	A	█	M	A	N	H	O	L	E
C	E	N	S	E	D	█	R	I	G	█
A	D	O	P	T	█	V	O	D	K	A
P	A	W	E	R	█	S	P	I	E	D
S	T	L	E	O	█	O	P	E	D	S

134

A	T	E	█	I	M	P	█	A	R	T
R	E	X	█	T	E	A	█	L	O	U
M	E	T	█	A	D	S	█	L	A	P
A	I	R	█	L	I	T	█	I	R	E
D	N	A	█	I	T	S	█	G	E	L
A	G	O	R	A	E	█	D	A	D	O
█	R	U	N	R	I	O	T	█	█	█
J	A	D	E	█	R	O	C	O	C	O
O	B	I	█	F	A	D	█	R	O	B
G	U	N	█	A	N	I	█	P	U	S
G	S	A	█	L	E	D	█	E	R	E
E	E	R	█	S	A	E	█	A	S	S
D	R	Y	█	E	N	S	█	R	E	S

135

P	E	T	I	T	█	T	O	R	U	S
E	V	A	D	E	█	A	R	E	T	E
L	I	C	I	T	█	L	I	N	A	C
F	L	O	O	R	C	L	O	T	H	█
█	█	C	A	R	O	L	█	█	█	█
P	L	O	Y	█	T	W	E	L	V	E
E	E	R	█	█	█	█	A	I	M	█
A	U	B	U	R	N	█	O	C	A	S
█	█	P	O	I	L	U	█	█	█	█
█	R	U	M	B	L	E	S	E	A	T
M	A	N	O	R	█	A	T	R	I	A
A	V	I	S	O	█	S	E	G	N	O
G	E	T	T	Y	█	T	R	O	T	S

136

A	R	C	H	A	I	C	█	█	█	█
L	O	R	E	T	T	A	█	H	C	H
A	B	Y	S	M	A	L	█	A	R	A
N	O	S	H	█	N	E	R	V	E	S
O	T	T	E	R	█	█	I	E	S	T
N	S	A	█	E	S	S	E	N	C	E
█	█	L	E	F	T	O	U	T	█	█
S	U	B	S	I	D	Y	█	A	C	H
I	S	A	O	█	█	S	O	C	L	E
M	U	L	L	A	H	█	F	L	A	M
O	R	L	█	N	U	R	T	U	R	E
N	Y	S	█	A	G	R	E	E	O	N
█	█	S	O	S	A	█	█	█	█	█

Solutions

137

S	E	C	T	█	█	P	O	S	E	R
A	C	H	E	█	D	A	R	K	L	Y
S	H	A	H	█	A	E	D	I	L	E
H	O	R	R	I	B	L	E	█	█	█
█	█	L	A	C	█	L	A	N	C	E
C	R	A	N	E	█	A	L	E	R	T
L	I	T	█	█	█	█	█	F	A	A
A	G	A	R	S	█	S	T	A	B	S
M	A	N	I	A	█	A	I	R	█	█
█	█	█	S	U	R	P	R	I	S	E
P	E	T	I	T	E	█	█	A	O	N	E
A	T	O	N	E	D	█	D	U	A	L
D	A	N	G	S	█	█	E	S	P	Y

138

S	T	U	P	E	█	█	W	A	G	E
S	O	N	O	M	A	█	S	S	N	S
W	I	C	K	E	D	█	W	H	A	P
█	█	O	Y	E	R	S	█	W	R	Y
N	A	N	█	R	E	N	T	E	█	█
A	I	D	E	█	P	O	O	D	L	E
P	R	I	M	P	█	T	E	N	E	T
A	S	T	A	R	E	█	D	E	S	I
█	█	I	G	O	R	S	█	S	E	C
E	C	O	█	B	A	A	E	D	█	█
X	E	N	O	█	O	C	T	A	D	S
E	B	A	Y	█	F	R	A	Y	E	D
C	U	L	L	█	█	A	S	S	E	S

139

I	M	I	N	E	█	█	B	R	O	S
T	A	N	E	Y	█	L	E	O	V	I
A	S	F	A	R	█	E	L	L	E	N
S	K	I	L	I	F	T	█	L	R	G
C	E	N	█	E	L	S	█	O	D	E
A	D	I	O	█	O	U	T	F	O	R
█	█	T	E	N	S	P	O	T	█	█
O	P	E	R	A	S	█	A	H	A	S
D	A	S	█	S	I	G	█	E	M	I
O	R	I	█	D	E	R	I	D	E	D
N	E	M	E	A	█	A	G	I	R	L
T	R	A	N	Q	█	B	O	C	C	E
O	S	L	O	█	█	S	T	E	E	R

140

A	N	I	█	R	Y	A	█	S	L	Y
C	E	N	T	A	U	R	█	T	A	O
R	E	F	O	R	M	A	T	O	R	Y
E	M	O	T	E	█	B	U	N	K	O
█	█	█	A	B	Y	S	S	E	S	█
T	H	A	L	I	A	█	H	A	P	S
W	E	N	█	T	H	E	█	G	U	T
O	L	D	S	█	O	R	N	E	R	Y
█	S	A	P	P	O	R	O	█	█	█
D	I	N	A	R	█	A	P	I	A	N
I	N	T	R	A	C	T	A	B	L	E
E	K	E	█	D	A	I	L	I	E	S
T	I	S	█	O	R	C	█	S	E	T

Solutions

141

```
S O P R A N O ■ A D M
E S I A S O N ■ R I A
A I R M A T T R E S S
N E A P S ■ H O Y A S
C R T S ■ L E N O R E
E S E ■ T E D I U M ■
■ ■ D I X O N ■ ■ ■
■ H E R M I T ■ S U E
M O V I E S ■ D U M A
C R E E L ■ G I B B S
C A N D I D A T U R E
O C T ■ N E U T R A L
Y E S ■ E N R O B E S
```

142

```
A P T ■ ■ S K A T E
G R A B ■ S H O W E R
H E R O ■ T U R N E R
A P P O S I T E ■ ■
■ G A L ■ A D O S
B E S I D E S ■ I L O
O R I E L ■ A G A I N
A G O ■ Y U L E L O G
T O N E ■ K O I ■
■ ■ P L A N G E N T
P A T O I S ■ E M I R
I C I C L E ■ R U N E
T E C H Y ■ ■ S E E
```

143

```
■ P R O S ■ I N C A S
A L A R M ■ M O O R E
D E S T I N A T I O N
D U P ■ T E G ■ N U S
E R E ■ T W O ■ E N E
D A D O E S ■ O D D S
■ ■ I N P U T ■ ■
B U R L ■ A N T I C S
E R A ■ U P S ■ M O P
D A T ■ N E T ■ P S I
I N T E R R O G A T E
M I A M I ■ P A L E D
S A T U P ■ S L E D ■
```

144

```
H U L U ■ A L C A P P
I N A S ■ R E U S E S
R A Y B R A D B U R Y
E P T ■ I M O ■ N F C
S T O O D I N ■ D U H
■ ■ M E S ■ H E M E
T A P E S ■ C A R E D
A L A N ■ S E I ■ ■
R I N ■ D U N G E O N
B E A ■ A C S ■ S N O
U N C O N C E R N E D
S E E N T O ■ P E A U
H E A T E R ■ I S L S
```

Solutions

145

```
O F F S ■ I C I C L E
S I L T ■ B E M O A N
T R O I ■ I A M B I C
E S P R E S S O ■ ■ ■
R T E ■ L E E R S A T
■ R A C K S ■ T I T O
L A R A S ■ C A N T O
U T E P ■ G U L C H ■
S E D A R I S ■ E E E
■ ■ C A R P A R T S ■
R E M I N D ■ B E I T
P U T T E E ■ A L M A
G R A Y E R ■ T Y E S
```

146

```
B O S C ■ A S S O R T
R I A A ■ M O P U P S
I N X S ■ B A R R I E
O K I E ■ U S E ■ ■ ■
■ F L U S ■ E L M O
K A R A C H I ■ I E R
O Z A W A ■ L O T T A
B U G ■ L A Y I T O N
E R E I ■ B A L E ■
■ N A S ■ C R T S
A V I A T E ■ A B R A
P U L L I N ■ K O O L
P E L L E T ■ E X I T
```

147

```
A S C A P ■ R U B O N
S T O L E ■ O T A R U
E A R E D ■ S T R A T
A N D R E W W E I L ■
■ H O O S I E R ■
N O V ■ I L L U M E
S P A T S ■ L Y S O L
C E N S O R ■ S R O
■ E V E N B E T ■
■ C A L I F O R N I A
E E N I E ■ M I A M I
S C O O T ■ A N T E D
C A S T S ■ D E E R E
```

148

```
C O M D R ■ D I D I
E X I L E ■ S A B I N
S T A R W I T N E S S
A A S ■ E N E ■ R S T
R I M ■ D I R T I E S
E L A L ■ K N E A D ■
■ A L A S S ■
M A D A M ■ H O S S
P O K E M O N ■ N O H
A L I ■ A Z O ■ S N O
C I T I Z E N K A N E
E N A T E ■ O S L E R
R E S T ■ S U E T S
```

Solutions

149

	A	G	H	A		P	A	N	S	Y
P	L	I	E	D		A	G	A	P	E
H	E	M	A	L		S	E	T	I	N
D	E	P	R	E	S	S	I	O	N	
		T	R	E	K	S				
A	L	P	S		A	E	T	H	E	R
R	E	V		P	L	Y		A	K	A
P	I	C	A	R	O		A	M	E	N
		G	O	F	O	R				
	D	I	R	T	F	A	R	M	E	R
D	O	N	E	E		R	O	O	M	Y
D	U	K	E	S		E	Y	R	I	E
T	R	Y	S	T		D	O	E	R	

150

G	E	E		M	A	N		V	F	W
T	I	M	P	A	N	I		E	R	O
I	S	S	U	I	N	G		L	E	V
	G	L	E	E			A	Y	E	
A	L	A	S	S		R	E	R	A	N
D	A	E		E	I	N				
J	A	C	T	I	T	A	T	I	O	N
	S	C	H				G	M	C	
P	I	Q	U	E		D	I	N	A	R
O	S	U		D	U	R	A			
R	E	I		T	R	A	G	E	D	Y
E	E	E		E	N	F	O	R	C	E
S	A	T		A	S	T		B	C	S

151

A	L	I	C	E	S		T	H	A	I
F	A	N	O	U	T		S	O	P	S
B	A	N	G	L	E		K	E	P	T
	U	S	E		C	T	R	L	S	
C	O	E		R	N	A	S			
O	L	N		U	N	K	N	O	T	
L	L	D		M	R	I		A	C	T
T	A	O	I	S	M		M	H	O	
	B	R	I	M		E	S	P		
B	L	E	E	P		I	F	S		
O	R	C	A		P	A	L	A	T	E
L	O	O	M		H	O	O	K	U	P
A	N	N	S		D	W	E	E	B	S

152

S	O	L	O	S		A	N	I	L	S
Q	U	A	R	T		S	E	R	A	L
U	T	T	E	R		P	O	R	N	O
A	L	I		I	C	E		E	D	O
B	E	N		V	I	N		C	A	P
S	T	A	V	E	S		P	L	U	S
	M	E	N		P	E	A			
I	B	E	X		M	A	R	I	N	E
N	O	R		M	A	S		M	O	N
S	U	I		O	P	T		A	D	D
I	N	C	U	R		I	M	B	U	E
S	C	A	L	P		M	U	L	L	A
T	E	N	T	H		E	M	E	E	R

Solutions

153

K	E	P	I	█	A	R	I	S	E	S
I	L	L	D	O	M	Y	B	E	S	T
P	O	A	C	H	E	D	E	G	G	S
█	█	T	A	R	R	E	R	█	█	█
█	H	O	R	O	█	R	I	N	K	Y
R	A	N	D	B	█	S	A	O	N	E
D	W	I	█	█	█	█	R	U	N	█
A	S	S	A	M	█	P	I	T	T	S
S	E	T	T	O	█	A	S	H	E	█
█	█	M	O	B	C	A	P	█	█	█
R	E	S	O	L	U	T	I	O	N	S
C	A	E	S	A	R	S	A	L	A	D
A	P	A	T	H	Y	█	H	E	M	I

154

D	A	N	L	█	R	A	M	S	A	Y
A	L	E	A	█	O	L	I	N	D	A
S	T	A	Y	█	S	I	D	L	E	R
H	I	R	T	█	I	E	R	█	█	█
█	█	L	O	O	T	█	I	N	G	A
H	A	Y	█	H	A	M	B	U	R	G
O	P	A	R	T	█	O	S	M	I	C
O	I	L	H	O	L	E	█	E	D	Y
P	A	L	O	█	I	S	A	R	█	█
█	█	D	A	O	█	D	O	H	A	█
E	N	S	I	G	N	█	W	U	S	S
S	U	T	U	R	E	█	A	N	I	S
D	I	S	M	A	L	█	R	O	A	N

155

M	U	D	S	█	A	R	L	O	S	█
I	L	E	A	█	I	M	E	L	D	A
S	E	A	U	█	N	O	T	B	A	D
C	E	L	T	I	C	█	U	S	S	R
█	█	M	E	D	I	A	N	█	█	█
G	B	E	█	I	N	F	E	R	N	O
M	R	I	█	O	E	R	█	E	A	N
S	I	N	A	T	R	A	█	C	B	S
█	█	I	S	A	I	A	H	█	█	█
A	S	T	R	█	T	D	B	A	N	K
W	E	E	P	I	E	█	E	R	G	O
A	G	E	O	L	D	█	A	G	O	N
D	A	M	P	S	█	M	E	S	A	█

156

G	R	I	P	S	█	S	A	M	S	A
N	O	F	E	E	█	A	R	Y	A	N
A	S	Y	E	T	█	A	I	S	L	E
R	A	O	█	R	A	B	A	T	█	█
█	U	M	A	S	S	█	E	D	M	█
J	U	D	I	T	H	█	B	R	E	A
I	M	O	N	E	█	L	A	Y	E	R
L	P	N	S	█	K	E	R	N	E	L
L	S	T	█	I	N	T	R	O	█	█
█	W	I	L	T	S	█	V	A	N	█
A	M	A	T	I	█	E	N	E	M	Y
M	A	N	S	E	█	A	S	L	I	P
O	C	T	A	D	█	T	A	S	E	D

Solutions

157

A	S	T	E	W			I	R	E	N	A
C	L	O	T	H			N	O	N	O	S
D	O	G	C	A	T	C	H	E	R	S	
C	P	A		T	A	O		R	I	N	
		O	N	E	G	I	G				
P	E	T	R	O	L		N	I	P	S	
A	S	E	A	T		N	A	Z	I	S	
H	A	M	M		M	I	N	E	T	A	
		P	A	L	A	C	E				
A	Y	E		I	R	T		P	A	Y	
B	A	R	R	E	L	A	L	O	N	G	
E	L	E	N	I		T	O	N	T	O	
D	U	R	A	N		E	L	D	E	R	

158

Y	A	W	P			C	O	B	R	A
E	L	A	T	E		O	N	I	O	N
A	T	T	A	R		D	O	R	S	A
T	H	E		M	B	A		D	E	L
S	O	R	T	I	E			O	H	O
		S	I	N	G	E		F	I	G
C	H	O	S	E		S	A	P	P	Y
O	A	F		S	E	P	I	A		
P	I	T			G	O	D	S	O	N
I	R	E		L	O	U		S	U	E
E	N	N	U	I		S	H	A	G	S
R	E	E	F	S		E	I	G	H	T
S	T	R	O	P			P	E	T	S

159

R	U	B	E		N	E	A	T	E	R
A	P	R	S		O	N	S	I	D	E
R	I	A	A		N	T	E	S	T	S
A	N	G	U	L	A	R				
		E	M	E	R	I	T	I		
C	A	N	I	N	E		O	S	H	A
A	R	E	C	A		I	B	S	E	N
V	I	V	E		E	L	B	O	W	S
A	P	E	L	I	K	E				
		O	B	T	R	U	D	E		
D	E	B	O	N	E		Y	S	E	R
S	E	A	A	I	R		A	D	A	S
M	O	N	T	A	G		S	A	N	T

160

O	A	T	S		G	A	G	G	E	D
B	L	O	T		A	G	O	U	T	I
I	O	W	A		N	U	A	N	C	E
S	E	N	T	I	N	E	L			
		S	U	R	E		I	S	I	S
O	F	F	S	E	T		E	C	R	U
B	I	O						R	O	D
E	L	L	S		P	A	T	E	N	S
Y	O	K	E		A	N	E	W		
		E	N	V	I	A	B	L	E	
F	O	S	S	A	E		B	A	A	L
A	U	P	A	I	R		A	L	M	S
T	R	A	W	L	S		G	L	E	E

Solutions

161

```
D U F F · · S F C S ·
O S R I C · H A O L E
L A U G H · A N N U L
O U I · I S R · C D R
O S T · T A P · E G O
P A Y S · Y E N N E D
· P I A N I S T · ·
K L E P T O · C R A B
C A B · A T C · A P O
A M B · L O L · T I L
R O L L O · A M I C I
S U E T S · W O O E D
· R S S S · E N S E
```

162

```
A L O F T · · V A T ·
L A G O O N · T O R A
I M A R E T · A T M S
G O U T · H A B E A S
H U G H · T A R D E
T R E E · M I S S A L
· · R E B E C · ·
B O D E G A · O A K S
A R A C E · S N E E
I G N O R E · A D E E
L A I R · S L U R P S
O N E D · D E C E I T
R A L · Y E S N O
```

163

```
B A S R A · C A S A S
O N H E R · O B A M A
T O O L E · N O T I N
H A V A N A C U B A ·
· E T A P E ·
U G L I · I D I O C Y
N U E V E · E N N I S
E N D E A R · C E I L
· S E R I O ·
P H O E B E S N O W
B U E N O · A I O L I
M T W T F · D O N A T
W A S O F · A N E N T
```

164

```
C B S · P E A ·
H O W · L O G · S E E
A N E M O N E · P A P
I N E R T · S C A R E
N I T S · A C N E
S E T · A C T R E S S
· A F F A I R S ·
P A L E T T E · T A B
L I K E · N A G A
A M I S S · M O T E L
T E N · I M A G I N E
E R G · T E C · O D E
· E W E · N A N
```

Solutions

165

M	A	C	E	D	■	T	R	U	E	S
E	P	O	D	E	■	H	O	M	M	E
D	E	M	O	B	■	R	A	B	I	D
U	M	P	■	A	D	O	R	I	N	G
S	E	A	T	T	L	E	■	L	E	E
A	N	N	I	E	S	■	N	I	M	S
■	■	I	N	S	■	R	O	C	■	■
B	B	O	Y	■	D	E	T	A	I	L
I	A	N	■	L	A	J	O	L	L	A
A	R	A	P	A	H	O	■	C	D	S
F	I	B	E	R	■	I	N	O	U	T
R	U	L	E	D	■	C	I	R	C	E
A	M	E	S	S	■	E	N	D	E	D

166

C	C	L	E	F	■	S	W	A	G	E
O	R	A	R	E	■	H	A	L	E	D
M	I	L	L	I	S	E	C	O	N	D
E	S	A	■	N	A	P	■	M	I	I
A	T	L	■	T	V	S	■	A	A	E
T	O	A	T	E	E	■	U	R	L	S
■	■	■	E	D	S	E	L	■	■	■
T	E	C	S	■	T	S	T	R	A	P
U	T	E	■	C	I	S	■	A	P	R
R	E	M	■	A	M	E	■	M	O	A
G	R	E	E	N	E	N	E	R	G	Y
I	N	N	E	S	■	C	O	O	E	E
D	E	T	O	O	■	E	N	D	E	R

167

C	E	D	E	S	■	S	A	L	E	■
A	L	O	F	T	■	P	O	E	T	■
S	A	N	T	A	M	A	R	I	A	■
T	N	T	■	R	E	N	T	■	■	■
■	■	A	F	T	■	A	L	S	O	■
S	P	E	C	I	E	S	■	A	H	A
E	A	V	E	S	■	U	D	D	E	R
E	R	E	■	H	A	R	N	E	S	S
D	A	N	K	■	R	C	A	■	■	■
■	■	A	G	U	E	■	M	B	A	■
P	Y	R	O	M	A	N	I	A	C	■
T	O	M	E	■	S	O	L	A	R	■
A	D	A	R	■	E	R	O	S	E	■

168

S	O	R	B	E	T	■	I	C	I	■
T	R	O	I	K	A	■	I	N	O	N
A	M	U	L	E	T	■	R	E	N	D
R	O	T	L	■	A	P	I	E	C	E
T	R	E	O	■	I	S	D	U	E	■
S	E	R	F	■	C	S	H	A	R	P
■	■	R	A	H	A	B	■	■	■	■
G	I	V	I	N	G	■	R	A	P	T
A	L	I	G	N	■	O	P	A	H	■
B	O	O	H	O	O	■	G	A	R	R
L	I	L	T	■	S	T	U	C	C	O
E	L	I	S	■	T	E	E	H	E	E
S	O	N	■	E	A	S	E	L	S	■

Solutions

169

C	A	T		M	T	N			
O	F	A	S	O	R	T		W	T	S
S	T	R	I	D	E	S		A	H	H
T	E	A	M		A	B	U	S	E	R
A	R	M	P	I	T		S	T	L	O
	E	A	S	E	L		B	E	A	V
R	F	S		R	I	M		D	D	E
A	F	A	R		K	A	T	E	Y	
T	E	L	E		E	V	E	N	I	F
S	C	A	L	E	D		G	E	N	L
O	T	T		P	I	Z	A	R	R	O
N	S	A		O	R	A	N	G	E	S
				S	T	P		Y	D	S

170

S	T	A	P	H		F	L	E	S	H
R	I	L	E	Y		L	E	N	T	O
I	M	P	R	E	C	A	T	I	O	N
			K	N	O	T		D	A	K
A	C	T		A	R	T	S			
I	R	I	S		T	E	L	U	G	U
D	E	N	O	M	I	N	A	T	O	R
S	W	E	A	R	S		B	A	R	N
			P	R	O	S		H	E	S
G	A	T		I	N	C	H			
E	X	A	G	G	E	R	A	T	E	D
M	O	R	P	H		U	V	U	L	A
S	N	O	O	T		B	E	N	D	Y

171

S	C	I	S	S	O	R		S	S	A
C	A	S	C	A	D	E		T	O	T
H	P	L	O	V	E	C	R	A	F	T
E	L	A	T	E	D		I	N	T	I
M	E	N	S		A	S	N	E	R	
E	T	D		T	A	K	E	O	N	E
		K	E	F	I	R				
V	I	T	A	M	I	N		R	O	M
I	C	E	U	P		D	E	N	Y	
R	O	A	R		B	E	E	P	A	T
I	N	S	I	D	E	S	T	O	R	Y
L	I	E		T	A	P	E	S	U	P
E	C	T		S	T	Y	R	E	N	E

172

O	R	B	S		K	N	E	E	S	
R	O	U	E		N	U	T	M	E	G
A	B	R	A	C	A	D	A	B	R	A
T	I	P		E	V	E		A	I	M
E	N	S	U	R	E		R	O	E	
			R	E	S	T		G	U	T
S	A	U	N	A		A	R	O	S	E
A	N	N		L	O	T	H			
L	O	S		S	T	O	L	I	D	
S	I	N		G	P	O		O	N	E
A	N	A	C	H	R	O	N	I	S	M
S	T	R	I	A	E		O	R	E	O
	S	L	A	T	Y		W	E	T	S

Solutions

173

B	A	S	S		A	D	S	O	R	B
A	L	U	M		B	E	A	R	E	R
R	O	S	E	K	E	N	N	E	D	Y
R	E	P	R	O		T	E	G	A	N
		E	S	S	A	Y	S			
S	I	N	H		A	N	T	C	O	W
E	L	D		E	N	E		O	C	A
R	A	S	H	A	D		M	A	T	S
			A	T	E	O	U	T		
C	C	L	V	I		A	S	T	R	A
H	E	L	E	N	O	F	T	R	O	Y
O	D	D	I	T	Y		N	E	V	E
P	I	S	T	O	L		T	E	E	S

174

G	U	P	T	A		T	B	I	L	L
A	T	R	E	E		O	L	L	I	E
S	E	E	R	S		M	O	I	R	A
		T	R	O	N		O	A	R	S
J	O	E		P	O	N	D			
E	L	E	E		V	E	R	N	A	L
S	I	N	C	E		P	E	O	N	S
U	N	S	A	I	D		D	A	N	A
		U	N	C	O		H	O	T	
T	V	A	D		L	T	D	S		
E	I	L	A	T		O	R	A	R	E
T	I	L	T	S		E	A	R	T	H
R	I	S	E	R		S	Y	K	E	S

175

C	A	S	H		A	L	T	I	M	A
C	A	P	A		K	O	A	L	A	S
C	R	A	C	K	E	R	J	A	C	K
P	E	S	K	I	E	R				
		N	A	M	E	T	A	G	S	
B	A	B	E	S		S	O	C	L	E
O	S	A	Y			N	E	U	E	
T	I	B	E	T		A	I	R	E	R
S	P	U	D	W	E	B	B			
		O	L	E	A	R	Y	S		
S	T	U	F	F	E	D	S	O	L	E
H	E	I	D	E	N		I	L	E	T
O	M	E	A	R	A		L	O	M	A

176

P	I	C	A	S		G	L	I	B
H	O	B	N	O	B		M	E	N	U
I	N	S	I	N	U	A	T	I	N	G
		M	A	R	C					
A	S	T	E	R		I	S	N	T
C	H	I		O	D	I	O	U	S
H	E	A	R	T	H	S	T	O	N	E
E	R	R	O	R	S		K	E	G
	D	A	T	A		B	A	S	S	O
		P	E	E	L				
B	E	S	T	S	E	L	L	E	R	S
A	R	I	A		C	O	A	T	E	E
D	A	R	N		W	Y	A	T	T

Solutions

177

T	E	S	H	■	■	S	H	E	E	N
A	L	L	O	F	■	A	A	N	D	E
M	O	O	N	L	I	G	H	T	E	R
T	I	O	■	E	L	E	N	O	R	E
A	S	P	H	A	L	T	■	M	L	I
M	E	S	A	■	S	E	A	B	E	D
■	■	■	P	A	E	A	N	■	■	■
I	N	E	S	S	E	■	O	A	S	T
S	O	L	■	H	Y	U	N	D	A	I
A	V	I	A	T	O	R	■	U	R	L
D	I	S	G	R	U	N	T	L	E	D
O	C	H	O	A	■	E	S	T	E	E
R	E	A	D	Y	■	■	R	S	S	S

178

R	I	D	G	E	■	L	A	C	T	I
O	N	E	A	D	■	E	I	L	A	T
W	I	N	T	E	R	G	R	E	E	N
■	■	■	O	L	E	■	B	O	L	O
C	A	B	S	■	M	D	A	■	■	■
A	L	A	■	O	B	E	S	E	L	Y
S	I	L	V	E	R	B	E	L	L	S
A	I	M	E	D	A	T	■	I	B	E
■	■	■	S	S	N	■	U	S	S	R
S	C	O	T	■	D	E	R	■	■	■
C	H	R	I	S	T	M	A	S	S	Y
A	G	O	G	O	■	I	L	O	N	A
N	E	N	E	H	■	T	S	L	O	T

179

E	C	O	L	I	■	M	A	P	L	E
R	U	N	A	T	■	E	D	I	C	T
D	E	C	K	O	F	C	A	R	D	S
A	D	E	E	■	A	C	H	■	■	■
■	■	E	T	N	A	■	D	S	S	■
P	O	I	R	O	T	■	S	E	E	A
P	A	N	I	C	A	T	T	A	C	K
S	H	O	E	■	S	H	A	F	T	S
S	U	R	■	I	T	E	M	■	■	■
■	■	I	N	I	■	P	I	P	S	■
S	P	A	R	E	C	H	A	N	G	E
U	S	A	I	R	■	S	C	R	A	M
N	T	E	S	T	■	I	T	I	S	I

180

S	E	N	N	A	■	I	F	T	H	E
C	R	O	O	N	■	D	E	W	A	R
H	O	R	S	E	■	E	D	I	T	S
■	■	M	I	S	S	■	E	C	H	T
P	A	A	R	■	C	E	R	E	■	■
I	G	N	■	R	O	T	A	T	E	S
C	U	C	K	O	O	C	L	O	C	K
T	A	O	I	S	T	S	■	L	O	Y
■	■	U	L	E	E	■	I	D	L	E
A	H	S	O	■	R	E	S	T	■	■
R	A	I	T	A	■	A	N	A	I	S
A	M	N	O	T	■	S	E	L	L	S
Y	E	S	N	O	■	T	R	E	E	T

Solutions

181

N	O	S	E		W	A	R	G	O	D
U	G	L	Y		A	L	U	M	N	A
T	R	U	E		L	E	N	T	E	N
S	E	R	F		K	E	N			
			U	R	I		Y	A	M	S
A	P	P	L	I	E	D		L	E	U
G	U	E	S	S	T	I	M	A	T	E
E	R	A		C	A	B	A	R	E	T
S	E	L	F		L	S	D			
		L	E	K		D	O	L	E	
S	A	F	A	R	I		I	D	E	A
O	N	L	I	N	E		N	O	G	S
S	T	Y	L	E	S		G	R	O	T

182

A	C	T	S		L	A	M	B	S	
C	L	I	O		A	M	O	R	A	L
C	O	N	T	A	M	I	N	A	T	E
E	T	H		S	E	A		V	I	A
S	H	A	C	K		B	L	E	N	D
S	E	T	A		C	L	A	S	S	Y
			B	O	R	E	D			
L	E	M	O	N	Y		L	A	D	E
E	M	O	T	E		S	E	R	A	L
A	P	R		T	A	R		C	I	A
S	I	G	N	I	F	I	C	A	N	T
T	R	A	U	M	A		A	N	T	E
	E	N	T	E	R		B	A	Y	S

183

I	B	O	S		C	R	E	P	E	S
M	A	L	E		H	E	N	R	Y	I
A	R	E	D		A	C	C	O	R	D
C	I	G	A	R	S	T	O	R	E	
			K	O	M	O	D	O		
L	E	M	A	N	S		E	G	A	N
A	L	A						U	L	U
P	S	T	S		C	H	I	E	F	S
		U	N	C	L	E	S			
	T	R	I	L	O	B	I	T	E	S
T	I	E	P	I	N		T	A	D	A
I	N	S	A	N	E		M	R	I	S
P	O	T	T	E	D		E	N	T	S

184

I	N	S	P		O	N	C	D	S
T	O	O	T	H		A	G	A	M	E
I	N	P	U	T		T	O	R	A	S
		H	I	T	E	M		P	J	S
R	A	I		P	L	E	B	E		
S	P	E	C		F	A	T	T	E	D
S	I	S	I	S		L	U	C	I	E
S	A	C	R	E	D		S	L	R	S
	H	O	C	U	S		E	E	K	
O	B	O		E	B	O	L	A		
T	R	I	A	D		U	A	N	D	I
T	Y	C	H	E		P	T	E	R	O
O	N	E	A	D		S	R	I	S	

Solutions

185

W	A	X		M	G	S		N	E	B
A	B	M		T	I	E		A	I	R
I	R	A		E	R	A	S	U	R	E
F	I	R	S	T	L	E	T	T	E	R
	K	I	N		E	R	I			
T	E	S	T	A		L	I	C	I	T
R	A	T	T				P	A	S	A
U	N	H	I	P		A	I	L	E	Y
	E	G	S		R	E	M			
W	A	S	H	E	R	D	R	I	E	R
N	E	P	T	U	N	E		L	G	E
B	O	O		D	A	N		E	I	N
A	N	T		O	S	T		S	S	A

186

P	A	P	A		M	A	D	C	A	P
E	G	O	S		A	R	E	O	L	A
R	A	W	S		S	A	L	M	A	N
U	R	D	U		T	N	T			
	E	R	N	E		A	B	E	D	
C	A	R	E	E	R		S	E	R	E
A	R	K		T	S	P		T	O	N
L	I	E	D		A	R	R	E	S	T
M	A	G	I		T	O	O	N		
	E	R	A		L	O	A	D		
C	A	U	S	E	R		L	I	K	E
I	N	S	E	A	M		E	R	I	E
S	T	A	L	L	S		R	E	N	D

187

M	I	L		N	S	A		A	S	H
C	R	I		B	L	T		D	E	A
C	A	L	M	W	E	A	T	H	E	R
V	E	A	U		E	X	E	D	R	A
		S	A	T	Y	R				
I	B	I	S	E	S		Z	B	A	R
T	I	M	O	R		I	A	M	S	O
A	P	P	L		U	N	R	I	P	E
		I	S	S	E	I				
S	H	A	N	I	A		M	G	R	S
M	O	W	I	N	G	L	A	W	N	S
O	Y	L		K	E	Y		A	A	R
G	A	S		S	S	S		R	S	S

188

T	I	B	I	A		N	I	K	O	S
V	I	L	L	E		O	R	I	Y	A
A	S	A	I	R		N	A	M	E	S
	C	A	I	N	E		K	R	S	
E	L	K		A	E	T	N	A		
N	I	H	I	L	O		O	R	L	Y
C	R	A	M	S		O	R	D	I	E
Y	E	W	S		U	N	N	A	I	L
	K	O	A	L	A		S	I	P	
B	E	D		R	A	J	A	H		
A	R	O	S	E		U	T	I	C	A
L	E	W	I	S		R	O	A	R	K
L	I	N	G	O		Y	E	N	T	A

Solutions

189

B	M	W	S			S	B	A	R	R	O
L	E	H	R			W	O	N	O	U	T
I	R	A	S			O	R	G	A	N	O
P	C	T			H	O	I			R	A	E
		I	O	N	E	S	C	O			
O	F	F	I	S	H			B	A	S	S
R	U	I	N	S			R	E	L	O	S
A	L	T	O			W	A	S	A	B	I
		N	E	A	T	E	N	S		
I	E	D			S	K	A			A	T	L
S	T	E	P	P	E			A	L	O	E
A	R	E	Y	O	U			B	D	R	M
W	E	T	M	O	P			C	A	Y	S

190

E	N	U	R	E			A	F	T	E	R
B	E	R	E	A			S	O	A	V	E
B	E	E	P	S			K	O	R	E	A
S	M	A	R	T	S			D	O	R	M
		E	S	T	O	P		
B	A	S	H			Y	A	R	R	O	W
O	R	I	E	L			T	O	I	L	E
T	E	N	N	E	R			C	O	D	E
		S	E	N	S	E		
H	I	F	I			A	N	S	W	E	R
A	D	O	B	E			O	S	A	K	A
F	E	L	L	A			R	O	G	E	T
T	A	K	E	R			T	R	E	S	S

191

R	I	A			S	A	L			K	E	R
A	N	A			O	C	A			E	D	O
C	U	R			C	T	N			E	D	M
E	R	O	S	I	V	E			P	I	A
M	E	N	L	O			O	L	S	E	N
E	S	S	O			G	N	E	I	S	S
		P	U	P	T	E	N	T		
A	L	E	G	R	E			A	I	M	S
D	E	L	H	I			A	P	N	E	A
D	O	L			M	A	K	E	M	A	D
L	I	I			A	W	N			I	N	I
E	I	N			T	A	E			N	I	S
D	I	G			E	Y	E			D	E	M

192

A	L	L	A			H	O	B	N	O	B
M	O	E	T			I	N	L	O	V	E
B	L	V	D			G	E	T	M	A	D
I	L	I	A			H	A	S	S	L	E
		T	W	O	P	M		
P	L	A	N	A	R			I	R	K
T	O	T			T	E	Y			M	O	A
A	C	E			S	E	A	N	C	E
		A	S	O	L	O		
O	R	M	O	L	U			O	T	O	S
D	I	E	T	E	R			N	Y	N	Y
E	C	A	R	T	E			Z	O	O	S
R	E	L	O	A	D			O	U	S	T

Solutions

193

A	P	E	R	C	U		O	D	D	S
D	O	R	I	A	N		W	E	R	E
S	L	E	E	P	W	A	L	K	E	R
			L	E	A	F		A	W	E
C	L	A	S	S	R	O	O	M		
A	I	R			R	O	W	E	R	S
P	E	R	I	P	A	T	E	T	I	C
O	N	E	M	A	N			E	M	U
		S	P	U	T	T	E	R	E	D
P	I	T		S	A	U	L			
O	L	I	V	E	B	R	A	N	C	H
M	I	N	I		L	I	N	E	A	R
P	A	G	E		E	N	D	O	W	S

194

S	I	B	S		L	E	G	A	T	O
C	N	E	T		I	N	E	S	S	E
O	F	N	O		E	S	T	H	E	R
R	U	E		O	N	U	S			
E	N	D	O	W		E	R	A	S	E
		I	R	E		D	I	M	E	S
R	E	C	D				D	I	S	C
A	N	T	I	S		B	O	N		
F	L	I	N	T		O	F	O	L	D
			A	R	T	S		A	A	R
R	O	D	N	E	Y		A	C	R	O
S	P	A	C	E	K		N	I	C	O
S	T	P	E	T	E		A	D	H	D

195

A	L	O	N	G		N	I	N	T	H
R	I	F	L	E		E	M	O	R	Y
R	E	F	E	R		E	A	T	U	P
A	N	Y		A	N	D		H	S	N
U	S	O		L	U	S		I	T	O
			U	S	D	T		O	N	E	I
C	U	R	I	O		P	A	G	E	D
I	N	R	E		D	I	R	T		
T	S	O		S	E	C		O	L	E
A	T	C		O	A	K		L	O	L
D	A	K	A	R		S	T	O	G	Y
E	G	E	S	T		O	A	S	I	S
L	Y	R	E	S		N	I	E	C	E

196

M	Y	O	P	I	C			S	U	P
P	O	T	A	T	O		P	P	S	S
H	U	B	C	A	P		I	E	S	T
			I	N	T	E	G	E	R	S
A	S	O	F		S	L	O			
L	O	R	I	S		L	U	C	A	S
T	I	N	C	T		I	T	C	H	Y
A	R	E	C	A		S	O	L	O	N
			O	R	A		N	I	T	S
B	E	P	A	R	T	O	F			
U	T	E	S		E	L	O	I	S	E
L	A	I	T		A	D	O	R	E	E
G	S	N		R	E	D	E	A	L	

Solutions

197

B	A	R	B	A	R	A		E	M	U
U	N	O	I	L	E	D		R	E	S
G	I	B	B	O	N	S		T	A	P
			L	E	A		E	N	S	
E	L	B	E		M	I	D	S	T	
D	A	U	B		E	R	E			
O	C	T	E	T		K	A	P	P	A
		L	E	U		T	R	A	P	
	F	A	T	A	L		H	O	L	E
C	A	D		T	A	R				
H	U	M		M	I	N	A	R	E	T
A	N	A		E	M	O	T	I	V	E
P	A	N		G	O	N	E	B	A	D

198

I	N	S	T		M	A	S	S	E	D
D	A	T	E		I	L	L	U	S	E
E	T	A	L		T	W	E	N	T	Y
S	O	R	E	H	E	A	D			
		S	C	A	R	Y		M	A	P
A	L	I	A	S		S	M	A	L	L
C	I	G	S				A	G	U	E
M	O	N	T	H		P	R	I	M	A
E	N	S		O	P	T	I	C		
			J	A	L	A	P	E	N	O
C	E	S	U	R	A		O	Y	E	R
H	O	U	N	D	S		S	E	A	T
I	N	M	E	S	H		A	S	P	S

199

P	R	O	M	O		P	I	P	E	T
U	N	G	A	R		E	M	E	E	R
M	A	R	I	A	H	C	A	R	E	Y
A	S	E		L	E	T	T			
			G	E	R	I		C	H	G
		H	A	R	D	N	O	S	E	D
A	L	A	I			R	C	M	P	
S	P	A	N	G	L	I	S	H		
A	N	S		I	T	N	O			
			L	A	R	A		P	J	S
U	N	C	O	N	S	C	I	O	U	S
A	T	E	I	T		A	R	R	A	N
W	H	E	N	S		B	A	N	N	S

200

S	H	U	T	S		O	O	H	S	
T	O	N	Y	A		O	B	E	Y	S
P	U	R	P	L	E	H	E	A	R	T
E	D	E		S	N	L		N	I	E
T	O	S	T	A	D	A		E	A	R
E	N	T	R		E	L	A	Y	N	E
			I	S	A	A	C			
A	S	I	M	O	V		M	O	S	H
R	P	M		R	O	B	E	R	T	A
U	R	E		T	R	L		M	E	R
M	I	L	L	I	S	E	C	O	N	D
S	E	D	A	N		E	R	R	O	L
	R	A	N	G		P	O	E	S	Y

Solutions

201

S	A	K	E	S		L	A	V	A	S
I	R	E	N	A		A	T	I	L	T
S	E	E	D	Y		S	E	R	T	A
T	O	P		S	O	C		G	A	B
E	L	I		T	U	A		I	R	S
R	A	T	A		T	R	A	N		
S	E	A	L	S		S	C	R	I	P
		S	L	U	E		R	E	L	O
A	A	E		C	C	S		C	O	M
U	F	C		C	G	I		O	V	A
N	O	R	S	E		C	E	R	E	D
T	R	E	A	S		E	D	D	I	E
S	E	T	T	S		M	A	S	T	S